ELDER LAW

IN A NUTSHELL

FOURTH EDITION

By

LAWRENCE A. FROLIK
Professor of Law
University of Pittsburgh

RICHARD L. KAPLAN
Peer and Sarah Pedersen Professor of Law
University of Illinois

THOMSON

WEST

Mat #40453051

Nutshell Series, In a Nutshell, the Nutshell Logo and West Group are trademarks registered in the U.S. Patent and Trademark Office.

COPYRIGHT © 1995 WEST PUBLISHING CO.
© West, a Thomson business, 1999, 2003
© 2006 Thomson/West
        610 Opperman Drive
        P.O. Box 64526
        St. Paul, MN 55164–0526
        1–800–328–9352
Printed in the United States of America

ISBN–13: 978–0–314–16777–4
ISBN–10: 0–314–16777–3

TEXT IS PRINTED ON 10% POST CONSUMER RECYCLED PAPER

In loving memory of my parents
L.A.F.

To my parents,
whose memory is a blessing
R.L.K.

*

PREFACE

This brief volume is intended to introduce the reader to one of the fastest growing and significant legal specialties—elder law. This title increasingly is used to describe the multitude of legal concerns faced by older Americans as they plan their later years and seek to maximize their personal autonomy. These concerns range from age discrimination in employment, to housing alternatives and options, to ensuring control of one's financial affairs, to financing one's medical needs, and ultimately to determining the scope of medical care that one desires. In many ways, elder law is a response to extended life expectancy, in contrast to more traditional "estate planning" with its largely after-death orientation.

Accordingly, this book should be of interest to anyone who has regular contact with older persons: lawyers and law students needing an overview of some particular subject, social workers, certain medical personnel, gerontologists, retirement planners, and the like. We address this book to all these audiences with the hope that it clarifies the issues and sets forth a framework for informed action and understanding.

The authors express their appreciation to their respective secretaries, Patricia Blake and Ann

Perry, for their inestimable help in bringing this project to fruition, and to their families, for their interest, encouragement, and support.

LAWRENCE A. FROLIK
RICHARD L. KAPLAN

Pittsburgh, Pennsylvania
Champaign, Illinois
August, 2006

OUTLINE

Chapter 4.   Medicare and Medigap

OUTLINE

Chapter 7. Nursing Homes, Board and Care Homes and Assisted Living Facilities

Page

Chapter 8.   Housing Alternatives and Options

Chapter 14. Pension Plans

Chapter 15. Age Discrimination in Employment

Chapter 16.   Elder Abuse and Neglect

*

TABLE OF CASES

References are to Pages

TABLE OF CASES

ELDER LAW

IN A NUTSHELL

FOURTH EDITION

*

CHAPTER 1

INTRODUCTION: THE SCOPE AND DIVERSITY OF ELDER LAW

§ 1.1 The Development of Elder Law as a Specialty

The development of a specialty devoted to the legal needs of older Americans has several distinct origins. First, people are living longer due to medical advances, better nutritional habits, and improved living conditions generally. People who reached age 65 in 2002 had an average remaining life expectancy of 16.6 years for males and 19.5 years for females. As a consequence, there are more people attaining ages that have historically been characterized as "old." For example, the cohort of persons aged 75–84 years increased from the 1990 to the 2000 Census by 22.9%. Meanwhile, the cohort of persons aged 85 years and older, the so-called "old-old," increased by 37.6% during this period and is projected to increase another 36.5% by the year 2010.

Second, increasing age usually means increasing medical costs. Since 1965, much—though not all—of the medical care costs of older persons has been a Federal responsibility. The increasing numbers of

1

older persons combined with significantly escalating costs of medical care generally have caused the scope of this Federal responsibility to explode. As a result, bureaucratic rules and regulations have been promulgated to implement and manage this Federal responsibility over an ever-enlarging patient pool.

Third, increasing age usually means increased caregiving burdens. At the same time, broad demographic trends have meant that those family members who have historically shouldered this burden are no longer doing so. Delayed childbearing has produced the "sandwich generation" phenomenon of caring for young children and old parents simultaneously, increased economic opportunity for women has diminished the ranks of potential caregivers lacking careers outside the home, and general economic trends have meant geographic dispersion of adult children and their siblings. The result of these trends is that more care of older persons is being "contracted out" to institutions or other third party "providers." The involvement of such caregivers necessarily raises legal questions relating to the rights of care recipients, the responsibilities of care providers, how these arrangements are to be monitored, and how they are to be financed.

Fourth, older Americans have more accumulated wealth than ever before, and their level of education is increasing steadily. The result of these twin phenomena is increased political visibility and organized political clout. Quite simply, the needs of these people are being articulated more clearly than ever before when questions of public benefits are debated, and those programs have, not coincidentally, expanded as well.

Additional factors could be adduced, but the point is that older Americans face an increasing number of legal questions involving entitlement to public benefits, protection of property interests, utilization of medical resources, health care decisionmaking, and interaction with legal and financial institutions of various sorts.

§ 1.2 Scope of Elder Law

This book begins with a chapter devoted to the special challenges faced by those who advise older persons. Ethical conflicts faced when advising more than one generation are typical, in addition to questions involving a client's legal "capacity" or the mental ability to make legal decisions.

The next chapter involves the most pivotal issue in elder decisionmaking—namely, deciding which medical procedures should be employed when a person is no longer able to make such decisions or to communicate the decisions made. This subject involves variously named legal forms, including living wills, health care proxies, powers of attorney for health care, and other forms of advance directives. This area is not an exclusively "elder law" subject, because persons of any age can find themselves in the circumstances that these documents address. In fact, the most celebrated court decisions on the "right to die" have involved young adults. Nevertheless, in recognition of elder law's general focus of enhancing an older person's control over his or her circumstances, the subject of medical care decision-making has evolved into a core element of this area.

Next follows three chapters dealing with different mechanisms for financing health care. The prominence of this subject is attributable both to the variety of programs that address this issue and to the fact that for many older persons, their single greatest fear is becoming impoverished by rising health care costs. The first of these chapters deals with Medicare, the Federal program that pays for hospital care and physician expenditures, as frequently supplemented by privately insured "Medigap" policies. The second chapter considers the joint Federal and state medical care program for the poor, Medicaid. Most older persons are not poor, of course, but many are and still others become poor as medical costs not otherwise covered gradually consume their resources. Medicaid is not restricted to older persons, although the largest portion of Medicaid's expenditures is attributable to older claimants. The final chapter in this sequence deals with the phenomenon of private insurance to cover long-term custodial care—a newer development that responds to Medicare's omissions while seeking to avoid Medicaid's deficiencies regarding this important, and costly, aspect of medical care.

Most long-term care is provided in nursing homes. While paying for such care is a prime consideration, the nursing home setting also poses a variety of legal issues relating to admission contracts and criteria, rights of patients, responsibilities of the institution to the patient, and liability for mistreatment. Those issues are addressed in Chapter 7, which also considers a similar but less medically intensive alternative—assisted living facilities.

Next is an overview of other housing alternatives. These alternatives include so-called "continuing care retirement communities," subsidized older-adult apartments, reverse mortgages, and other means of utilizing the equity of older homeowners in their existing residences. The Federal tax consequences of these arrangements are considered here as well, including the sale of the older person's home.

Then follows two chapters dealing with how individuals can control their financial affairs. Few matters are more sensitive to older people and have a greater impact on their sense of well-being than the day-to-day control of their assets. For individuals who are unable to handle these matters, the state can appoint a guardian or conservator to fulfill this function, although the person appointed, the process involved, and the procedures required may not necessarily accord with any particular older person's preferences. Chapter 9 describes the guardianship process, while Chapter 10 considers the major alternatives available to those who can plan ahead of necessity—including joint tenancy, durable powers of attorney, and revocable (or "living") trusts.

The next sequence of chapters focuses on issues of older persons' income. Chapter 11 examines Social Security benefits and their taxability. These benefits, as adjusted for early or delayed retirement, and as modified when a retiree continues to work after retirement, comprise the major source of income for over a third of older Americans. The next two chapters deal with other categories of public benefits—namely, Supplemental Security Income (in Chapter 12), and veterans' benefits (in Chapter 13). The final chapter in this sequence considers pension plan benefits, their common payout options, and their Federal income tax treatment.

Many older people seek additional income by working. When these people face discrimination by potential employers because of their age, securing employment may be quite difficult. The remedies that are provided by the Age Discrimination in Employment Act are the focus of Chapter 15.

This book's final chapter deals with elder abuse and neglect, the statutory response, and the various agencies that try to deal with this phenomenon.

None of the chapters in this book purports to be a definitive exposition of the subject covered. Nor does this book attempt to examine every possible "elder law" subtopic. Consumer fraud, for example, is not discussed herein, even though victims of such fraud are disproportionately older persons. The legal elements of proving such claims, however, are the same as for younger victims.

Similarly, Federal income tax ramifications for older taxpayers are not considered in any systematic fashion. Tax consequences of certain topics are, however, considered in connection with their basic coverage; e.g., deductibility of long-term care insurance premiums (Chapter 6), sale of a principal residence (Chapter 8), Social Security benefits (Chapter 11), and pension plan distributions (Chapter 14). But no attempt is made to catalog every income tax provision that might be of specific interest to older persons.

Finally, this book does not discuss estate planning in any real depth or Federal estate tax minimization at all. In part, this omission reflects the fact that fewer than 1% of decedents owe any Federal estate tax. But it also reflects the focus of elder law on maximizing the comfort of, and control by, the older person as he or she lives longer, rather than the tax burden faced by that person's heirs. The reader is referred to the separate titles in this Nutshell series for "Estate Planning" and "Federal Estate and Gift Taxation" when information on those topics is desired.

CHAPTER 2

ETHICAL CONSIDERATIONS IN DEALING WITH OLDER CLIENTS

§ 2.1 Ethics in Context

In elder law, most of a lawyer's ethical considerations revolve around two critical questions: who is the client, and is the client competent? Each of these questions, in turn, has particular facets. For example, identifying the client may have implications regarding the lawyer's duty to preserve confidentiality, the lawyer's duty to avoid conflicts of interest, and even from whom the lawyer may receive payment of his or her fees. Similarly, questions of client competence will determine whether communication difficulties preclude the creation of a lawyer-client relationship, or may limit the scope of permissible actions that may be implemented by the client.

Of course, many of these concerns are endemic to any type of legal practice that involves individuals as clients. Nevertheless, the nature of elder law—with its specific focus on *older* individuals—seems to make these concerns particularly problematic. For example, older persons generally do not meet with an attorney by themselves. More typically, a

8

spouse, an adult child, a friend, or a neighbor accompanies them. The question then becomes what role do these people play in the deliberations of the lawyer and the older person. Similarly, although the law presumes that all adults have sufficient decisionmaking capacity, older adults are peculiarly susceptible to certain age-related diseases that can limit, or even eliminate, the ability to function as clients and to transact legal business. Thus, this Chapter considers some of the ethical considerations that have particular significance when the client in question is an older person.

§ 2.2 Who Is the Client

A central question in elder law is identification of the client. It is to the client, after all, that the attorney owes the various obligations imposed by the Model Rules of Professional Conduct. For example, a lawyer "shall act with reasonable diligence and promptness in representing *a client*." Rule 1.3 (emphasis supplied). Similarly, a lawyer must "reasonably consult with *the client* about the means by which *the client's* objectives are to be accomplished" and must "keep *the client* reasonably informed about the status of the matter." Rule 1.4(a)(2), (3) (emphasis supplied). Finally, a lawyer "shall not reveal information relating to representation of *a client* unless *the client* gives informed consent." Rule 1.6(a) (emphasis supplied). Thus, a clear determination of who is the client is imperative in avoiding, or at least minimizing, ethical difficulties.

As a general proposition, the older person is the client, because it is that person's situation that is being addressed. Accordingly, it is to the older person that an elder law attorney owes the above-delineated duties of diligence, communication, and confidentiality. Yet, older persons often appear before a lawyer in the company of some other person. Is this other person there simply to physically transport the older person to the lawyer's office? Or is this person there to translate or explain what is going on to the older person? Alternatively, the other person might be there as a co-owner of properties being discussed, or as the likely designee of some contemplated decisionmaking proxy. Perhaps, the person is there as the older person's caregiver or as a source of moral or financial support. The precise role that this person plays, therefore, must be determined in setting the limits of the lawyer's interaction with that person.

This inquiry is necessitated, in part, by a lawyer's duty of loyalty to the client. That is, a lawyer may not generally represent someone whose interests conflict with the older person's interests. And yet, this precept seems somewhat contrived in an elder law context, where the older person's family is often very supportive, cohesive, and motivated by honorable intentions.

Although the Model Rules do not contemplate "the family" as a client, they do permit representation of multiple persons, or even multiple generations, as long as there is no "concurrent" conflict of interests. If there is such a conflict, the lawyer may represent the client, but only when "the lawyer reasonably believes that the lawyer will be able to provide competent and diligent representation to each affected client," and each client gives "informed consent, confirmed in writing." Rule 1.7(b)(1), (4). In this regard, the official commentary to this Rule requires a lawyer to consider whether a potential conflict of interest will "materially interfere with the lawyer's independent professional judgment" in proposing alternative courses of action. Comment 8 to Rule 1.7.

One solution is disclosure. In fact, the official commentary explains that the reason a client's consent must be confirmed in writing is "to impress upon clients the seriousness of the decision the client is being asked to make." Comment 20 to Rule 1.7. Similarly, a lawyer may represent the older person even though the legal costs are being paid by someone else, if the older person is so informed and consents. Rule 1.8(f)(1). But the lawyer must also determine that this payment arrangement will not interfere "with the lawyer's independence of professional judgment or with the client-lawyer relationship." Rule 1.8(f)(2).

Such situations, however, are inevitably fraught with difficulty. For example, if Mother creates a joint bank account with Son to facilitate his handling of her financial affairs, her plan to split her estate between Son and Daughter may be jeopardized by Son's ability to drain the account for his own benefit.

Moreover, the possibility of "undue influence" must always be considered. Does Mother really want to make Son a co-signer on her bank account, or is this arrangement primarily Son's idea? If Mother is currently living in Son's home, there is a further likelihood that Son is overreaching, or pressuring Mother, into adding his name to her account. In such circumstances, overt threats are often unnecessary. Ongoing behavior patterns may be sufficient to manifest undue influence, or even abuse in extreme situations. Such considerations cannot be easily disregarded, even when their detection is difficult.

Virtually any multi-generational representation, or multi-person representation even within the same generation, can create dilemmas like those described above. In such circumstances, an attorney might consider withdrawing from the engagement. The Model Rules, however, also require that withdrawal not have a "material adverse effect" on the interests of the family members involved. Rule 1.16(b)(1).

These ethical dilemmas rarely admit to fully satisfactory solutions, and efforts to make the legal profession's ethical guidelines more responsive to the type of family situations encountered in elder law still have a way to go.

§ 2.3   Client Competency

Once the older person is identified as a client, the question of legal capacity must be considered. In fact, the lawyer may not be able to establish a lawyer-client relationship if the older person does not have sufficient legal capacity. The ability of the putative client to understand what is being discussed, to comprehend the need for a particular document, and to understand its general operation is essential if that document is to have any legal effect. Such is the case whether the instrument is a living will, a health care proxy, a durable power of attorney, joint ownership of property, a transfer of assets, or a contract. Without the requisite legal capacity, much of the planning that elder law might involve is simply not available, and guardianship must be considered. See generally Chapter 9.

The law's general presumption of client competency may be inaccurate in many common situations involving older clients. When adult children or a worried spouse bring an older person to the lawyer, they often are doing so because of some observed events or behaviors that suggest—to them at least—a decline in mental faculties. Such non-clinical observations are not determinative, of course, but they raise the question of requisite legal capacity.

In an elder law context particularly, capacity must be understood as not simply a yes-or-no question. Some clients may be losing capacity slowly, but irreversibly, due to a degenerative illness like Alzheimer's disease. Others may be depressed because of a natural decline in certain mental capabilities—like recognizing faces or associating names with faces—but still have more than enough competency to satisfy legal standards. Still others may experience periods of lucidity and relative confusion, such periods lasting for days at a time, or alternatively, for certain parts of the day. Mornings, for example, may be a time of maximum understanding. Still other clients might be the unwitting victims of less than optimal combinations of medications. Altering dosages or providing substitutes may reduce or even eliminate the confusion that is raising questions of legal competency.

In any case, determining a client's capacity is not easy. There is no standardized procedure or even a universally accepted definition. Some attorneys rely on their personal observation of the older person plus comments from those who spend time with the older individual. Such comments can be biased, however, by various factors including possible financial gain. Moreover, legal incompetency must be distinguished from a pattern of making decisions that the lawyer believes are unwise or inappropriate. Legal capacity, in this sense, is not the same as rationality determined according to an attorney's predilections. While bizarre or inexplicable behavior is often interpreted as evidence of diminished capacity, eccentricity is not the same as incompetency. To be sure, in practice, the dividing line may be exceedingly difficult to draw.

On this point, the official commentary to the Model Rules merely admonishes lawyers to "consider and balance such factors as: the client's ability to articulate reasoning leading to a decision, variability of state of mind and ability to appreciate consequences of a decision; the substantive fairness of a decision; and the consistency of a decision with the known long-term commitments and values of the client." Comment 6 to Rule 1.14.

To avoid such an impressionistic approach, some lawyers prefer to administer simple "mental status" examinations that test a person's attention span, memory recall, elementary reading and writing skills, and language comprehension. Other lawyers, finding such examinations either degrading to the examinees or beyond the scope of their training to interpret, prefer to have mental health professionals assess the older person's mental capacity. Indeed, the official commentary to the Model Rules indicates that a lawyer "may seek guidance from an appropriate diagnostician." Comment 6 to Rule 1.14. This approach is no panacea, however, since a medical diagnosis of "dementia" can vary enormously, depending upon the particular diagnostic methodology being used. Given the pivotal significance of legal capacity, such variation in determining its presence or absence can be very discomforting to a lawyer faced with a possibly impaired client.

In part, this discomfort is attributable to the fact that legal capacity itself is not a single standard. The ability to understand a situation, make choices, and communicate those choices will vary with the importance of the legal task one is asked to do. The capacity needed to reinvest dividends is quite different from the capacity required to make a will, to execute a limited power of attorney dealing with Federal tax matters, or to designate a proxy for deciding the extent of life-extending medical care that will be provided. See Comment 1 to Rule 1.14 regarding the handling of "routine financial matters."

Lawyers sometimes alter their practice styles to maximize older clients' capacity. Some techniques include having shorter meetings rather than lengthy client conferences, preparing documents in larger type, reducing ambient noise and background glare, facing the client during interviews, and speaking more slowly than usual. Others use open-ended questions, rather than questions that require only "yes" or "no" answers. Videotaping is more controversial, with proponents and detractors equally confident of their position's merits.

Some circumstances require more drastic measures. The Model Rules direct that a lawyer "may take reasonably necessary protective action" for a client with "diminished capacity" who is "at risk of substantial physical, financial or other harm." Rule 1.14(b). Such action might include petitioning a court for the appointment of a "conservator or guardian." In this connection, the Model Rules provide that a lawyer may reveal information about the client that would otherwise be confidential, "but only to the extent reasonably necessary to protect the client's interests." Rule 1.14(c).

Guardianship is not the only alternative, and the official commentary to the Model Rules recognizes that appointing a guardian "may be more expensive or traumatic for the client than circumstances in fact require." Comment 7 to Rule 1.14. Instead, a lawyer is advised to consult with family members, support groups, or adult protective services. Comment 5 to Rule 1.14. See § 16.8 regarding those services. As one might suspect, "the lawyer's position in such cases is an unavoidably difficult one." Comment 8 to Rule 1.14.

Alternatively, a lawyer might simply follow the client's instructions, as long as this action does not harm any other person or that client's interests. While this approach appears to place great value on a client's autonomy, a truly incompetent client has little autonomy in the usual sense of that word. The Model Rules, after all, direct the attorney to take "protective action" when the client "cannot adequately act" in his or her own interest. Rule 1.14(b).

In any case, the Model Rules instruct the lawyer to "as far as reasonably possible, maintain a normal client-lawyer relationship." Rule 1.14(a). But in an emergency when a person's "health, safety, or a financial interest . . . is threatened with imminent and irreparable harm," a lawyer may act on that person's behalf, even though that person is "unable to establish a client-lawyer relationship." Comment 9 to Rule 1.14. Nevertheless, the lawyer can act "only to the extent reasonably necessary to maintain the status quo or otherwise avoid imminent and irreparable harm." Comment 9 to Rule 1.14.

CHAPTER 3

HEALTH CARE DECISIONMAKING

§ 3.1 The Doctrine of Informed Consent

Patients have the right to control their medical treatment. In consultation with their physician, they can determine the course of their medical care, choose the kind of treatment they wish and correspondingly refuse treatment they do not want. Of course, if the patient requests treatment that the medical personnel consider inappropriate, it may not be provided. Nevertheless, for the most part, patients can initiate care and refuse it.

The right of patients to control their medical care arises from the doctrine of informed consent, which has as its goal patient autonomy and self-determination. Personal autonomy reflects individuals' ability to control their own bodies and is an essential component of personal liberty. To be autonomous, individuals must be able to freely control their bodies by having the right to initiate or refuse medical care treatment.

Merely having the right to control treatment decisions is not sufficient, however. To make a meaningful decision, the patient must have enough information to understand the consequences of the decision, its risks and benefits, and the possible alternatives. This then is the essence of the doctrine of informed consent: the patient must be provided with sufficient information to be able to give meaningful consent to proposed medical care.

a.   Development of Case Law

The common law doctrine of informed consent arose in the 1914 New York case of *Schloendorff v. Society of N.Y. Hospital* (N.Y.1914) in which Justice Cardozo wrote: "Every human being of adult years and sound mind has a right to determine what shall be done with his own body; and a surgeon who performs an operation without his patient's consent commits an assault." Over time this requirement became known as "informed consent" and was gradually adopted by every state through common law or by statute.

Several state courts have decided that the informed consent doctrine is constitutional and foundational. Relying upon prior United States Supreme Court's decisions, courts have concluded that the Federal constitutional right of privacy means that individuals must be allowed to control their own bodies and, therefore, their medical treatment. The first state to so hold was New Jersey in 1976 in the *Matter of Quinlan* (N.J.1976). In 1990 the United States Supreme Court implied in *Cruzan v. Director, Missouri Dept. of Health* (S.Ct.1990) that the United States Constitution may grant an individual a constitutionally protected right to refuse life-saving treatment. To date, however, the Supreme

Court has yet to hold that informed consent is constitutionally guaranteed. However, several state constitutions specifically protect the right of privacy. In these states, individuals enjoy state constitutional protection of the right of informed consent.

Enforcement of the doctrine of informed consent rests upon the patient's right to sue a physician or other medical care provider who fails to obtain the patient's consent prior to providing medical treatment. A physician who provides medical care to a patient who has not given consent may be guilty of assault and battery or medical malpractice.

The need for informed consent is not absolute. It gives way in the case of an emergency if the patient is incapable of giving consent or receiving information and yet is in serious danger and need of immediate care. In such cases the doctrine does not apply. For example, when an individual is brought to the hospital directly from an auto accident unable to communicate, the hospital can take action to stabilize the patient even without consent from the patient or, for that matter, anyone else. Under these conditions the patient's consent is said to be "implied," but it is probably more accurate simply to admit that there is no need for consent in an emergency situation in which a delay in treatment could either endanger the patient's life or result in serious bodily harm.

Informed consent is also waived if the physician invokes "privilege" based upon the belief that the disclosure of the information necessary to obtain consent would so upset the patient that he or she would be unable to make a rational decision. This exception is increasingly narrowly interpreted. It cannot be used, for example, to justify not telling a patient of a fatal diagnosis even though such information naturally would be upsetting. Patients may also waive the right to informed consent by telling the physician that they do not want to hear anymore about their treatment and prefer to let the physician make the treatment decisions. However, physicians generally prefer to involve patients in decisionmaking and often attempt to override expressions of refusal to participate.

b. *The Right of a Competent Patient to Die*

One of the more thorny questions in medicine is to what extent a competent individual can refuse medical treatment even if it means death. Though the state has an interest in its citizens' continued lives, no state has a law against suicide. Still, courts recognize that the state has an interest in protecting the health, safety and welfare of its citizens. The question is: how to balance the state's interest in life against the individual's right of personal autonomy?

The classic statement of the state interest in its citizens' lives arose in the 1977 Massachusetts case, *Superintendent of Belchertown State School v. Saikewicz* (Mass.1977). The court listed four state interests: 1) the state's general interest in the preservation of life; 2) the protection of the interests of innocent third parties, in particular minor children;

3) the prevention of suicide; and 4) the maintenance of the ethical integrity of the medical profession. This exposition of the state's interests is routinely cited by other courts, although it has rarely been invoked to deny an individual's right to refuse medical care.

It is generally accepted that a competent adult may refuse medical treatment even if that decision results in death. Absent some special circumstances, the countervailing state interests are not sufficient to warrant overturning the patient's autonomous decision. Courts have come to recognize that a competent patient's refusal to accept life-sustaining medical treatment or to request that such treatment be terminated does not constitute suicide, because death comes as a result of the disease, not because of a self-inflicted injury. A refusal to consent to medical treatment is not suicide, because an individual is under no obligation to prevent the natural course of illness even if it might result in death. Several of the cases that have permitted patients to terminate their medical care involved patients suffering from amyotrophic lateral sclerosis (commonly known as ALS or Lou Gehrig's disease). ALS affects the nerve responses to muscles and gradually results in total paralysis, respiratory failure, and death. An individual suffering from this disease in some cases prefers to avoid its final stages and therefore refuses intervening medical treatment even though that will hasten death. Courts have agreed that such a decision is protected under the rubric of the informed consent doctrine.

§ 3.2   The Mentally Incapacitated Patient

Some elderly patients suffer from diminished mental capacity and so are unable to give informed consent to medical treatment decisions. This brings up two questions. First, how do we determine who is incapacitated or put another way, how do we determine who is capable of giving informed consent? Second, who makes decisions for an incapacitated patient who is unable to give informed consent?

Mental competency, or as it is increasingly known, mental capacity, is a legal term that refers to the capability of an individual to make a reasonable decision based upon an understanding of reality. The law presumes that all adults are competent, a presumption can only be rebutted by clear and convincing evidence of a lack of mental capacity. Competency is situational, however, and so the degree of mental capacity required for legal competence depends on the proposed act. For example, a relatively low level of competency is required for someone to create a valid will. Greater capacity may be required to grant informed consent to medical care. Conversely, a person might be considered too incapacitated to handle his or her investments, but still have sufficient capacity to give consent to medical care.

The capacity required to give informed consent depends upon how well the individual can function in the particular setting. Individuals react differently based upon the decision to be made and their own relative level of capacity. At the extreme, an unconscious patient will have absolutely no capacity. Absent a comatose state, however, almost every individual possesses some level of comprehension and ability to communicate. The question arises whether that level of comprehension is sufficient to participate in the proposed medical treatment decision. The answer is not easy, and it is difficult to give general rules. In order to give informed consent, the individual must understand the supplied information, comprehend the consequences of acting on that information, be able to assess the relative benefits and dangers of the proposed action, and be able to provide a meaningful response to the question of what should be done. (For a discussion of mental capacity, see § 2.3, Client Competency.)

In assessing capacity, the fact finder must determine whether the patient has the mental ability to make a choice that is based either on rational reasons or on personal, though generally accepted, values. The individual's decision should be based upon an appreciation of reality and not be a consequence of phobia, panic, depression or a reaction to medicine. For example, a patient who believes that the physician is an agent of the devil is not competent to give informed consent. Conversely, a patient who refuses to consent to an operation because he or she believes that the physician is inept does not demonstrate a lack of capacity even if mistaken about the physician's capabilities.

Patients also must be capable of understanding information: they need sufficient capacity to understand what they are told. For example, suppose a physician tells her patient that he is suffering from a tumor pressing against his brain. If the patient cannot understand what the term "tumor" means, if the words simply have no meaning for him, no informed consent is possible. It is difficult to state how much the patient must understand of the proposed course of action. Ideally the patient would have a sophisticated understanding of what is being proposed and what would happen if the physician's recommendation were not followed. Realistically, many patients lack the ability to weigh the relative costs and benefits of the proposed medical treatment. Given the stress and confusion that often surround medical decisions, it is highly probable that even competent patients often understand only the larger issues and fail to grasp the details of what is being proposed.

§ 3.3 Surrogate Decisionmaking for the Incapacitated Patient

a. *Use of Guardians*

The doctrine of informed consent requires that for every patient there must be a decisionmaker. Normally that would be the patient who, in consultation with the medical provider, determines the course of treatment. However, if the individual is unable to grant consent because of a lack of capacity, an alternate decisionmaker must be identified. There are several ways of achieving that. The formal solution requires that a guardian be appointed. (Guardianship is fully discussed in Chapter 9.)

Upon the filing of a guardianship petition with the appropriate court, a hearing is held to determine whether the patient is legally incapacitated. If the individual is found to be incapacitated, the court will appoint a guardian of the person to make medical decision treatments for the incapacitated person.

In most cases the guardian will be able to make all decisions required, but occasionally a guardian will be called upon to make a medical treatment decision for which the guardian believes court guidance or prior approval is necessitated. For example, if a guardian has to make a determination to terminate life-sustaining treatment, the guardian may believe it prudent to go to the court for approval. Whether such prior approval is necessary will depend upon the law of the particular jurisdiction.

For the great majority of situations, however, the guardian will make decisions on behalf of the incapacitated person without specific court guidance or approval. The guardian's decisions are imputed to the incapacitated person so that, in effect, he or she continues to control medical decisions, albeit through the use of a guardian. Thus, the doctrine of informed consent continues to be honored, although the consent comes from the guardian on behalf of the incapacitated person.

Often no formal guardianship is sought even though the patient is incapacitated. Instead, family members make medical treatment decisions for an incapacitated spouse or relative. Spouses commonly grant approval for medical treatment of their husband or wife without any legal justification for doing so. Similarly, parents often decide for adult incapacitated children and, conversely, adult children make decisions for incapacitated older parents. Whether such an informal arrangement will suffice depends upon the medical provider. Technically these informal arrangements have no standing, and, therefore, the medical provider is acting without informed consent. Some physicians and hospitals are willing to act in consultation with the family, but some medical providers are reluctant to accede to such informal arrangements. They therefore require that surrogate decisionmakers have a legal basis for their involvement such as having been appointed as guardian or appointed as the surrogate health care decisionmaker in an advance health care directive.

b.   *Advance Health Care Directives*

The term, advance health care directive, refers to written directives that give direction or guidance as to an individual's future medical care in the event of mental incapacity. The term can apply either to attempts to specifically state the kind of treatment the patient wishes to have, or it can refer to an attempt to appoint a surrogate decisionmaker who will have a greater or lesser amount of discretion as to the form of health care to be given to the maker of the directive. Some directives do both; not only do they provide specific instructions as to health care under certain circumstances, they also appoint a surrogate decisionmaker to act as to health care decisions not governed by the directive.

Advance care directives come in a variety of forms, some quite specific, others very general and vague. Some follow state statutes, others are the creation of a lawyer or even by individuals themselves. The validity of these documents and the interpretation, of course, depends upon state law and the response of courts. But even more importantly, the effect they have will depend upon the medical care provider and the friends and family of the patient. If those concerned with the patient's well-being wish to follow the advance directive, the courts will probably not be resorted to. On the other hand, if everyone concerned decides not to follow the directive, then the court may never learn of the refusal to follow the instructions. Courts generally only hear those cases where there has been a disagreement, either within the family or between the family or caregiver and the health care provider.

Despite the widespread availability of statutory created advance directives, many individuals fail to create them. In response, many states have passed surrogate decision making statutes, many modeled on the Uniform Health Care Decisions Act—these state laws identify who may make health care decisions for incapacitated patients who have not previously appointed a surrogate. The statutes contain a list that creates an order of priority of those persons who may act as surrogate decisionmakers in regard to medical treatment decisions. These, in effect, are "statutory created advance directives," which automatically take effect without prior court approval. Generally these laws name the spouse as the initial surrogate with adult children next, followed by more distant relatives and friends. Beyond spouses and children, state statutes vary considerably in the order of priority and whether the statute lists individuals, such as domestic partners, as surrogates.

Typically, the state law requires the surrogate to act in a manner consistent with how the patient would have behaved in the circumstances, that is, a substitute judgement standard. A few states permit the surrogate to employ a best interests test, that is, do what is best for the patient, particularly if the desires of the patient are not well enough known to employ substitute judgement.

Finally, in all states, individuals have the right to create a "living will." Unfortunately named, the document represents the right of an individual to give instructions as to how they should be treated in the event that they become terminally ill or in a permanently unconscious state.

§ 3.4 Living Wills

The term "living will" or, as it is probably better called, "natural death instructions," is a document by which individuals attempt to control their medical care in the event that they become mentally incapacitated. Living wills usually contain treatment instructions in the event the individual becomes either terminally ill or is in a persistent vegetative state (permanently unconscious). The living will explains the type of medical care desired by the individual, and under what condition life-sustaining treatment should be initiated or discontinued.

Every state has a statute that provides for living wills, the first being passed in 1976 in California. Living will legislation was a response to the concern as to whether individuals would dictate their health care treatment after the onset of incapacity. The living will laws respond to individuals' desire to avoid life-sustaining treatment where it would be hopeless, which might be the case if they are terminally ill or in a persistent vegetative state. In theory, the laws also permit a living will to state an individual's desire for continued treatment, but in an overwhelming number of cases individuals use the document to request termination of treatment under appropriate conditions.

Although state laws differ, certain factors are true for any living will. First, it applies only in situations in which the individual becomes incapacitated. As long as an individual is competent to participate in their health care decisionmaking, the living will has no authority. Second, living wills are designed to control health care decisionmaking in the future. That is, they are documents that are signed today, but take effect only upon the onset of incapacity. Third, although the statutes vary greatly, all purport to permit a declarant to terminate life-sustaining treatment in the case of terminal illness or persistent vegetative state.

a. Contents

A living will should contain two essential elements. First, a statement that if incapacity occurs, the instructions in the document should determine the form of treatment provided. Second, the living will should state under what conditions life-sustaining treatment should be terminated. Usually this will be in the case of a terminal illness or persistent vegetative state.

Living wills are not designed as total health care decisionmaking documents. Under most statutes, they apply only to the special conditions of terminal illness or persistent vegetative state. If an individual has hope for recovery, the living will is generally not applicable. Whether individuals can direct that life-sustaining treatment be terminated if they are under conditions not terminal or not in a persistent vegetative state is not clear. Almost no living will statute expressly permits termination of life-sustaining treatment under conditions other than terminal illness or persistent vegetative state. Nevertheless, many commentators believe that the statutory limits are not the constitutional limits for health care decisionmaking. Since individuals, as long as they have capacity, can refuse life-sustaining treatment, it is argued that the onset of incapacity should not terminate this constitutional right. Therefore, it is maintained by many that an individual who clearly expresses a wish in the event of incapacity to permit his or her surrogate the authority to terminate life-sustaining treatment must have those wishes respected and obeyed.

b. Terminal Illness

Even the permitted condition, "terminally ill," can pose difficulties. In most states the term is defined as a situation in which the patient will die "shortly" regardless of the continuation of medical treatment. These statutes envision a situation very close to end of life, the idea being that if patients are soon to die, they may request that their treatment be terminated and that no additional treatment be instituted. In lay persons' terms this is often referred to as "pulling the plug."

Other state statutes are less clear in defining the term terminal. Some require death to be imminent, and a few even define it to mean that death will occur within a certain number of days. Whether any physician can make such a precise prediction is unclear. For example, an individual may be suffering from irreversible cancer, yet no physician can be certain that death will occur within x number of days. If the statute requires that medical treatment must be provided unless death is expected to occur shortly, aggressive life-sustaining treatment may continue to be provided, even though the patient's condition is hopeless, merely because no one can accurately predict death. Most commentators and most patients would prefer the word terminal to be given a more open meaning. They would prefer to terminate life-sustaining treatment for an incapacitated patient who is certain to die even if death itself is not imminent. Many patients would prefer to terminate life-sustaining treatment prior to the time that the statute might allow. Whether an individual can write a valid living will that permits termination prior to the time specified in the statute is unclear. If the right to die is a constitutional right, presumably that right supersedes state statutes. Conversely, if the state can statutorily define the right to die, the statute might be held to be enforceable despite explicit patient wishes to the contrary.

c. *Persistent Vegetative State*

The requirement that the patient be terminally ill does not cover the situation of an individual in a persistent vegetative state because individuals in that condition can survive for years. Unlike the phrase "terminally ill," a persistent vegetative state has a precise meaning. It results from a partial death of the brain and differs from a coma from which a patient can awake. Because brain cells cannot regenerate, an individual in a persistent vegetative state will never recover and will remain in that state until death. The only issue is the adequate identification of the condition. Generally, the diagnosis requires days, if not weeks to pass before the patient is considered to be in a persistent vegetative state. Once the physician is satisfied that the patient is in a persistent vegetative state or permanently unconscious (the terms have the same meaning), many statutes permit the living will to take effect, and no further life-sustaining treatment need be provided if that is what the patient requested in the living will.

Termination of life-sustaining treatment for patients in a persistent vegetative state often means removing them from a ventilator or respirator or not treating them with antibiotics. In many cases this will cause the death of the patient. However, not all patients in a persistent vegetative state require a ventilator, many are able to breath on their own. But they are fed through artificial tubes inserted either through the nose or directly through the stomach wall (nasogastric tube or gastrostomy). If kept on a feeding tube, individuals in a persistent vegetative state may survive for months or even years totally unaware of their surroundings and impervious to pain. Whether the patient can request in the living will that artificial nutrition and hydration be terminated in the event of his or her being in a persistent vegetative state depends on state law. Most states permit such termination under a living will. (See discussion in "e. Termination of Artificial Nutrition and Hydration" below.)

Some patients would also like the living will to take effect if they have a serious mental incapacity, such as Alzheimer's Disease, but which itself is not terminal. If an intervening illness occurs, they would prefer not to be treated for that intervening illness, since they are already irrevocably incapacitated from Alzheimer's. For example, an individual who is mentally incapacitated because of severe Alzheimer's comes down with a form of operable cancer. Prior to the incapacity, the patient stated that he would prefer to die from the intervening cancer, with appropriate pain relief, rather than being treated, only to sink even deeper into the depths of dementia caused by the Alzheimer's. Unfortunately, state statutes do not explicitly permit termination of health care under such circumstances. It is therefore not clear whether a court would necessarily honor such a request inserted into a living will.

d. Brain Death

If the degree of mental incapacity is severe enough, the individual is considered clinically dead. Because death is a definitional reality and not an actual description of a biological event, what constitutes death has changed over time. In the past, a finding of death was linked to the cessation of the individual's circulation and respiration. Persons who ceased to breathe were considered to be dead. This was known as a systemic definition of death, one that did not concern itself with the fact that, though circulation and respiration may cease, other biological activity may continue. Conversely, even though circulation continues, the individual's brain may be dead. The introduction of artificial ventilators and respirators further complicates the problem because respiration can be continued almost indefinitely. With the continuation of respiration, circulation continues and so an individual technically would be considered alive regardless of the amount of brain damage.

In order to deal with the issue of individuals who have suffered massive, irreversible brain damage and yet who can be maintained on a respirator, the concept of "brain death" was fashioned. Today, every state has statutorily adopted a definition of death that includes brain death. The Uniform Definition of Death Act (UDDA) defines brain death as the "irreversible cessation of all functions of the entire brain, including the brain stem." UDDA, 12 U.L.A. 292. Brain death is determined by a flat electroencephalogram (EEG).

Brain death is now considered to be the functional equivalent of death. If a patient is brain dead, artificial respiration is turned off because there is no reason to continue health treatment for a deceased individual. Brain death is different from a persistent vegetative state. The latter involves the partial death of the brain, generally the higher or cerebral regions that control consciousness, voluntary actions and some involuntary responses. This is in contrast to the brain stem that controls the vegetative functions such as breathing and other involuntary biological activity. An individual who is in a persistent vegetative state has suffered the death of the upper cerebral hemispheres, but the brain stem has remained intact and is functioning. The individual is not brain dead because the entire brain has not died, though the condition is permanent and irreversible.

e. *Termination of Artificial Nutrition and Hydration*

A serious issue that arises with living wills is whether the document can call for the termination of artificial nutrition and hydration. Individuals who are in a persistent vegetative state require tube feedings either through the nose or through insertion directly into the stomach. Terminating life support systems in the case of these individuals often means the termination of artificial nutrition and hydration, which is considered a form of medical treatment according to the American Medical Association. (Several courts have also concurred that nutrition and hydration are medical treatment and thus come within the purview of an informed consent doctrine.) Nevertheless, some state statutes do not permit the termination of artificial hydration and nutrition despite such an instruction in a living will. The enforceability of such statutes is not clear. If artificial nutrition and hydration are a form of medical treatment, it would seem that a patient can request their termination under the appropriate conditions.

Some state statutes are silent as to the issue and leave the decision to be resolved by the courts. Increasingly, however, individuals and legislators have come to recognize that the termination of hydration and nutrition is an option that should be allowed to the patient. Most state statutes and court decisions permit termination of artificial hydration and nutrition if the patient has clearly evidenced a desire that it be done. Even if the state statute denies the right, the courts may overrule the statute and permit termination on the theory that the state has no authority to force medical treatment upon an unwilling patient.

The courts often require "clear and convincing" evidence of the patient's intent before permitting termination of life-sustaining treatment and, in particular, the termination of artificial nutrition and hydration. A living will can provide the necessary evidence of such intent, but it need not be the only source of such evidence. Other forms of written intent and even oral statements may be sufficient to allow termination of life-sustaining treatment. Still, where states permit the use of a living will it is advisable to create a written document that declares the individual's attitudes towards when and if termination of life support is appropriate. Whether that document must meet the formal requirements of a living will to be effective is less clear. Presumably, if the writing clearly shows the patient's intent, it may be sufficient to permit the patient's wishes to be carried out.

f. Formalities of Execution

Because a living will is a formal legal document, state laws require it to meet certain formal requirements. At a minimum, the document must be in writing and signed by the patient. Most statutes require the document to be witnessed, and many require notarization. Individuals who have a conflict of interest such as spouses, potential heirs, or even an attending physician are usually barred from acting as witnesses. Some states bar employees of health care facilities from witnessing living wills. A few states have special rules if the patient is in a medical institution such as a nursing home. For example, in California, if the declarant lives in a skilled nursing home, the living will must be witnessed by a patient advocate or state ombudsman.

Many state living will statutes contain a model form, and a few states require that the model form be used. Usually, however, use of the statutory model form is optional.

g. *Duration of a Directive*

A few states have statutes that cause the living wills to automatically terminate after a given number of years. In the great majority of states, however, living wills remain valid until specifically revoked. Individuals can terminate a living will at any time. Most states are very liberal in the manner which it can be revoked. Physical destruction, cancellation, written revocation and most importantly, verbal revocation are all effective. The revocation is effective upon notification to the physician. Almost any statement will suffice to revoke a living will. Subsequent inconsistent statements or instructions will be considered to overrule or at least supersede a living will. A few states even permit incapacitated individuals to revoke prior living wills, although the logic of this is not apparent. What is apparent is that most states are very concerned that individuals not be bound by a living will if they should have a change of mind.

h. *Validity in Other Jurisdictions*

It is not always clear whether a living will valid in State A is necessarily valid in State B. Unfortunately, there is no general reciprocity for recognizing out-of-state living wills. State A can require that a living will meet State A's requirements before State A will recognize the validity of the living will. Individuals who anticipate spending any amount of time in more than one state should create separate living wills to meet the requirement of each state.

i.   *Living Wills are Valid and Operative Only if Communicated to the Attending Physician*

The Federal Patient Self–Determination Act of 1990 requires hospitals and nursing homes to advise patients upon admission of their rights under state law to refuse medical treatment. As a practical matter, hospitals now routinely provide living wills or advance health care directives to their patients. Nevertheless, in theory, it is the patients' obligation to inform the medical provider if they have signed a living will.

State laws provide legal immunity to health care providers who follow the instructions of a living will. They cannot be subject to either civil or criminal liability for following a valid, unrevoked declaration even if they permit a patient to die. Many states provide rights for physicians or other health care providers who for reasons of conscience cannot effectuate the living will's directive to discontinue treatment. Generally these statutes require that the patient be transferred to a different facility or to a different physician who will carry out the instructions contained in the living will.

Few states provide any significant penalties for failure to obey a living will. There may be civil liability and a few states provide criminal penalties, but the enforcement of these provisions is seemingly nonexistent to date.

Although legal documents, living wills are rarely the subject of litigation. For the most part they are used by the spouse, family or friends of an incapacitated patient to help determine what course of medical action should be taken. Whether the instructions in living wills are actually followed is unknown. If a living will is ignored and life-sustaining treatment is continued in opposition to the patient's wishes, probably no one will ever know. Conversely, even if the document is somehow flawed procedurally, it may nevertheless be used by the family and physician to determine treatment. Again, if no one complains about the course of action, the lack of legal validity of the document is irrelevant.

§ 3.5   Advance Health Care Directive

In addition to or in lieu of a living will, patients increasingly are executing advance health care directives, sometimes known as health care proxies or durable powers of attorney for health care. These documents attempt to name a surrogate decision-maker with authority to act in the event of the incapacity of the creator of the document. Every state has enacted a statutory durable power of attorney for property management. Whether such a general power of attorney for property can also be extended to health care is not clear. Most states have separate laws permitting the appointment of a surrogate health care decisionmaker. Others have allowed the appointment of a proxy health care decisionmaker as part of a living will. Still other states have statutes that permit the use of a single durable power of attorney for both property and health care. A few states have a statutory form that must be used to appoint a surrogate decisionmaker for health care.

Because the statutes vary from state to state and because the extent of the powers that can be delegated is unclear, it is difficult to generalize. As with the living will, any individual desiring to create a surrogate health care decisionmaker should consult the appropriate state statute.

Most statutes permitting the creation of a surrogate health care decisionmaker are less onerous than those for living wills. They usually require little other than that the document be in writing and signed by the declarant. Most states require that the directive be witnessed, but only a few require that the signatures be notarized. As a practical matter, however, a health care directive should be witnessed and, if possible, notarized. In many cases the agent will also sign the document to provide a sample of his or her signature.

The extent of the powers that can be delegated to the health care agent vary from state to state. A few states specifically forbid the termination of artificial nutrition and hydration by the agent. Whether such limits are constitutional is unclear. Since the declarant could decide on his or her own behalf to refuse artificial hydration and nutrition, it can be argued that he or she has a constitutional right to delegate that power to an agent.

Most states provide for what is known as a "springing" power that goes into effect only upon the mental incapacity of the declarant. A few statutes provide that the grant of power to the agent takes place upon execution of the document, although as a practical matter the agent will be able to act only in the event of the declarant's incapacity.

Some statutes permit the nomination of a potential guardian in the durable power of attorney for health care. This permits persons to name who should be their guardian in the event one is needed.

The Uniform Health Care Decisions Act (UHCDA) is a model statute for surrogate decisionmaking for health care. The UHCDA is an attempt to create a statute that combines the often fragmented state laws that govern living wills, powers of attorney for health care, and family surrogate decisionmaking. It permits any adult or emancipated minor to create an advance health care directive that can either be a durable power of attorney for health care or an "individual instruction," the Act's term for a living will. If the individual fails to create an advance health care directive, the UHCDA provides that a statutorily identified surrogate can make the incapacitated individual's health care decisions.

The UHCDA permits the delegation of extensive decisionmaking rights to the surrogate, including the authority to terminate or bar the initiation of life-sustaining treatment, defined to encompass artificial nutrition and hydration. The surrogate's powers are limited only to the extent that the surrogate not act contrary to the patient's express wishes and always act in the patient's best interests. If the patient has not named a surrogate decisionmaker, one will be appointed for him or her. The UHCDA lists a priority of appointment of the surrogate: the spouse, followed by an adult child, parent, adult brother or sister, another relative or friend who exhibited special care and concern for the patient, or anyone orally designated by the patient as surrogate decisionmaker.

§ 3.6   Termination of Life Sustaining Treatment Without a Formal Advance Directive

Many individuals who lack mental capacity to make medical treatment decisions fail to appoint a surrogate decisionmaker prior to the onset of the incapacity. In the past, the only solution was to appoint a guardian of the person to make medical decision treatments for the incapacitated ward. If the medical treatment decisions do not rise to the level of whether or not to terminate life-sustaining treatment, guardianship is an acceptable solution, although less desirable than if the individual had named a surrogate decisionmaker. However, if the question is whether to terminate treatment, the guardian may lack authority or fear that he or she lacks authority to make such a decision. Alternatively, even if the guardian is willing to terminate treatment, the hospital or treating physician may refuse to do so because they are unsure whether the guardian has the authority to terminate life-sustaining treatment. Moreover, there have been some instances of third-party intervention when family or guardians attempt to terminate life-sustaining treatment. These outside interveners attempt to bar the termination of treatment claiming that it violates either the law or a higher moral code. It is always preferable, therefore, to be able to rely on a formal surrogate decisionmaking document prepared by the patient, which approves of the termination of treatment, rather than relying on a court appointed guardian.

Physicians and family members, of course, often decide to terminate life-sustaining treatment and do so even in the absence of a formal written directive from the patient directing such action. If the physician and family feel comfortable with their mutual decision, and the hospital or treating facility does not object, the treatment can be terminated and the individual allowed to die. But the danger always exists that such informal arrangements will break down, either because of disagreement between the family, fear of litigation by the physician, or a demand by the treating facility for better evidence of the patient's desires. When the parties are unable to reach accommodation, they must turn to the courts.

a. *In Re Quinlan (355 A.2d 647 (N.J.1976))*

Modern case law dealing with termination of life sustaining treatment can be traced to the 1976 New Jersey Supreme Court case of *In re Quinlan*. Twenty-two-year-old Karen Ann Quinlan fell into a persistent vegetative state because of her cessation of breathing for at least two fifteen-minute periods. She was eventually stabilized on a respirator and survived by way of artificial nutrition. After several months, her father requested that the respirator be turned off, believing there was no reason to continue life-supportive measures under such conditions. Because his request was opposed by the doctors, the hospital, the county prosecutor, the state of New Jersey and Karen's court-appointed guardian ad litem, the father sued to have his wishes implemented. The New Jersey Supreme Court consented to the removal of the respirator at the father's request. Interestingly enough, although the respirator was removed, Karen Quinlan did not die. She survived for several years, being kept alive by a feeding tube that her father never requested to have removed.

The New Jersey Supreme Court held that an individual had a right to have life support terminated on the basis of the right to privacy guaranteed under the Federal Constitution as elucidated in *Griswold v. Connecticut* (S.Ct.1965). The court held further that the New Jersey Constitution also guaranteed a right to privacy. As a result, if Karen had been competent, under her right to privacy she could have requested termination of life support.

Unfortunately, she never expressed a coherent opinion about this issue prior to becoming incompetent. Nevertheless, her father, who was her legal guardian, was permitted to assert her right to privacy and request termination of life support. Specifically, the court held that upon concurrence of the guardian and her family, the respirator could be terminated if the attending physicians concluded that there was no reasonable possibility of her ever emerging from her comatose condition. If the parties agreed, they should consult with the hospital "ethics committee" or a similar institution. If they too agreed that there was no reasonable possibility of recovery, then termination of life support systems could occur with no civil or criminal liability.

b. *Barber v. Superior Court of State of California (Cal.App. 2 Dist.1983)*

Fear that criminal prosecution could result from termination of life support systems has largely been erased by the *Barber* case. This 1983 California case involved a family agreeing with physicians that the patient, who was in a deeply comatose state from which she was unlikely to recover, should not continue to receive medical care. As a result, the respirator and other life-sustaining treatment was removed, eventually the intravenous feeding tubes were discontinued; as a result the patient died.

Subsequently the physicians who had been involved in the termination of life support were charged with murder by the county prosecutor. On appeal, the case involved whether the physicians' acts constituted a criminal behavior. The appellate court held that under the circumstances the decision to terminate treatment, even though intentional and with knowledge that the patient would die, was not an unlawful failure to perform a legal duty. The physicians were not guilty of any criminal activity for terminating life support to a comatose patient who had no hope for recovery.

Since the *Barber* case there has been almost no criminal prosecution of medical personnel for termination of life-support systems. The cases instead have focused on whether there is authority to terminate the life-support systems.

c. Termination Based Upon Prior Statements of the Incompetent Patient: Substitute Judgment

Many individuals do not leave written treatment instructions detailing how they want to be treated in the event that they become incapacitated, but have made oral statements about the issue of life-sustaining treatment. The question arises as to what weight should be given to these oral statements of values and treatment preferences. The courts have adopted a variety of responses.

The issue of how to treat prior oral statements often emerges when a guardian, statutorily appointed surrogate or other third party wishes to terminate the life-support systems of an incapacitated patient. The court will ask whether there been any evidence of what the patient would have wanted under these conditions. If the patient did express a preference, how specific was it? Is any statement sufficient, or must there have been clear and convincing evidence of the patient's intentions concerning termination of life-sustaining treatment? In determining what the patient would have done, almost any prior statements are used, but the value of such evidence varies depending on the specificity, remoteness, consistency and thoughtfulness of the prior statements. Reliance upon the expressed wishes of the incapacitated person is known as the doctrine of substituted judgement.

In most states guardians or surrogates may terminate life support without prior court approval so long as they base their decision on what the patient would have done under the conditions. The patient's prior statements and as well as the patient's values and lifestyle must be considered in the attempt to determine what the patient would have wanted.

In general, courts have adopted the approach of using whatever evidence is available and making a case-by-case decision as to its probative value. Not all courts, however, have been so liberal. A few states, including Delaware, Michigan, Missouri and New York, require that there must be clear and convincing proof of that the incapacitated patient would want the treatment terminated.

The most significant case ruling on the interpretation of prior statements is *Cruzan v. Director, Missouri Department of Health* (S.Ct.1990). Nancy Cruzan, age 25, was rendered mentally incapacitated when she suffered severe injuries in an automobile accident. Due to a temporary lack of oxygen, she suffered permanent brain damage that left her in a persistent vegetative state. She was maintained alive by artificial feeding and hydration equipment with no hope of recovery given the extent of damage to her brain.

Her parents eventually asked the hospital to terminate the artificial nutrition with the view toward hastening her death. The hospital refused and the parents sued in an attempt to force the hospital to remove the feeding tube. The trial court held that Nancy's prior oral statements about not wanting to continue to live in case she was severely injured provided sufficient support for terminating her life support. On appeal, however, the Supreme Court of Missouri reversed, holding that her oral statements were "unreliable" and insufficient to permit her parental guardians to exercise substitute judgment on her behalf and terminate care.

The case was appealed to the United States Supreme Court, which affirmed the Missouri court and refused to permit termination of life support treatment. In a lengthy opinion the Court held that incapacitated patients did have a right under the informed consent doctrine to control their own medical care. Since the incapacitated party could not make their own decisions, the doctrine of substitute judgment must be relied upon. The right of a guardian to terminate life-sustaining treatment was not absolute, however. According to the Supreme Court, under the Federal Constitution a state could re-

quire clear and convincing evidence of the patient's
wishes prior to allowing a guardian to terminate
life-sustaining treatment. The case did *not* hold that
states had to adopt a clear and convincing standard
of the patient's intent. Rather, the case merely
stands for the proposition that states are permitted
under the Federal Constitution to do so. A few state
courts have adopted the clear and convincing requirement, but many have continued to rely on a
less onerous standard of proof.

d. Termination of Life–Sustaining Treatment When the Patient Has Not Made Prior Statements of Intent: Best Interests Test

If an incapacitated patient is terminally ill or in a
persistent vegetative state and has never expressed
an opinion as to when and if he or she would want
termination of treatment, may a guardian or other
surrogate nevertheless terminate treatment? In
many states guardians and surrogates are permitted
to terminate life-support systems under the doctrine known as the best interests test.

The best interests test arose in 1977 in the Massachusetts case of *Superintendent of Belchertown
State School v. Saikewicz* (Mass.1977). In that case
an elderly, severely retarded man was suffering
from leukemia. The question brought before the
court was whether to provide a painful, though not
life-saving, treatment that might extend his life.
The guardian of the patient requested that the
treatment not be given on the basis that it would
not save the patient's life, and that the patient

would not comprehend why he was subjected to the painful treatment. The court concurred that it was proper for the guardian to attempt to act in the best interests of the patient, and that the patient would not be well served by a non-lifesaving, painful treatment. It was therefore proper for the guardian to rely on what was best for the patient.

§ 3.7   Assisted Suicide and Euthanasia

Assisted suicide refers to giving aid to an individual who wishes to end his or her life. Most commonly that entails a physician or other individual supplying a patient with sufficient drugs so that the patient can commit suicide by ingesting the drugs. Assisted suicide is illegal in all states except Oregon. Where illegal it is often prosecuted as a form of manslaughter or as an independent legal act. In separate law suits the laws that barred physician-assisted suicide in New York and Washington state were challenged as being unconstitutional. In 1997, in *Washington v. Glucksberg* (S.Ct.1997), the United States Supreme Court upheld both state statutes and stated that there is no constitutional protection or right of physician-assisted suicide.

In 1994, Oregon voters passed Measure 16, which authorized physician-assisted suicide for some patients under limited circumstances. Entitled the Oregon Death With Dignity Act, the initiative permits qualified patients who suffer from terminal disease to voluntarily request a prescription for medication to end their lives in a humane and dignified manner. The initiative has a complex set of steps that must be followed. The patient must be suffering from a terminal disease and have six months or less to live. The patient must make an oral request for a prescription for medication to end life and then wait fifteen days. At the end of that time, if the patient's physician determines that the patient has the capacity to make his or her own health care decisions and is acting voluntarily, the physician asks the patient to notify his or her next of kin. The physician then refers the patient to a consulting physician who verifies the attending physician's diagnosis and prognosis. Either physician can stop the procedure and refer the patient to counseling if they believe that the patient is suffering from a psychiatric illness or depression. Finally, the patient must sign a written request witnessed by two people, at least one of whom is not a relative or an heir. The patient must restate the oral request for medication. No sooner than 48 hours after the written request, the patient will receive the prescription for medication to end his or her life. The patient can withdraw a request at any time in any manner. The Oregon Act can be used only by Oregon residents; it specifically forbids mercy killing and lethal injection.

After a series of court challenges, the Oregon Act took effect in 1998.The act was challenged in 2002 by the United States Attorney General as being in violation of federal laws that control the use of potentially lethal drugs, but the Act was upheld as not violating the federal law.

Euthanasia refers to a consensual termination of a patient's life. In the past, the term euthanasia referred to both active measures, such as giving the patient a lethal dose of drugs and to passive responses, such as terminating treatment and allowing death to occur. Today the term euthanasia is generally reserved for active acts such as a lethal injection. The mere termination of life-sustaining treatment is today not considered euthanasia. Euthanasia is permitted in the Netherlands, and has its advocates who believe that it alleviates suffering and allows death with dignity for individuals.

The goal of euthanasia is to put a consenting individual painlessly to death who is suffering from an incurable disease. Euthanasia is seen as an act of mercy at the request of a dying patient who would prefer to terminate existence rather than proceed to a painful death. Most individuals who wish to terminate their life need the help of another, for example, to inject the necessary drug. Even patients who intend to ingest drugs will often need others to acquire the drugs for them, because if they are terminally ill, they are often physically incapable of acquiring the means to terminate their own life.

Active euthanasia, even with the full consent of the patient, is illegal in the United States. Even if it is a so-called "mercy killing," it is homicide, and the actor who participates in such acts can be expected to be prosecuted either for homicide or for the crime of assisted suicide.

CHAPTER 4

MEDICARE AND MEDIGAP

Fewer issues are more central to older persons' concerns and apprehension than the availability and cost of medical care. The inevitabilities of the aging process dictate that on average, older people will need more medical attention than younger people and that this attention will become increasingly more expensive. Indeed, ongoing developments in medical technology and research have made these natural tendencies only more likely as life expectancy increases and life-ending maladies become newly treatable. This is the case today and it was already the case in 1965, when the Federal government created a major health care program for older citizens entitled "Medicare."

Medicare basically pays for acute care for persons aged 65 years and older without regard to their health status or financial resources. It consists of three major programs: Part A covers hospitalization, short-term nursing home care, and some home health services; Part B mainly covers physician fees; and Part D covers prescription drugs. Certain medical costs, however, are not covered or are covered only in part by Medicare, thereby leaving older people to pay these costs themselves. In response, private insurance companies have developed so-called "Medigap" policies to cover some of the costs that Medicare does not.

The Medicare program just described covers approximately seven out of eight older Americans. The rest have chosen a variant of managed care in the context of Medicare or some other alternative. These options are collectively described as Medicare Part C or "Medicare Advantage."

In addition to Medicare, there is another governmental health care financing program called Medicaid. This program is not limited to older people but applies to low-income persons of any age and covers certain costs—primarily long-term institutionalization—that Medicare generally does not. Because of this more extensive coverage, some older people will need to consider Medicaid in addition to Medicare. See generally Chapter 5.

§ 4.1   Eligibility

Medicare is part of the Social Security system in terms of both its authorizing statute and its implementation. See 42 U.S.C. § 1395 et seq. Accordingly, participation in Medicare is tied most directly to eligibility for Social Security benefits.

a.   Part A Eligibility

Any person who is at least 65 years old and is eligible for Social Security benefits is entitled to Medicare Part A without charge. The Part A program is financed through a 2.9% payroll tax on all wages and self-employment income, which in the case of employees is collected one-half from the employee and one-half from the employer. In this respect, the financing of Medicare Part A is like that of Social Security, except that there is no annual wage cap beyond which Medicare taxes are not assessed, unlike Social Security.

Although Medicare eligibility is tied to Social Security benefit eligibility, a person need not actually be collecting Social Security benefits to "enroll" in Medicare. Thus, even if a person has not yet retired or has otherwise chosen to defer receipt of Social Security benefits, mere eligibility for such benefits confers Medicare Part A entitlement. Indeed, such a person *should* enroll in Medicare Part A upon attaining age 65, since there is no financial incentive to defer enrollment, unlike the deferral options available in Social Security. See generally Chapter 11. Conversely, someone receiving early Social Security benefits, i.e., between ages 62 and 64, is not entitled to Medicare, because that person has not yet attained age 65. Both requirements—age 65 and Social Security eligibility—are necessary. Incidentally, for these purposes, Federal Railroad Retirement benefits are treated as Social Security benefits.

A spouse, widow, or widower of someone who was eligible for Social Security benefits (or Federal Railroad Retirement benefits) is also entitled to Medicare Part A coverage. Such persons must still attain age 65 in their own right, however, so the younger spouse of a Medicare enrollee will not be covered by Medicare until he or she reaches age 65.

A divorced spouse who has not remarried can qualify for Medicare via a former spouse's Medicare entitlement, but only if their marriage lasted at least ten years. A late-in-life divorce, in fact, might cause a person to lose Medicare benefits if the marriage lasted less than ten years and the divorced spouse is not otherwise entitled to Medicare—either on the basis of his or her own work history, or via a previous marriage. On the other hand, if the person's former spouse remarries, that fact does not affect the divorced spouse's Medicare eligibility. For example, Eric and Jane were married for 14 years before getting divorced. Eric has now married Katherine, but Jane has not remarried. Both Jane and Katherine are eligible for Medicare benefits on the basis of Eric's work record.

In addition, certain workers aged 65 years are entitled to Medicare even though their employment was not covered by Social Security. This category primarily applies to employees of state and local governments who were hired after March 31, 1986, who are liable for Medicare's 2.9% payroll tax but not for Social Security's payroll tax.

Persons aged 65 and over who are not otherwise entitled to Medicare Part A may voluntarily enroll in the program and pay a monthly premium. This premium is adjusted annually and in 2006 was $393 per month. Eligible enrollees must reside in the United States and be either U.S. citizens or resident aliens who have lived in this country during the preceding five years. Such persons are also required to obtain Part B coverage if they want to enroll in

Part A. In other words, one may not voluntarily enroll in Part A only. A person who is eligible to enroll in Part A but chooses to defer enrollment beyond age 65 will pay a 10% surcharge, in addition to the monthly premium, when that person subsequently does enroll. This surcharge then applies for a period based on the length of the delayed enrollment. Essentially, the surcharge continues for two years for each 12–month period of delayed enrollment. For example, if Helen deferred enrolling in Medicare Part A for 38 months, there are three 12–month periods of deferred enrollment. Her premiums, therefore, will be augmented by 10% during the first six years of her Medicare enrollment.

Finally, some persons are entitled to Medicare even if they are not yet 65 years old. Persons who have received Social Security disability payments for at least 24 months and persons with "end stage renal disease" are in this category. These persons are usually not within the scope of "elder law," so further details about their Medicare eligibility are not discussed in this volume.

b. *Part B Eligibility*

Eligibility for Medicare Part B coverage is distinct from, but related to, eligibility for Part A. Part B is financed through monthly premiums and general Federal revenues, rather than by a payroll tax. To obtain Part B coverage, one must generally be entitled to Medicare Part A. Alternatively, a person aged 65 years can obtain Part B coverage if he or she is either a U.S. citizen or a resident alien who has lived in this country during the preceding five years. A person can buy Part B coverage without buying Part A, even though a voluntary purchaser of Part A must also buy Part B.

Part B enrollees pay a monthly premium that is adjusted annually (in 2006, it was $88.50 per month) that covers 25% of the program's costs. See 42 U.S.C. § 1395r(a)(1), (3). The Federal government, in other words, covers 75% of Part B's costs from general tax revenues. Accordingly, almost all older people enroll in Part B either directly or through a former employer. Some older people who are still employed do not purchase Part B, because their employer provides similar coverage, either directly or through an independently insured program.

The 25%–75% allocation of Part B expenses between enrollee premiums and Federal tax revenues is modified for upper-income enrollees, starting in 2007. 42 U.S.C. § 1395r(i). This modification is being phased in over three years and by 2009, the percentage of Part B program costs paid by these enrollees will depend on their income for Federal tax purposes according to the following table:

Annual Income	Cost Percentage
Under $80,000	25
$80,001 to $100,000	35
$100,001 to $150,000	50
$150,001 to $200,000	65
Over $200,000	80

For example, assume that the regular Part B premium is $160 per month, representing 25% of the Medicare program's projected monthly cost of $640. If Marla's income is $170,000, her monthly premium will be $416 ($640 × 65%), rather than $160.

The testing figure for this purpose is "adjusted gross income" as determined for Federal income tax purposes, *plus* any tax-exempt interest income received. 42 U.S.C. § 1395r(i)(4). This income figure is determined for the second preceding calendar year. In other words, the Part B premium for 2011 will be based on an enrollee's income in 2009. Furthermore, the income parameters shown in the preceding table apply to unmarried individuals. For married couples, those parameters are doubled. Thus, a married couple will not owe increased Part B premiums unless their annual income exceeds $160,000 ($80,000 initial parameter × 2). Finally, these parameters are to be indexed for inflation for years after 2007.

Persons who do not buy Part B coverage when they first enroll in Part A can secure such coverage at a later date. But when they do so, their premiums are *permanently* increased based upon the length of time they chose not to enroll. This penalty does not apply, however, if they were covered in an employer group health plan available to current employees, *not* retired personnel. All other late enrollees face monthly premiums that are increased by 10% for each 12–month period during which they could have, but did not, enroll in Part B. For example, if Jack delays enrollment for 55 months after his "initial enrollment period," there are four 12–month periods to be considered. As a consequence, when he does enroll, his monthly premiums will be 40% higher (four years × 10% per year) than they would otherwise have been. Moreover, when the Part B monthly premium is raised the following year, Jack will pay that new rate plus 40%. The penalty differential, in other words, is a permanent feature and will increase annually as the Part B premium itself is raised.

§ 4.2   Enrollment Procedures and Coverage Periods

Persons who are age 65 and are receiving Social Security (or Federal Railroad Retirement) benefits are automatically enrolled in both parts of Medicare. No separate application procedure is required. If such a person chooses to decline Part B coverage, he or she must affirmatively do so. Medicare coverage starts with the first day of the month in which a person reaches age 65 and continues through the last month of that person's life.

Persons who are not receiving Social Security benefits, but are otherwise eligible for Medicare, must apply for such coverage. This requirement applies to people, for example, who have chosen to defer receipt of Social Security benefits until they are older. It also applies to Medicare-covered government employment (i.e., state and local governmental employees hired after March 31, 1986), certain disabled persons, and persons with end-stage renal disease.

Additional rules apply to persons who voluntarily enroll in Medicare Part A. Such persons may enroll within a seven-month period that begins with the third month before attaining age 65. For example, if Susan's 65th birthday is June 20, her "initial enrollment period" is March 1 through September 30. Any person who fails to enroll during this period can enroll later during a "general enrollment period," namely, January 1 through March 31 of each year.

The date on which one applies for such coverage affects both the premiums charged and the coverage's effective date. As explained in § 4.1(a), a person who enrolls after the "initial" seven-month enrollment period may face premium surcharges for a certain period of time. Moreover, the effective date of Medicare coverage is delayed until July 1 for persons who apply during a "general enrollment period," while coverage can begin as early as the month of a person's 65th birthday if that person enrolls before that month. Enrollment after reaching age 65 can also delay Medicare's effective date, even if it occurred within the "initial enrollment period."

Enrollment in Medicare Part B generally follows this same pattern. Most people are enrolled automatically. Those who must apply for Part B coverage can do so during the same seven-month "initial enrollment period" or any subsequent "general enrollment period," with premium surcharges being imposed for delayed enrollment, as described in § 4.1(b). For persons who are covered as employees under an employer group health plan, however, special rules apply. The seven-month, no-penalty "initial enrollment period" for such persons begins on the first day of the first month in which the person is no longer covered by the employer group health plan.

Medicare coverage for such persons becomes effective on the first day of the first month of the special enrollment period, unless enrollment occurred later in the period, in which case coverage becomes effective the next succeeding month. For example, assume that Joseph's employer group coverage ceases on April 30. His initial enrollment period is May 1 through November 30. If he enrolls during May, his Medicare coverage takes effect on May 1; but if he enrolls in June, the effective date becomes July 1. Enrollment after this special "initial enrollment period" may also trigger the increased premiums described previously for late enrollees.

§ 4.3 Coverage Under Part A

The Medicare Part A program covers medical care received as an inpatient in a hospital, a skilled nursing facility (SNF), at home, and via a hospice agency. Each such category has its own set of restrictions, medical requirements, and limitations. Medical care received as an outpatient or at home and physicians' charges are covered by Medicare Part B. Both Parts of Medicare, moreover, are subject to a general requirement that the medical care be "reasonable and necessary" for the diagnosis or treatment of illness or injury, or the improvement of a malformed body member's functioning. 42 U.S.C. § 1395y(a)(1). This requirement tends to exclude various "medically unproven" or experimental procedures, a category whose composition changes as medical research advances. Other general programmatic exclusions are described in § 4.5.

Within the categories of Medicare Part A's coverage are several institutional settings. In general, Medicare pays for semiprivate rooms, meaning at least one other patient. Private rooms are invariably more expensive, and Medicare will pay the corresponding extra charge only if a private room is "medically necessary." This test means either that a patient's condition requires isolation from other patients, that a facility has no semiprivate or less expensive rooms, or that a facility has such rooms, but all of them are occupied and immediate hospitalization is necessary.

In addition, benefits in some settings, namely hospitals and skilled nursing facilities (SNF), have limits based on the number of days spent in these institutions. Generally, the day limits are calibrated per "spell of illness." A "spell of illness" begins with admission to the facility in question and ends when the patient has been out of a hospital, SNF, or other facility providing rehabilitation services for a period of 60 consecutive days, counting the day of discharge. 42 U.S.C. § 1395x(a). Even if someone stays in a SNF or facility providing rehabilitation services indefinitely, a "spell of illness" ends when that person stops receiving "skilled care" for 60 days in a row. After a "spell of illness" concludes, any new "spell of illness" will effectively restart the per-day limitations, as well as any corresponding deductibles that are tied to the "spell of illness" rubric.

For example, assume that Anita enters a hospital on March 15 and is discharged on March 31. If she returns before 60 days have elapsed—i.e., before May 30, Anita will be within the same "spell of illness," even if her return is for a medically distinct and unrelated problem. Similarly, if Anita enters a hospital on June 1, this admission begins a new "spell of illness," even if this admission was medically precipitated by, or even a relapse of, the episode of last March.

a. Hospitalization

In a hospital setting, Medicare pays for all relevant services during the first 60 days of a single "spell of illness." There is a deductible per spell of illness that is adjusted annually. The deductible in 2006 was $952. After a patient satisfies this deductible, Medicare covers practically all other costs, including meals, special diets, nursing services (but not a private duty nurse), special care units (e.g., intensive care or coronary care units), pharmaceuticals used in the hospital, laboratory tests, medical supplies, diagnostic procedures billed by the hospital, room charges, and costs of hospital-based therapies, such as radiation therapy, physical therapy,

occupational therapy, and speech pathology. 42
U.S.C. § 1395x(b). Blood transfusions are also covered after the first three pints of blood, which
remain a patient's responsibility—either by payment or by arranging replacement. In essence, virtually all hospital costs other than television
charges and telephone expenses, are covered by
Medicare.

Given Medicare's general orientation to cover
acute care requirements, Medicare coverage of hospital costs declines once a hospital stay extends
beyond 60 days. For the 61st through 90th day in a
hospital during a single "spell of illness," Medicare
pays all costs after a per-day deductible. In other
words, for these 30 days, a patient pays the deductible each day, and Medicare covers the excess. This
amount is one-fourth of the initial deductible; thus,
in 2006, it was $238 per day. Hospital stays beyond
90 days may tap into a patient's "lifetime reserve"
of 60 additional days. As this title implies, this
"lifetime reserve" is established for each patient
and is not reset for a subsequent "spell of illness."
These lifetime reserve days are themselves subject
to a per-day deductible that is one-half of the initial
deductible. In 2006, therefore, that deductible was
$476 per day. On the other hand, the average
length of a hospital stay for an older patient is less
than six days according to available data.

To summarize, a patient is generally entitled to
90 days of hospital coverage (with only partial coverage for the last 30 days) per "spell of illness" and
60 additional days to be used over the patient's

lifetime. This provision is subject to a further limit, however, if a patient is in a psychiatric hospital. Medicare pays for a maximum of 190 days of inpatient psychiatric hospital care *per patient*; this 190–day limit, in other words, is a lifetime cap. See 42 U.S.C. § 1395d(b)(3).

b. *Skilled Nursing Facilities*

As to skilled nursing facilities (SNF), often referred to as nursing homes, the Medicare Part A benefits are quite limited. No fewer than four major requirements must be satisfied for Medicare to cover SNF expenses.

First, the facility itself must be Medicare-approved. This means that the specific facility meets various Medicare standards concerning quality of care, staff training, residents' rights, and health and safety. Any state law standards that exceed Federal mandates must also be satisfied for a facility to be Medicare-approved. Additionally, the facility must have a transfer agreement with at least one hospital that provides for the transfer of patients and the interchange of medical information between the two institutions. Finally, the SNF must be "participating" in the Medicare program, a requirement that limits the rates that a SNF can charge for certain services.

Incidentally, there are similar Medicare requirements for hospitals, but they are less consequential from an older patient's perspective, because most hospitals are Medicare-approved. Many nursing homes are not, or have only certain portions of their facility that are Medicare-approved.

Second, admission into a SNF must follow discharge from a hospital within 30 days of that discharge. Persons who go directly from their homes to a SNF without an intervening hospital stay, which often happens with older persons, do not satisfy this requirement. Nor can patients simply "drop by" a hospital on the way to the SNF because of the third major hurdle—namely, the preceding hospital stay must have been at least three consecutive calendar days in length. 42 U.S.C. § 1395x(i). Thus, if Peter falls, goes to an emergency room for X-rays, but broke no bones or otherwise presented any need for hospitalization beyond perhaps overnight observation, he will not be eligible for Medicare benefits when he enters a SNF after being discharged from the hospital. In this context, by the way, the date of discharge does not count as a hospital day.

The fourth and strictest requirement for Medicare coverage of SNF charges is that a patient must need skilled nursing or skilled rehabilitative services that can be provided only in a SNF. A medical professional must certify that the patient requires and is receiving such care on a daily basis. Furthermore, care in the SNF must be for a condition that was treated in the hospital or is medically related to that condition. "Skilled nursing care" involves services, ordered by a physician, that require the skills of technical or professional personnel; e.g., a licensed practical nurse, registered nurse, physical therapist, etc. Also, these services must be provided

directly by, or under the supervision of, such professionals. Specific examples of "skilled" care include
most injections, catheters, gastronomy feedings,
dressings with prescription medications, administration of medical gases, and so forth. This level of
care corresponds roughly to the highest level of care
(usually called "skilled care") offered by nursing
homes. See generally Chapter 7. Medicare also requires that a patient receiving this level of care
must need such care on a daily basis; twice-weekly
therapy sessions, for example, do not by themselves
constitute "skilled nursing care." Relatively few
nursing home residents receive this level of care.

If a patient satisfies all of these conditions, then
Medicare will pay—at its stipulated rates—for a
semiprivate room, including special meals, drugs,
therapy, medical supplies, and appliances. Even
then, however, there is a limit on the length of
coverage per "spell of illness." Medicare covers all
costs for 20 days and costs in excess of a per-day
deductible for 80 more days. This per-day deductible
is one-eighth of the initial "spell of illness" deductible. In 2006, therefore, it was $119 per day. After
these 100 days (20 days of full coverage + 80 days
of partial coverage), SNF benefits under Medicare
Part A cease. In this connection, it should be noted
that Medicare Part B provides no SNF benefits and
that private "Medigap" insurance applies only to
the per-day deductible on days 21–100. See § 4.4
and § 4.8. Special insurance called "long-term care
insurance" responds to this situation. See generally

Chapter 6. But the point remains: Medicare covers only the first 100 days of a SNF treatment period.

c. *Home Health Care*

Medicare also provides a limited range of home health services for persons who are confined to their homes. 42 U.S.C. § 1395d(a)(3). These services are provided in a person's house, apartment, or even a home for the aged, but not a hospital or SNF. To be eligible, individuals must be unable to leave their home except with assistance from other people or by using devices such as wheelchairs, walkers, or canes, and must rarely leave home except to obtain medical treatment.

The home health services must be provided by a home health agency pursuant to a written plan of care established by a physician and reviewed by such physician at least once every two months. A home health agency can be either public or private, but it must "participate" in the Medicare program and must specialize in providing skilled nursing or therapeutic services in patients' homes.

Covered services include physical, occupational, and speech therapy, medical supplies, durable medical equipment, and "part-time or intermittent" nursing care. See 42 U.S.C. § 1395x(m). Such nursing care must be provided by, or under the supervision of, a licensed nurse and can include home health aides if the services ordered by the physician do not require the skills of a licensed nurse. Moreover, "part-time or intermittent" services consists of "reasonable and necessary" care of less than eight hours per day and no more than 28 hours per week (possibly 35 hours per week in individually reviewed circumstances).

Medicare's coverage of home health care does not, however, extend to various forms of assistance that older persons often need to remain at home. Specifically, Medicare does not cover 24–hour nursing care provided at home, drugs, meals delivered to one's home, and homemaker services such as shopping, laundry, and meal preparation.

For the services it does cover, Medicare picks up the entire cost. There are no general deductibles or co-payments other than a 20% co-payment on "durable medical equipment." Such equipment includes wheelchairs, hospital beds, traction equipment, walkers, and an ever-changing variety of other devices.

In addition to these limitations, Medicare Part A has two further requirements. If these Part A requirements are not satisfied, the home health services are covered by Medicare Part B instead. See § 4.4. But if a person is not enrolled in Part B, the services remain covered by Part A. See 42 U.S.C. § 1395d(a)(3).

The first of these requirements mandates that the individual have been hospitalized for at least three consecutive days, or have received post-hospital extended care services in a skilled nursing facility (SNF). In either case, the home health services must begin within 14 days after being discharged from the hospital or the SNF.

Second, coverage is limited to 100 visits within a "home health spell of illness" benefit period. This period begins with the first day on which a person receives home health services and continues until 60 days after the person is no longer receiving such services and has not been an inpatient in a hospital or a SNF. 42 U.S.C. § 1395x(tt)(2). Thus, if the need for home health care is ongoing, Medicare Part A's coverage ceases after the 100th home visit.

d. *Hospice Care*

The final category of Medicare Part A coverage is hospice care. Hospice care is a combination of home care and occasional inpatient institutionalization, plus certain services not generally covered by Medicare. See generally 42 U.S.C. § 1395d(d). This coverage applies to persons who have been certified by a physician as having no more than six months remaining life expectancy. The basic idea of a hospice is to provide pain relief and symptom control, instead of active medical intervention to address the underlying terminal illness. To that end, Medicare pays for doctors and nursing services, home health aides, homemaker services, medical supplies, drugs, other custodial care items, and counseling. Typically, these services are provided by a "hospice," a public agency or private organization that makes these services available around the clock as its primary mission. Hospices are usually not separate facilities, in most circumstances.

Patients choose to receive hospice care instead of standard Medicare benefits when they enter the hospice program. Medicare will cover two separate hospice periods of 90 days each, plus additional 60–day periods if needed. These periods may be used consecutively but need not be. During these periods, the patient forgoes his or her right to the curative services that Medicare usually provides, except for conditions that are unrelated to that patient's terminal illness. If a patient changes his or her preference, standard Medicare benefits can be reinstated, but any days remaining in the particular hospice period are lost. For example, if Harold decides on the 72nd day of his first 90–day hospice period to return to the main Medicare program, he may do so, but the 18 days remaining in this hospice period are forever lost. His second 90–day period and his 60–day periods are still available, however, for future use.

The hospice care program of Medicare Part A pays for all costs incurred by a Medicare-approved hospice, with two exceptions. First, a patient must pay 5% of the cost of outpatient drugs or $5 per prescription, whichever is less. Second, a patient must pay 5% of the "respite care" provided by a hospice. Respite care is very short-term institutionalization of a patient—no more than five consecutive days—undertaken to afford the patient's regular caregiver some relief. This benefit enables the caregiver to take a short family vacation or some other short-term "respite." The Medicare-approved rate for such care varies somewhat by geographic region, but Medicare picks up 95% of this cost, whatever that rate might be. Beyond these co-payments for outpatient drugs and respite care, there are no deductibles or other patient expense in Medicare's hospice care program.

§ 4.4　Coverage Under Part B

Medicare Part B covers a range of outpatient services, focusing most particularly on doctors' charges. See 42 U.S.C. § 1395k(a). In fact, when an older person receives medical care in a hospital setting, the relevant costs will be split, with Part A covering the room charges imposed by the hospital and Part B covering the charges of the physicians who provided treatment in the hospital. Of course, Part B is not limited to hospital settings. Office visits to medical specialists, diagnostic tests performed in doctors' offices (or in hospitals on an outpatient basis), drugs that cannot be self-administered, and even second opinions about proposed surgery are all covered by Medicare Part B. A particularly important benefit for older persons is Medicare's coverage of ambulance services, since older persons are often susceptible to falls at home and other unplanned medical events.

As noted in § 4.3(c), Part B also covers some home health services that Part A limits. This coverage would apply to home health services that were not preceded by a hospital or SNF stay, or that have extended beyond 100 home visits during a "home health spell of illness." Part B also pays for some home health services if an older person is not enrolled in Part A.

a. Scope of Benefits

Each benefit category has its own limitations and restrictions. For example, ambulance services are covered only if that form of transportation is necessary from a medical standpoint; i.e., any other form of transportation would endanger the patient's health. Further, ambulance service is allowed only for trips between a person's home and a hospital or skilled nursing facility. Trips to a doctor's office are usually not covered.

Similarly, "routine" examinations by physicians, dentists, and podiatrists are not covered, although some services are covered if they are needed as part of a larger medical treatment plan. For example, there is a distinction in podiatric care: injuries and foot diseases, including treatment of ingrown toenails and bunion deformities, are covered, but nail trimming, corn and callus removal, and hygienic care are not. Cosmetic surgery is also generally excluded, although such surgery is covered if done in connection with an accidental injury or an effort to improve some bodily function. As to Medicare's general programmatic exclusions, see § 4.5.

Medicare does cover an "initial preventive physical examination" that must be performed within the first six months of an enrollee's coverage under Part B. 42 U.S.C. § 1395x(ww). This examination is intended to promote health and detect diseases before they worsen and "includes education, counseling, and referral with respect to" a wide variety of screening tests. The exam generally does not cover clinical laboratory tests, but Medicare does cover annual influenza vaccinations, mammograms, and prostate cancer screenings. Medicare also covers periodic screening for colorectal cancer and cardiovascular disease, as well as pap smears and pelvic examinations.

In addition, Medicare Part B covers outpatient blood transfusions, medical supplies like splints and casts, durable medical equipment, and outpatient physical and occupational therapy. While the exact details of coverage change periodically and are contained in voluminous program manuals, certain limitations can be usefully noted here. Outpatient therapies, for example, must be prescribed by a physician who periodically reviews the prescribed plan. Furthermore, for some therapy providers, there is an annual billing cap that applies to their services. 42 U.S.C. § 1395*l*(g)(1). Similarly, a doctor's prescription is necessary for Medicare to cover durable medical equipment such as seat lift chairs (and then only the lift mechanism is covered, not the chair), electrical nerve stimulators, power-operated vehicles, wheelchairs, and other items that primarily serve a medical purpose. 42 U.S.C. § 1395x(n).

Some distinctions seem unfathomable to nonmedical people (and often to medical people as well). Medicare, for example, pays for prosthetic devices like artificial limbs and braces on the arm, leg, back, and neck. But orthopedic shoes are not covered unless they are an "integral part" of leg braces and their cost is included in the cost of such braces.

Corrective lenses are usually not covered, but if they are needed after a cataract operation, Medicare covers their cost. Similarly, breast prostheses are covered following a mastectomy, even though they would not be covered if considered cosmetic surgery. Finally, immunosuppressive drugs are covered by Part B for one year following discharge from an inpatient hospital stay during which an organ transplant was performed.

Even these details, it should be noted, may be changed as health care cost containment measures and various versions of health care rationing are implemented. But at least they convey some sense of Part B's present scope of coverage.

b.   *Financial Responsibility of Patients*

A patient's financial obligations under Medicare Part B are very different from those under Part A. In general, a patient pays an annual deductible that is adjusted every year. In 2006, this deductible was $124. The annual deductible applies to the first costs covered by Part B, without regard to the specific components of those costs. For example, if Jocelyn is treated in 2006 by an internist who charges her $100 and a gastroenterologist who charges her $125, she would owe the internist's bill and $24 of the gastroenterologist's bill. Alternatively, if she obtains a leg cast that costs $250, her annual deductible is satisfied from the first $124 (in 2006) of this charge. Once the annual deductible is met, costs are then split between Medicare Part B, which pays 80%, and the patient, who pays the other 20%.

This general scheme is subject, however, to a major complicating factor—the concept of Medicare-approved "reasonable charges." That is, for every medical service, supply, procedure and other covered item, Medicare establishes an "approved" charge. These "approved" charges are adjusted periodically to reflect changing costs of medical care, as well as changing governmental budgets and economic priorities. In other words, sometimes the Medicare "approved" charges do not correspond to emerging health cost patterns, because the budget process of the Federal government has dictated cost reductions due to fiscal constraints. As a result, the Medicare "approved" rate is frequently, if not usually, less than the amount that is customarily billed by the health care provider.

The significance of the "approved" rate, moreover, is that Medicare pays 80% of this figure, regardless of the amount actually billed by the provider. 42 U.S.C. § 1395*l*(a). For example, assume that Doctor bills $155 for a procedure that Medicare has "approved" a charge of only $100. Medicare pays 80% of the "approved" charge, or $80 in this case.

The extent of the patient's financial responsibility, however, cannot be determined without knowing whether Doctor "participates" in Medicare. If Doctor does "participate," or "takes assignment" as it is sometimes called, the Medicare-approved amount of $100 is all that the physician will collect—$80 from Medicare and $20 (the 20% co-payment) from the patient. The difference between Doctor's $155 billing and Medicare's $100 "approved" amount is simply written off and of no consequence to the patient. This mandatory write-off is of concern to Doctor, of course, but not to the patient covered by Medicare. To the extent that Doctor can shift this $55 uncollected amount to patients who are not covered by Medicare, Doctor may or may not try to do so. But the extent of the Medicare patient's liability is clear: a 20% co-payment computed on the Medicare's "approved" rate schedule.

This limitation on what Doctor can collect might suggest to Doctor—or any other health care provider, including ambulance services—that he or she may prefer not to "participate" in Medicare. In some states, physicians do not have this choice, because participation in Medicare is required as a condition of their licensure. But in most states, a physician can choose not to "participate" in Medicare.

As a nonparticipant, Doctor is not limited to Medicare's "approved" rates. Doctor can collect from the patient an additional amount up to 15% of the Medicare-approved amount. In the preceding example, the amount that can be "balance billed," as it is sometimes called, is $15 (Medicare-approved amount of $100 × 15%). In this case, the patient is responsible for the $20 co-payment plus the $15 additional billing, for a total of $35. Even in this situation, Doctor has not collected his or her full billing. Instead, Doctor is receiving a total of $115 ($80 from Medicare + $35 from the patient) for a procedure billed at $155. This $40 difference is, once again, written off (or possibly shifted to non-Medicare covered patients) as part of the cost of doing business with Medicare—note, *even* as a non-participant.

Although the preceding description applies to most services covered by Medicare Part B, there are exceptions in which Medicare's payment structure is more generous from a patient's perspective. For example, clinical diagnostic laboratory tests are covered in full by Medicare. That is, the annual deductible does not apply, and the 20% co-payment is waived. Medicare still imposes its established fee schedule on the test providers, but a patient owes nothing for these tests. Similar treatment is extended to home health services, except that durable medical equipment still bears a 20% co-payment. The no annual deductible/no 20% co-payment treatment also applies to the cost of second opinions for surgery (and to third opinions if the first two opinions disagree), expenses for pneumococcal vaccine, and to charges incurred by kidney transplant donors.

On the other hand, Medicare pays only 50%, rather than 80%, of "approved" costs of outpatient treatment for mental, psychoneurotic, and personality disorders. The patient then owes the remaining 50%. This limitation applies to physicians' charges and to any supplies or items that are furnished in treating the patient. Hospitals, skilled nursing facilities, and home health agencies are not subject to this 50% rule. Charges subject to this rule, moreover, must still be applied against the annual Part B deductible, if the patient has not already satisfied that obligation.

§ 4.5 General Medicare Exclusions

In addition to specific exceptions pertaining to particular benefits, Medicare Parts A and B have several general exclusions. The most pervasive, and in many ways the most nebulous, exclusion pertains to services that fail the "reasonable and necessary" standard. 42 U.S.C. § 1395y(a)(1). That is, Medicare covers only services and items that are medically appropriate for the diagnosis and treatment of illness or injury, or that improve the functioning of a body member. Various medically suspect or experimental procedures fall outside this criterion, including acupuncture, cellular therapy, transsexual surgery, and a host of specific treatments for specified disorders. The parameters of this exclusion necessarily change over time; e.g., heart transplants have been acceptable only since 1987.

A second major exclusion applies to services provided outside the United States. 42 U.S.C. § 1395y(a)(4). Medicare does, however, cover emergency inpatient hospital services furnished in Canada or Mexico to U.S. border residents and to persons traveling through Canada between Alaska and the mainland United States. In these specific circumstances, physicians' charges and ambulance services are covered as well. On the other hand, a ship or aircraft is not considered within the United States once it departs the geographic territory of the United States, even if that ship or airplane is of U.S. registry.

A third general exclusion applies to personal comfort items. 42 U.S.C. § 1395y(a)(6). This exclusion refers to charges for telephone, television, beauty and barber services, and the like. Minimal grooming, however, in a long-term institution may be covered if these services are not billed separately and seek to achieve a basic level of hygiene and presentability. More extensive procedures, such as professional manicures, are clearly excluded.

Cosmetic surgery is excluded from Medicare coverage, unless it is required for the prompt repair of an accidental injury or to improve the functioning of a malformed body member. 42 U.S.C. § 1395y(a)(10).

From an older patient's perspective, however, the most significant exclusion from Medicare pertains to routine care. Most dental services are not covered; nor are routine eye and ear examinations, eyeglasses, hearing aids, routine podiatric services (nail trimming, removal of corns and calluses, use of skin creams), orthopedic shoes, most immunizations, and routine physical examinations after the initial Medicare enrollment examination. See 42 U.S.C. § 1395y(a)(7), (8), (12), (13). Many generally healthy older persons spend many of their medical visits on precisely the items described above. To be sure, serious medical procedures in all of these areas are usually covered; e.g., treatment of glaucoma, cataracts, permanent prosthetic lenses, dental reconstruction of a bridge done in connection with tumor removal surgery. But many medical maintenance procedures are excluded from Medicare's coverage.

This noncoverage of basic medical care is nowhere more striking than Medicare's exclusion of custodial care. Other than hospice care, Medicare does not cover services that assist older persons in the so-called "activities of daily living"—walking, getting into and out of bed, bathing, dressing, feeding, toileting, and administration of ordinary drugs. Even if this care is provided in a skilled nursing facility, Medicare covers none of it. 42 U.S.C. § 1395y(a)(9).

Beyond certain ordering principles that exclude Medicare coverage for services covered by workers' compensation laws, automobile or liability insurance, and employer group health plans for current employees, one final exclusion bears mentioning. That exclusion applies to charges imposed by health care providers who are "immediate relatives" of the patient or members of that person's household. 42 U.S.C. § 1395y(a)(11). The phrase "immediate relative" includes: one's spouse; natural or adoptive parents, children, and siblings; stepparents, stepchildren, and stepsiblings; in-laws (parent, child, siblings); grandparents, grandchildren and the spouses of same. A person's household for this purpose extends to domestic employees and others who live together as a single family unit. The specific rules are subject to a variety of complex nuances. For example, in-law and step-relationships continue for purposes of this Medicare exclusion, even if the marriage upon which those relationships were premised ends in divorce or death of one of the persons involved. Be that as it may, Medicare does pay for out-of-pocket costs incurred by a patient's "immediate relative" in furnishing otherwise covered items, but there can be no profit element in such payments.

§ 4.6 Prescription Drugs

Although Medicare Part A covers prescription medications used during a hospital stay, most outpatient use of such medications was not covered by Medicare until Part D became effective in 2006. Even then, Part D is not the only source of prescription drug coverage for Medicare enrollees. Many enrollees have prescription drug coverage from their former employers as a retiree health benefit, while other enrollees have pharmaceutical coverage from pre–2006 "Medigap" insurance policies that included this feature. See § 4.8(c) regarding such coverage. Still other enrollees obtain drug coverage through a Medicare managed care plan. See § 4.9(a) regarding those plans.

In any case, Medicare Part D is organized very differently than the other Parts of Medicare and relies much more heavily on private companies for key coverage elements. For example, there is no fixed premium that applies to all plans. Instead, each Part D plan sets its own monthly premium.

Each plan also establishes its scope of coverage, subject to some overall "actuarial equivalent" standards that the government monitors. Accordingly, monthly premiums can range from under $2 to over $60, depending upon the specific package of plan benefits provided. Some plans use designated pharmacy networks while others provide mail-order refills. Even the specific drugs that a plan covers can vary considerably, and plan sponsors may discontinue coverage of a particular pharmaceutical during a plan year, as long as they provide 60 days' notice to current subscribers.

a. Delayed Enrollment Penalty

Plan D enrollment is voluntary and takes place during December of the preceding year. Medicare enrollees must, however, have some type of prescription drug coverage or they will face a delayed enrollment penalty if they eventually enroll in a Part D plan. This penalty is 1% for each month of delayed enrollment, with no limit, and is a permanent addition to the enrollee's monthly premium.

For example, assume that Peter chooses not to enroll in any Medicare Part D prescription drug plan during the first five years of his eligibility to do so. Five years is 60 months, so Peter will face a 60% penalty if he subsequently enrolls in a Part D plan. Assume further that he enrolls in a Part D plan during his sixth year and that the national average monthly premium at that time is $45. In this circumstance, Peter will pay a penalty of 60% of this $45, or $27, in addition to the monthly premium of the plan that Peter selects. This 60% surcharge, moreover, will continue as long as Peter is enrolled in any Part D plan. It never stops.

A delayed enrollment penalty will not apply, however, if the Medicare enrollee had "creditable coverage" during the time when that person was not enrolled in a Part D plan. For this purpose, "creditable coverage" can include an employer-sponsored plan that the agency administering Medicare determines to be "actuarially equivalent" to Medicare Part D. The enrollee should receive a letter indicating whether a drug plan that is sponsored by a former employer meets this standard. On the other hand, Medigap policies do not constitute "creditable coverage," because the Medicare administration contends that such policies are "not at least as good as" Part D coverage. Many Medicare managed care arrangements satisfy this standard. Moreover, enrollees in such plans must obtain drug coverage from these plans and are ineligible to purchase a separate Part D plan. Finally, military drug coverage, veterans' drug coverage (e.g., TRICARE), and Medicaid benefits all constitute "creditable coverage."

b. Plan Components

The Federal prototype plan has four dollar-based elements or layers of prescription drug coverage, and most Part D plans conform to this prototype. The dollar parameters at which the prototype plan's coverage changes are indexed for inflation, but the basic elements (in 2006) are as follows:

1.   Annual deductible of $250; i.e., the enrollee pays the first $250 of prescription drug costs incurred in a plan year.

2.   For the next $2,000 of annual drug costs, i.e., drug costs between $250 and $2,250, the plan pays 75% of the cost and the enrollee pays the other 25%. The maximum enrollee's cost for this coverage tier, in other words, is $500 ($2,000 × 25%).

3.   For the next $2,850 of annual drug expenditures, i.e., drug costs between $2,250 and $5,100, the plan pays nothing. This coverage gap is known colloquially as the "doughnut hole" and might represent an expenditure by the enrollee of as much as $2,850.

4.   For all annual drug costs above $5,100, the plan pays 95% and the enrollee pays the other 5%. There is no upper limit on this so-called "catastrophic coverage" tier.

A minority of Part D plans modify the plan elements in various ways. For example, some plans reduce or even eliminate the annual deductible, while other plans provide limited coverage within the "doughnut hole." Still other plans apply a fixed co-payment obligation (e.g., 20% of cost) to an enrollee's total drug expenditures without regard to which tier of coverage would otherwise pertain. Such plans typically offset this more generous coverage with higher-than-average monthly premiums.

Moreover, almost all Part D plans have restricted formularies. That is, the plans do not cover all pharmaceuticals, but Federal regulations require that they cover some drugs in each of several diagnostic categories. Within these broad mandates, however, plans can differentiate among drugs according to generic vs. brand names and can apply different levels of coverage. For example, a plan might cover generic drugs without any enrollee co-payment, preferred brand names for a nominal co-payment (e.g., $10 or 20% of cost), and nonpreferred brand names for a higher co-payment (e.g., $25 or 50% of cost). Some medications may not be covered at all. Most Part D plans further restrict dosage amounts or dosage frequency. That is, a plan might cover 600 milligrams of a covered pharmaceutical once a day but not 300 milligrams of the same pharmaceutical twice a day.

These various options are displayed on Medicare's website and are regularly updated to reflect changes in plan coverage. As noted previously, Part D plans may change their coverage of specific drugs even during a plan year, as long as they provide 60 days' notice to current subscribers. Those subscribers, however, may not change their enrollment once the plan year begins, regardless of changes in their plan's formulary, but they may petition their plan to maintain coverage of specific drugs based on medical necessity. In any case, Medicare enrollees may switch plans during the end-of-the-year re-enrollment period, effective the following January 1.

c. *Assistance for Lower–Income Enrollees*

Medicare enrollees whose financial resources are sufficiently low to qualify under the Medicaid program receive their pharmaceuticals through that program. See § 5.3 regarding Medicaid eligibility. But certain Medicare enrollees whose resources exceed Medicaid's eligibility criteria may obtain special Medicare Part D benefits that are more extensive than the prototype plan described in § 4.6(b). There are two categories of enrollees who may qualify for these benefits based on their resources and annual income.

The first category applies (in 2006) to people who have resources of no more than $6,000 if an individual or $9,000 if a married couple, and annual income of less than $13,230 if an individual or $17,820 if a married couple. For such persons, Part D provides the following benefits:

1.   No monthly premiums.

2.   No annual deductible.

3.   No "doughnut hole" coverage gap.

4.   Co-payments of $2 for a generic drug (or a preferred "multiple source" drug) and $5 for all other drugs, until an out-of-pocket limit of $3,600 (in 2006) is reached. After that point, there are no further co-payment obligations.

The second category applies (in 2006) to people who have resources of no more than $10,000 if an individual or $20,000 if a married couple, and annual income of less than $14,700 if an individual or

$19,800 if a married couple. For such persons, Part D provides the following benefits:

1.   Monthly premiums that are subsidized on a sliding scale depending upon income.

2.   Annual deductible of $50.

3.   No "doughnut hole" coverage gap.

4.   Co-insurance of 15% of drug costs—i.e., the enrollee pays 15% of drug expenses—until an out-of-pocket limit of $3,600 (in 2006) is reached. After that point, co-payments cannot exceed $2 for a generic drug (or a preferred "multiple source" drug) and $5 for all other drugs.

§ 4.7   Appeal of Claim Denials

As the preceding sections of this Chapter have demonstrated, Medicare is not a program of unlimited benefits. Some of these limitations are mathematical in nature and are easily determined. But many restrictions and exclusions are based on more nebulous and evolving criteria: medically reasonable and necessary; appropriate under the circumstances; no more than six months of remaining life expectancy; and so forth. These standards are inherently subjective. As a result, different conclusions may be reached by different health care providers and reviewers, thereby setting the stage for disputes about whether Medicare will pay for a given service in a particular situation, and to what extent. This section describes the mechanism for resolving such disputes.

a. Waiver of Patient Liability

At the outset, it should be noted that Medicare holds patients harmless in certain circumstances, even if Medicare does not cover the services being disputed. In these situations, the older person is not liable for the costs of the services provided. Rather, it is the health services provider who suffers the economic loss, *not* the patient. This so-called "waiver of liability" applies if a patient did not know, or could not have been expected to know, that Medicare would refuse to pay for the services in question. This standard usually requires written notice to the patient of Medicare's noncoverage.

Even then, the "waiver of liability" applies primarily to three categories of Medicare exclusions. Those exclusions are:

1.   The medical service was not "reasonable and necessary" under Medicare's current diagnosis and treatment standards.

2.   The care provided was "custodial care."

3.   In connection with home health services, the patient is not homebound or is not receiving skilled care on an "intermittent basis."

In most other circumstances, the patient is liable for any costs that Medicare fails to cover.

Moreover, even this limited "waiver of liability" does not excuse a patient from financial responsibility for services provided under Medicare Part B, if those services were provided by a nonparticipating provider who did not "take assignment" of the claim. This rule acts as a further incentive for Medicare enrollees to choose "participating" providers whenever possible.

But the "waiver of liability" provision does apply if the nonparticipating provider was a physician (rather than a hospital, SNF, health services agency, or other supplier), and the services were determined by Medicare to be "not reasonable and necessary." The only time the patient must pay for services in this situation is when the physician gives the patient written notice of the reason why Medicare will not cover the services at issue. Even then, this written notice must be given *before* the services are rendered, and the patient must agree, once again in writing, to pay for those services. Otherwise, the patient is not liable.

b. Appeals Procedures

Beyond the confines of the "waiver of liability" provision, a patient is financially responsible for health care providers' bills that Medicare does not cover. If Medicare declines to pay for services that arguably should be within its benefits, appeals may be made, both administratively and judicially. The precise procedure is usually described in the notice of noncoverage, or similar denial form, that is sent to the patient.

There are five distinct steps in the Medicare appeals process. First, the beneficiary seeks a "redetermination" by a "Medicare administrative contractor," an outside entity hired by Medicare to process Medicare claims. This entity must send the beneficiary a written redetermination within 60 days of receiving the redetermination request.

Second, the claim can be brought for "reconsideration" by a "qualified independent contractor" (QIC), a different outside organization hired by Medicare to handle appeals. The QIC must conclude its reconsideration within 60 days of receiving the request for reconsideration.

Third, appeals of an adverse decision by a QIC can be heard by an administrative law judge (ALJ) within the U.S. Department of Health and Human Services. To reach an ALJ, the claim must involve an amount that is adjusted annually for health cost inflation; in 2006, this threshold was $110. The ALJ must provide a written decision within 90 days of receiving the request for an ALJ hearing.

Fourth, an adverse decision by an ALJ can be appealed to the Medicare Appeals Council of the U.S. Department of Health and Human Services. This Council must decide the case within 90 days of receiving the request for its review.

Finally, a decision of the Council can be brought to Federal district court. To do so, the claim must involve an amount that is adjusted annually for health cost inflation; in 2006, this threshold was $1,090.

An increasing percentage of older patients receive their Medicare coverage through a "health maintenance organization," or HMO. An adverse decision of an HMO is appealable under similar procedures: first, request reconsideration by the HMO according to the HMO's internal grievance procedures. Unfavorable HMO reconsiderations are then appealable to an outside entity hired by the Medicare program called the Center for Health Dispute Resolution. Decisions by this organization are appealable within 60 days of receipt of its decision to an administrative law judge, then to the Medicare Appeals Council, and finally to a Federal district court, subject to the same amount-in-controversy thresholds described earlier.

Interestingly, a Medicare enrollee may represent him or herself in these appeals proceedings. Representation by a personal representative or by an attorney is also permitted. In addition, a patient can be represented by a physician or other health care provider, but with two caveats. One, there can be no question at issue involving the "waiver of liability" provisions described previously, because that situation would create an inherent conflict of interest. Two, the health care provider may not charge the patient for its services in representing the patient through the appeals process.

Medicare provides other appeals procedures exclusively for health care providers, but these mechanisms generally do not involve Medicare patients directly and accordingly are not covered in this volume.

§ 4.8   Private Medigap Insurance

As discussed above, Medicare has a significant co-insurance element for its enrolled participants. They must pay for various deductibles computed by benefit period, by day, and by year, plus co-payment obligations based upon percentages of "approved" charges. The scope of this financial exposure is difficult to estimate in advance, and most of its components increase every year as the related thresholds are indexed for inflation. Still other medical costs—principally pharmaceuticals, outpatient dental costs, and vision care—are not covered at all. As a result, Medicare is not complete coverage and does not apply to first-dollar expenditures.

Many older persons, however, want a way of limiting their exposure to unanticipated medical costs. To satisfy this demand, private insurance companies developed so-called "Medigap" policies to cover many of the costs that Medicare does not. These policies are entirely optional for older persons, and Medicare enrollees may abstain from securing any Medigap coverage, thereby choosing to pay the various deductibles and co-payments themselves.

a. *Standardization of Policies*

Medigap policies have been standardized into twelve different packages. These packages are identified by the letters A through L, with A being the least comprehensive. Any given benefit package, however, is identical across the spectrum of insurance companies. A prospective purchaser must still consider such factors as the premiums being charged, the financial strength of the insurer, the reputation of the insurer in terms of customer service, and the amount of medical information being sought in the application. But those are the only differentiating variables: an E package from one company, for example, covers the exact same items as an E package from any other company. Companies can choose to offer only certain packages, or to restrict the availability of certain packages according to an applicant's age, or to apply tougher underwriting criteria and investigative procedures in deciding whether to issue one policy or another. The contents of the packages themselves, however, are fixed.

b. *Consumer Protection Provisions*

Federal law provides several consumer protection features in addition to package standardization. First, Medigap policies must be guaranteed renewable; only nonpayment of premiums and material misrepresentation on an application constitute reasons for nonrenewal. 42 U.S.C. § 1395ss(q)(1). Of course, premiums may be increased annually, reducing the benefits of this protection somewhat.

Second, a Medigap applicant may not be denied a policy because of pre-existing conditions, if that person applies during the first six months of enrollment in Medicare Part B. 42 U.S.C. § 1395ss(s)(2)(A). This protection generally does not apply after that time, greatly increasing the incentive to obtain Medigap insurance during this particular period. In any case, specific claims relating to pre-existing conditions can be denied coverage, but only if they occur in the first six months after a policy's effective date. Some companies, in fact, limit this exclusion to even shorter periods, typically the first three months of a policy's term.

Another consumer protection provision precludes insurance companies from selling more than one Medigap policy to any one buyer. Federal law provides civil and criminal penalties if anyone knowingly sells a Medigap policy to someone who already has a policy with any of the same benefits. 42 U.S.C. § 1395ss(d)(3). Moreover, any premiums paid for a duplicative policy must be refunded to the buyer. Insurance sellers must obtain a written description from the buyer of any Medigap policies that the buyer currently has, plus a written commitment from the buyer that he or she intends to cancel any existing policies once the new policy takes effect. A buyer need not, however, actually cancel any policies until the replacement coverage becomes effective.

c. *Policy Benefits*

As to the Medigap policies themselves, the packages range from Plan A with its "core group of basic benefits" to more elaborate combinations. States may prohibit the offering of more elaborate packages, but all states must allow Plan A to be offered. Moreover, any given insurance company may choose not to offer every plan that is authorized in any specific state, but all companies operating in the state must offer Plan A.

The five "basic benefits" of Plan A include the following:

1. The Medicare Part A daily deductible for hospitalization days 61–90.

2. The daily deductible for 60 lifetime reserve hospitalization days.

3. An additional 365 lifetime hospitalization days at full coverage.

4. The first three pints of blood not covered by Medicare.

5. The 20% of approved Part B charges that represents the patient's share of these expenses.

Every plan contains these benefits. Plan A contains nothing else.

Plan B adds one feature that is included in all the plans "above" B as well: the Part A deductible on hospital admissions per benefit period. Plan C adds two further benefits that are also found in all plans "above" C: the daily deductible for skilled care in a SNF for days 21–100, and medically necessary emergency care in a foreign country.

Beyond these features, five other features are mixed and matched in various combinations. These five features include the following items:

1. The Part B annual deductible. (Plans C, F, and J.)

2. The balance billing portion of physician charges that a patient must pay if a physician does not "participate" in Medicare. Using the example of a Medicare-approved charge of $100, a nonparticipating physician may charge up to $115, requiring the patient to pay the $15 difference—in addition,

of course, to the 20% co-insurance portion of the Medicare-approved amount (here, $100 × 20% = $20). Actually, this feature comes in two versions: one, available in Plan G only, pays 80% of the excess charges (here, $15 × 80% = $12), with the patient owing the other 20% (here, $3); or, two, available in Plans F, I and J, pays the entire excess (here, $15).

Note that Plan F is more comprehensive with respect to this feature than either Plan G, which covers only 80% of excess costs, or Plan H, which does not cover excess costs at all. Plans G and H do, however, offer other features that are not found in Plan F. The point is that while "higher" lettered plans are generally more comprehensive than "lower" lettered plans, that pattern may not apply to every single feature.

3.   At-home recovery paying up to $40 per visit with a cap of $1,600 per year for short-term assistance in a patient's home with such activities of daily living as bathing, dressing, and personal hygiene. This feature facilitates recovery at home following an illness, injury, or sickness and might forestall a nursing home admission in certain circumstances. (Plans D, G, I, and J.)

4.   Prescription drugs, available in two versions: one, on Plans H and I, provides no coverage for the first $250 of prescription drugs per year, but then pays 50% of the cost of drugs thereafter, up to an annual limit of $1,250; two, available in Plan J only, has the same annual deductible and 50% co-insur-

ance requirement but with an annual limit of $3,000. Note that only medigap policies that were initially obtained before 2006 offer prescription drug benefits. See § 4.6 regarding Medicare Part D coverage of prescription drugs.

5.   Preventive medical care for physical examinations, influenza shots, hearing tests, diabetes screenings, cholesterol screenings, and thyroid function tests—all subject to a annual limit of $120. (Plans E and J.)

In addition, Plans F and J come in two versions: either as described above, or with a high deductible feature. The high deductible version does not pay for covered benefits until the policyholder satisfies an annual deductible of covered expenses. 42 U.S.C. § 1395ss(p)(11). This deductible is increased annually; in 2006, it was $1,790.

A very different approach is taken in Plans K and L. Both plans provide the same coverage of hospital co-payment obligations as Plans A through J provide. But Plan K covers only 50%, and Plan L covers only 75%, of the following five benefits:

1.   Part B's 20% co-payment obligation other than for preventive services, which are covered in full.

2.   Part A's spell-of-illness deductible ($952 in 2006).

3.   Part A's skilled nursing facility deductible for days 21–100 ($119 in 2006).

4.   Three pints of blood.

5.   Hospice care cost-sharing; see § 4.3(d).

For example, assume that Jamel incurs $2,500 of doctors' bills in connection with an operation. Assume further that Jamel has already satisfied this year's Part B annual deductible and that $2,500 is the Medicare-approved charge for this procedure. In this circumstance, Jamel would owe 20% of this cost, or $500. If Jamel has a Medigap Plan K, that policy would cover 50% of his $500 obligation, or $250. If Jamel had a Medigap Plan L instead, that policy would have covered 75% of his $500 obligation, or $375. By comparison, Medigap Plans A through J would have covered the entire $500 as one of the "basic benefits."

Plans K and L do, however, have an annual limit on a policyholder's out-of-pocket expenditures for covered services. After that limit is reached, all further deductibles, co-payments, and co-insurance obligations under Medicare Parts A and B (other than physicians' "balance billing" charges) are covered by the Medigap policy. This limit is adjusted annually and in 2006, it was $4,000 for Plan K and $2,000 for Plan L.

Beyond these features, Medigap policies do not go. In other words, Medigap policies fill *some* of the gaps in Medicare's coverage but by no means all. Vision care, eyeglasses, hearing aids, and dental care are not covered, except in connection with an injury. But the biggest gap of all is the absence of custodial care coverage—or for that matter, skilled care in a skilled nursing facility after the first 100 days. To address that need, one must examine an entirely different insurance product—namely, long-term care insurance. See generally Chapter 6.

§ 4.9 Managed Care and Other Alternatives

As noted previously, most of the Medicare-eligible population utilizes the programs described thus far in this Chapter. Approximately one in eight beneficiaries enroll in Medicare health maintenance organizations (HMO) or other forms of managed care. Other alternatives to "traditional" Medicare have recently become available as well. This section considers these options.

a. Managed Care

In contrast to traditional Medicare's fee-for-service orientation, Medicare managed care organizations collect a fixed payment per enrollee each month from the government. In addition, the enrollee generally pays the Medicare Part B premium to the HMO, plus an additional amount, which varies by plan. In return, the Medicare HMO provides all the services the enrollee requires (as determined by the HMO), without the array of deductibles, limitations, and co-payments that traditional Medicare imposes. Medigap insurance is also unnecessary in most plans. On the other hand, an enrollee is limited to a specified group of physicians, hospitals, pharmacies, and sometimes other providers as well.

Although managed care arrangements vary in their details, they typically provide additional benefits that are geared to patients' routine medical needs. For example, most plans cover prescription drugs, subject to a nominal co-payment and often to an annual dollar limitation. Many HMOs also cover eyeglasses, hearing aids, wellness programs, nutrition guidance, and even dental care in their benefit packages.

Similarly, physical examinations are provided on a regular basis in keeping with the HMOs' emphasis on preventive care. This orientation can translate into better health care for the enrollee by spotting problems early and by coordinating specialist care. Of course, the HMO also benefits if it manages to avoid the need for expensive medical treatments, because such treatments represent additional costs for the HMO. The flip side of this arrangement, however, is that the HMO may limit the range of treatments offered or may deny coverage for certain procedures. Medicare managed care, in other words, parallels managed care generally.

Medicare HMOs do have one incontrovertible advantage—simplicity. Managed care plans eliminate almost all of the paperwork associated with health insurance arrangements. Moreover, a retiree's financial exposure is generally limited to nominal co-payments for pharmaceuticals and in some plans, for office visits. But if a retiree needs medical care while outside an HMO's geographic service area, the retiree usually must file a claim for reimbursement. Coverage of such care varies by plan, but some hassle and out-of-pocket expense are not uncommon, especially if the care rendered was not "urgent."

Medicare HMOs must offer an appeals procedure for enrollees to challenge decisions that refuse reimbursement of nonplan services or that deny care generally. 42 U.S.C. § 1395mm(c)(5)(B). The HMO must notify enrollees within 30 days of a grievance's being received. An appeal can be made to an independent review organization, then to an administrative law judge, then to the Medicare Appeals Council, and finally to a Federal district court, according to the procedures described in § 4.7(b) for Medicare appeals generally. But an enrollee or a physician can request an expedited 72–hour review, if a longer wait would seriously jeopardize the enrollee's life or health. 42 U.S.C. § 1395w–22(g)(3).

Persons who enroll in a managed care plan when they first become eligible for Medicare benefits at age 65 may leave that plan in favor of "traditional" Medicare at any time during the first year of their enrollment. 42 U.S.C. § 1395w–21(e)(4) (final sentence). After that first year, a Medicare enrollee may switch managed care plans or elect "traditional" Medicare only once during the first three months of the plan year. 42 U.S.C. § 1395w–21(e)(2)(C)(i), (ii). Such changes take effect at the beginning of the next month. 42 U.S.C. § 1395mm(c)(3)(B). In addition, a person may switch plans whenever he or she moves out of a managed care plan's service area. 42 U.S.C. § 1395w–21(e)(4)(B). Finally, beneficiaries may switch plans during the annual re-enrollment period that begins on November 15, effective the following January. 42 U.S.C. § 1395w–21(e)(3)(B)(iv).

b. *Other Options*

Medicare beneficiaries have a variety of options that are collectively designated "Medicare Advantage" or Medicare Part C. 42 U.S.C § 1395w–21. Some of these options are slight modifications of the Medicare HMOs described above. For example, a Provider–Sponsored Organization is very similar to a Medicare HMO, but it is operated by doctors, hospitals, and other health care providers, rather than by insurance companies.

Another variant is the Preferred Provider Organization (PPO), which covers services rendered by its designated health care providers, but which also covers *part* of the cost of services rendered by other providers. PPO enrollees pay the remainder of the cost incurred, which operates as an incentive to stay within the PPO's network. This feature is also offered in some Medicare HMOs as a "point-of-service" option, for which an additional premium is usually charged by the HMO.

A very different alternative is the private fee-for-service insurance plan, which covers most Medicare services, plus routine physical examinations and prescription drugs. These plans can cover any health care provider, and charges for the services provided are not limited to Medicare's "approved" charges. See § 4.4(b) regarding such charges. Beneficiaries pay their Part B premiums plus an additional amount each month to the plan. Thus far, only a few areas of the country have such plans.

Plans can also be offered by "religious fraternal benefit societies." These plans must be offered exclusively to members of a church, association of churches, or affiliated groups of churches. 42 U.S.C. § 1395w–28(e)(2)(A). The "society" cannot limit membership based on health status, and the plans must provide health coverage to members who are not entitled to Medicare benefits. 42 U.S.C. § 1395w–28(e)(3)(C), (D).

c. *Medigap Insurance and Managed Care Options*

As indicated previously, persons who enroll in Medicare managed care typically do not need Medigap insurance. But if a person leaves managed care, the need for such insurance returns. The same situation can apply if a managed care plan leaves the Medicare program at the end of the year, a phenomenon that has increased dramatically in recent years. In either circumstance, the Medicare enrollee may want to acquire a Medigap policy but is probably beyond the first six months of Medicare eligibility during which Medigap policies cannot be denied for health reasons. See § 4.8(b). Certain protections do apply, however, depending upon the particular situation.

The first such situation involves a person who joined a managed care plan when he or she first became eligible for Medicare at age 65. If that person leaves the plan within the first year, the no-denial rule is still in effect, as long as the person applies for a Medigap policy within 63 calendar days after the managed care plan's coverage ceases. For example, Melony first became eligible for Medicare at age 65 on February 2, and she enrolled in a Medicare HMO at that time. She has now decided to leave that plan, effective September 30. She cannot be denied any Medigap policy for health reasons if she applies for such policy by December 2 (i.e., 63 days after September 30).

A different situation involves someone who *had* a Medigap policy, but dropped it to join a managed care plan, which he then leaves. If this is the first time that person enrolled in a Medicare managed care plan, and if that person left this plan within one year after joining, the enrollee may return to the same Medigap policy that he owned previously. Once again, application for the new policy must occur within 63 calendar days after the managed care plan's coverage ceases.

In all other situations, an enrollee's Medigap options may be limited by that person's medical condition, but Plans A, B, C, or F are always available. 42 U.S.C. § 1395ss(s)(3)(A), (B)(iii), (C)(i). See § 4.8(c) regarding those plans. Once again, enrollees must apply for a Medigap policy within 63 calendar days of losing their managed care plan's coverage. Among the persons covered by this provision are enrollees who lose their Medicare HMO coverage when they move outside the HMO's geographic service area, and enrollees who lose managed care coverage when their plan leaves the Medicare program.

CHAPTER 5

MEDICAID

§ 5.1 History

Created in 1965, Medicaid is a Federal program designed to pay for the medical expenses of low-income individuals who are aged, blind or disabled. Title XIX of the Social Security Act (42 U.S.C. § 1396 et seq.) delegates authority to the Department of Health and Human Services (DHHS) to approve state plans for medical assistance, which are to be paid for by both the Federal and state governments. The state cost of Medicaid varies from approximately 25% to 50%. Responsibility for administering Medicaid rests with the Centers for Medicare and Medicaid Services (CMS). The Center for Medicaid and State Operations (CMSO) focuses on the Medicaid program operated by the states. Medicaid does not provide medical services directly nor does it reimburse individuals for their out-of-pocket medical expenses. Instead, Medicaid, acting through state agencies, reimburses providers of medical care.

Participation in Medicaid by states is voluntary, but every state plus the District of Columbia has elected to do so. Most states refer to their programs as Medicaid, but some title it Medical Assistance, and California calls it Medical. By whatever name, all programs are part of the Federal Medicaid program and are governed by its rules. Though state laws and regulations (known as state Medical Assistance Plans) cannot be more restrictive than the Federal law, individual state Medicaid programs vary. Eligibility is established by Federal law, but eligibility issues that depend upon state family or property law are governed by state law. The Federal supremacy clause applies only if the state law would significantly conflict with Federal interests. Though each state has its individual approaches to Medicaid, it is a Federally governed program whose operation can be described in general terms. Unless otherwise noted, states must follow Federal law as to eligibility and what services they provide. The territories of Puerto Rico, the Virgin Islands, Guam, the Northern Mariana Islands, and American Samoa also participate in Medicaid, but operate under different programs. The following discussion may not be applicable to those programs.

§ 5.2 Available Benefits

In 2005, Medicaid provided benefits to over 53 million individuals at a combined Federal and state cost of over $330 billion. The Medicaid statute guarantees certain medical services for eligible individuals including the poor elderly. States may, at their expense, expand benefits, and many have done so.

Under Federal law, state medical assistance programs must provide the following services to older persons; inpatient hospital services (other than in a mental hospital); inpatient hospital services and nursing facility services for individuals age 65 or older in an institution for mental diseases; outpatient hospital services; rural health clinic services; laboratory and X-ray services; nursing facility services for individuals age 21 or older; physicians' services, medical and surgical services furnished by a dentist, midwife services, and medical care furnished by practitioners licensed under state law; home health care services; private duty nursing services; nurse practitioner services; clinic services furnished on or off-site under the directions of a physician; dental services; physical therapy services; prescribed drugs, dentures, prosthetic devices and eyeglasses prescribed by a physician or optometrist; diagnostic, screening, preventative and rehabilitative services; intermediate care facility services for the mentally retarded other than in an institution for mental diseases; hospice care; case-management services; and respiratory care services and any other medical care recognized under state law as specified by the Secretary of Health and Human Services.

Although Medicaid initially was envisioned as existing primarily for poor younger persons, it provides significant benefits to older persons in the form of required reimbursement of the costs of nursing home care. State Medicaid programs must also provide limited home and community care for functionally disabled elderly individuals. Medicaid mandates home health care only for the categorically needy, not for the medically needy (defined below) except for those who are entitled to skilled nursing care. Several states, however, do provide additional home health benefits for the medically needy. If the state does provide home health services it must include nursing services, home health aide services, and medical supplies, and equipment. Some states also provide personal care services in a recipient's home.

As a result of the high cost of institutionalization in a hospital or nursing home, many states, known as "waiver states," are provided special Federal funds, called "waivers," to provide Medicaid services to individuals who live at home or with a relative or friend. Most older persons much prefer to remain at home rather than being forced to enter a nursing home. The daily reimbursement amount for home care is less than what is paid for nursing home care, so that the provision of health care in the home is less costly than requiring the patient to receive care in a nursing home.

Waiver states can provide a variety of home services such as homemaker services, home health aides, personal care services, adult day care health services, habilitative services for the mentally retarded, respite care, case management, and other services approved by HCFA as being cost-effective.

§ 5.3 Eligibility Requirements

State Medical Assistance Programs must provide benefits for financially needy individuals who are known as the "categorically needy." They are defined as individuals who are: aged, blind, or disabled individuals eligible for Supplemental Security Income (SSI) (see Chapter 12, Supplemental Security Income) under Title XVI of the Social Security Act.

Under Federal law, other individuals who also are defined as being categorically needy include those who would be eligible for SSI, but for the 1972 and post-April 1977 cost of living increases in Social Security benefits; and those who are qualified Medicare beneficiaries (QMB), meaning those who qualify for Medicare Part A (hospital insurance, see § 4.1(a)) whose income does not exceed the Federal poverty line and whose resources do not exceed twice the SSI resource eligibility standard.

When SSI was adopted in 1974, it expanded eligibility for Medicaid. To permit states to avoid the correspondingly higher costs, Congress gave states the option to apply more restrictive eligibility standards than those permitted under SSI. States could elect to include only those individuals who were eligible for Medicaid before SSI was enacted. The states that elected the stricter eligibility rules are known as Section 209(b) states (named after the section of law that permitted the stricter eligibility requirements). These states use eligibility standards that are generally stricter than those under SSI. However, Section 209(b) states must create eligibility under the categorically needy standard for individuals who "spend down" their income on medical expenses. The mechanism of spend-down is described below in the description of the "medically needy" category.

The Section 209(b) states are: Connecticut, Hawaii, Illinois, Indiana, Minnesota, Missouri, Nebraska, New Hampshire, North Dakota, Ohio, Oklahoma, Utah and Virginia.

a. Financial Eligibility Requirements: Income

Individuals age 65 or older are eligible for Medicaid if they meet the income and resource tests. Except in Section 209(b) states, individuals are eligible for Medicaid if they meet the requirements for SSI. Individuals who are eligible for even one dollar of SSI qualify for Medicaid.

In 2006, the income limit for SSI eligibility was $603 a month for a noninstitutionalized individual and $904 for a noninstitutionalized couple. (The income limits are adjusted annually for inflation.) The determination of income for SSI purposes is fully discussed in § 12.1(a). What follows is a summary of the basic principles. Chapter 12, however, should be consulted for the specifics.

Income for SSI purposes is "anything you receive in cash or in-kind that you can use to meet your needs for food or shelter." (20 C.F.R. § 416.1102.) In-kind income is food or shelter or something that can be use to obtain these items. An item that is not food or shelter, or cannot be used to obtain them, is not income for determining SSI eligibility. (For a detailed list, see § 12.2.)

If a SSI recipient lives in the household of another and receives free food and shelter, the value of these items is held to be worth one-third of the

Federal SSI benefit rate ($603 in 2006), and the monthly benefit is reduced accordingly. The actual value of the items is irrelevant as the presumption of value is not rebuttable.

If the recipient receives food *or* shelter, but not both, a presumed value rule applies under which the value of the items is presumed to equal one-third of the SSI benefit plus any amount left of the $20 general income exclusion (explained below). This presumption, however, is rebuttable if the recipient can prove that the fair market value of the item is less than the presumed value. If the fair market value is more than the presumed value, the presumed value governs and the fair market value is ignored.

For example, assume Scott, an SSI recipient, lives with his brother rent-free, but pays for his own food. The fair market value of the rent is $150 a month. Because the presumed value of one-third the basic rate plus $20 ($\frac{1}{3}$ x $603 = $201 + $20 = $221), Scott's SSI will be reduced only by the actual value of the rent. If the fair market value of the rent was more than $221, the presumed value of $221 would be the amount of the reduction of monthly benefits.

Two types of income are excluded from the SSI determination of income: (1) a $20 general income exclusion; and (2) an "earned income exclusion." The $20 general income exclusion applies first to unearned income, and if unearned income is less than $20, then to earned income. Unearned income is any income other than wages, salary, wages from self-employment or any other payment for services whether in cash or in-kind. Typical unearned income includes pensions, Social Security benefits, interest, dividends, and rents.

After the $20 exclusion has been applied, the recipient may exclude earned income up to $65, plus one-half of the remainder of the earned income after the $65 exclusion. The amount of income left after the exclusion of the $20 any income amount and the earned income exclusion is referred to as countable income. It is the amount of a SSI recipient's countable income that determines the amount of the SSI payment and thus eligibility for Medicaid.

For example, Paul, age 70, earns $415 a month and receives $220 a month from Social Security for a total of $635. His countable income, however, is much less. First, he can exclude the $20 income exclusion from his unearned income, Social Security. Next, he can claim the $65 a month earned income exclusion and exclude one-half of the rest of his earned income for a total of $240 ($415 − $65 = $350 ÷ 2 = $175 + $65 = $240). His countable income is $635 less $260 ($20 unearned income exclusion + $240 earned income exclusion) or $375. In 2006, Paul would have been eligible for a monthly SSI benefit of $228 ($603 − $375), as well as being eligible for Medicaid.

b. *Financial Eligibility Requirements: Resources*

Resource eligibility limits are $2,000 for an individual and $3,000 for married couples if both apply for benefits. (Section 209(b) states may use a lower dollar amount.) Not all resources are counted in determining eligibility; whatever assets are excluded for SSI eligibility purposes are also excluded for Medicaid eligibility. The personal residence, if the individual's equity interest in the house is $500,000 or less ($750,000 if the state so elects), is an excluded resource as long as the individual lives in it, expects to return to it, or has a spouse living in it. If the equity value of the house exceeds $500,000 ($750,000 if the state so elects), the individual is not eligible for Medicaid. (The $500,000 and $750,000 will be indexed for inflation beginning in 2011.)

The value of household and personal belongings are excluded. Other exempt assets include an automobile necessary for transportation for the individual or a member of the individual's household (the equity value in a second automobile is counted as a resource); the cash surrender value of life insurance, if the face value of the policies does not exceed $1,500; and the value of burial plots and up to $1,500 specifically set aside for burial expenses. For a complete discussion of excluded assets, see the discussion in § 12.1(b).

The Deficit Reduction Act of 2005, effective February 8, 2006, extended eligibility for the Long–Term Care Insurance Partnership to all states. In general, the Partnership permits an individual who purchases state-certified long-term care insurance to become eligible for Medicaid after all benefits under the policy have been paid. The individual can retain a certain value of assets, typically up to the value of the benefits paid by the long-term care insurance and be eligible for Medicaid so long as the income eligibility requirements are met. (See § 6.7.)

c. *Qualified Medicare Beneficiary Program*

State Medicaid programs are required to pay the cost of Medicare (including HMO charges) for eligible low income persons, including Medicare premiums, copayments, and deductibles under a program called the Qualified Medicare Beneficiaries Program (QMB Program). Individuals qualify for QMB if their resources do not exceed more than twice the level for SSI beneficiaries, or $4,000 for an individual or $6,000 for an eligible couple. Their income cannot exceed the federal poverty level, which in 2006 was $9,800 for an individual and $13,200 for a couple. Individuals with income up to 120% of the poverty level are also eligible for is called the Specified Low Income Medicare Beneficiaries Program (SLMB Program),but the state Medicaid program will pay only the monthly Medicare Part B premium, not the other copayments or deductibles. Due to a lack of publicity by the states, the enrollment rates in the QMB and SLMB Programs are very low.

§ 5.4 Optional Coverage

Individuals who are not eligible for SSI may still qualify for Medicaid. Federal law permits states to extend medical assistance benefits to the optionally categorically needy including institutionalized individuals with limited incomes, and to provide home and community based benefits under a waiver program.

a.   The Optional Categorically Needy

The Federal Medicaid statute provides a dozen categories of individuals that, at the option of the state, may be included as individuals who are covered as being members of the categorically needy. They include individuals eligible for SSI benefits, but not receiving them, individuals who but for receiving state income supplements would be eligible for SSI, and institutionalized individuals whose incomes are low enough so that, but for being institutionalized, they would be eligible for SSI.

Also eligible as optional categorically needy are individuals for whom there has been a determination that they will require institutionalization in a hospital, nursing facility, or facility for the mentally retarded unless they are provided home or community-based services.

States may also extend Medicaid eligibility to individuals living in an institution (usually meaning a nursing home) who meet the resource eligibility requirements and whose income does not exceed 300% of the maximum SSI benefit for a single individual. States who adopt this eligibility standard are known as "income cap" states because institutionalized individuals are eligible for Medicaid only if their income is less than the amount of the income cap. The maximum SSI benefit is adjusted annually for inflation. In 2006, it was $603 and so the income cap was $1,809.

In 2006, individuals residing in nursing homes in income cap states who had monthly incomes of $1,809 or less could qualify for Medicaid if they met the resource test. Even if they had excessive resources, they could "spend down" their resources, that is, use their savings to pay the nursing home bills until the remaining savings meet the resource eligibility test. At that point, they could apply for Medicaid, which would pay for the cost of the nursing home to the extent that it exceeded their income.

For example, Jane, age 66 and a widow, has income from Social Security and a small private pension that total $1,100 a month. She lives in an income cap state. She enters a nursing home as a private pay patient at a monthly cost of $5,400. She does not own a home or a car (potentially exempt resources), but she has savings of $28,000. After five months of paying for the cost of her nursing home, Jane has exhausted her savings. Because her income is less than the cap, she is eligible for Medicaid. She pays her share of $1,070 (her monthly income less $30 a month allowed to her as her personal needs allowance), and Medicaid pays the balance of her nursing home expenses.

In states that use an income cap as a standard for optional eligibility, many individuals who cannot afford the costs of nursing homes are nevertheless ineligible for Medicaid because their income exceeds the cap ($1,809 in 2006). Excess income of even one dollar results in a loss of eligibility, and individuals cannot refuse a source of income merely to create

Medicaid eligibility. For example, an applicant for Medicaid cannot attempt to create eligibility by refusing to accept a private pension or Social Security. Because of the severity of the effect of excess income, some individuals who need nursing home care, but cannot afford to pay for it, move to states that apply the more liberal medically needy standard of eligibility. (Discussed below.)

b. *Medically Needy*

States are permitted to extend medical assistance to medically needy individuals. The medically needy category is an alternative to the option of using the income cap test to determine categorically needy eligibility. The medically needy standard is more liberal than the income cap test because no one is excluded from becoming eligible no matter how great their income. Even if their income exceeds the SSI eligibility limit, individuals can qualify as medically needy if they meet the applicable SSI resource test, and if their income is insufficient to pay for the cost of their nursing home or other medical care.

To qualify as medically needy, the individual must meet the resource limitations of $2,000 for an individual and $3,000 for married couples. Individuals with excess assets are permitted to spend down (pay for their medical care) until they meet the resource eligibility standard.

Over two-thirds of the states have medically needy programs that create Medicaid eligibility for noninstitutionalized individuals. Nine section 209(b) states also have medically needy programs.

In medically needy states, individuals become eligible for Medicaid by spending down their income in payment of their medical expenses until their remaining monthly income is below 133% of the applicable Aid for Families with Dependent Children (AFDC) payment. (In a few states the percentage limit is lower.) Though the 1996 welfare reform essentially eliminated the AFDC program, Medicaid continues to use the July 16, 1996 AFDC income levels as adjusted for inflation, to determine medically needy eligibility.

Since state AFDC payments varied greatly from state to state, so do the medically needy income eligibility requirements. For couples, the standard is income not in excess of 133% of the highest monthly payment for a family of the same size. For an individual, it is 133% of the payment that would be made to a family of two, i.e. a parent and a child. As an example of the creation of Medicaid eligibility in a spend down state assume that Alice, a 67 year old widow, lives in a state in which the AFDC payment for a mother and a child, for example, is $300 a month. The spend down income limit is therefore $400 a month (133% of $300). Assume that Alice has medical bills in June of $750. Her only income is a monthly payment of $850 from Social Security. Subtracting the minimum monthly income level of $400 from her income of $850, means that she must spend $450 on medical expenses to be eligible for Medicaid. After she pays for $450 of her medical expenses, Medicaid will pay the remaining $300.

The majority of states have a medically needy category that creates eligibility for institutionalized individuals whose incomes exceed the SSI eligibility limit. In these states, institutionalized individuals, who meet the resource requirements but have excess income, must spend down their income for medical expenses until their remaining income meets the eligibility requirements. The result is that the individual pays for as much of medical care as can be afforded with Medicaid paying whatever amounts remain. For example, Bruce has a monthly income of $2,750 a month, but monthly nursing home bills of $5,000. Assuming he meets the resource eligibility test, he qualifies for Medicaid as being medically needy, and Medicaid will pay the difference between his income and the cost of the nursing home. Bruce will retain $30 per month for his personal expenses and pay the remaining $2,720 to the nursing home. Medicaid will pay the difference between $2,720 and the amount that Medicaid will pay to a nursing home in that region. Typically, Medicaid pays less than the rate charged to a private pay resident.

The determination of eligibility is made each month, and an individual could be eligible in June, ineligible in July, if he or she had few medical expenses, and be eligible again in August if medical expenses were very high.

§ 5.5 Support for the Community Spouse

Many individuals apply for Medicaid because they are unable to afford the cost of a nursing home

facility. Known as institutionalized Medicaid applicants, these individuals, if married, face special
eligibility rules. These rules allocate a portion of the
couple's assets to the noninstitutionalized spouse,
referred to as the community spouse, and attempt
to provide the community spouse with income sufficient for his or her support. MCCA spousal support
rules come into play if the Medicaid applicant is
expected to be institutionalized for thirty days or
more.

The MCCA rules permit a married individual to
become medically eligible for Medicaid without requiring the community spouse to become destitute.
(42 U.S.C. § 1396r–5.) First, the community spouse
need not use his or her income to pay for the care of
the institutionalized spouse. If, for example, Judy
and Jim are married and Jim enters a nursing
home, Judy is not required to use any of her income
to pay for Jim's nursing home expenses. Second,
income belongs to the spouse whose name is on the
check. So, if Judy and Jim both receive Social
Security, each is considered the sole owner of his or
her respective checks. Judy's income from her Social Security is not considered available to pay the
cost of Jim's institutionalization. Checks payable to
both spouses are allocated according to their respective ownership interests, or if there is none, then
equally between them.

Third, the community spouse has a right to a
minimum monthly maintenance needs allowance
(MMMNA). If the community spouse's monthly income is less than the MMMNA, the community

spouse has a right to a minimum income allowance paid out of the institutionalized spouse's income. The MMMNA is equal to 150% of the official poverty level for a family of two ($1,650 as of July 1, 2006) plus an excess shelter allowance which when added to the MMMNA cannot exceed the MMMNA cap ($2,489 as of July 1, 2006). The amount is adjusted every July 1 for inflation. The excess shelter allowance is computed by totaling the community spouse's cost of shelter, including rent or mortgage payments, taxes, and utilities. To the extent that these expenses exceed 30% of the income allowance (30% of $1,604 or $482 in 2006), the community spouse has a right to an excess shelter allowance subject to the MMMNA cap. If the income of the community spouse is less than the MMMNA, the institutionalized spouse is required to contribute income to the community spouse. This will result in the institutionalized spouse having less income available to pay for the cost of institutionalization, and thereby increases the portion of the cost of institutionalization paid by Medicaid.

The amount of the MMMNA may be increased if a court has entered an order requiring the institutionalized spouse to provide a certain level of support of the community spouse. The community spouse also has a right to request a fair hearing and ask for additional income from the institutionalized spouse "due to exceptional circumstances resulting in significant financial duress." (42 U.S.C. § 1396r–5(d)(1)(c).)

The community spouse who is entitled to additional income obtains it from the institutionalized spouse by an income-first policy in which income of the institutionalized spouse is diverted to the community spouse to bring the community spouse's income up to the MMMNA. If diverting all the institutionalized spouse's income to the community spouse does not meet the MMMNA, then sufficient resources of the institutionalized spouse are transferred to the community spouse to create enough income to make up the shortfall in the MMMNA.

Finally, though the institutionalized spouse must spend down excess resources to establish eligibility, the community spouse has a right to retain some resources to assist in his or her support. The spouse of an institutionalized individual is permitted to retain a "community spouse resource allowance." The exact amount of resource that the community spouse can retain depends upon state law, but Federal law mandates that in 2006 the community spouse be permitted to retain a minimum of $19,908 of nonexempt resources (adjusted annually every January 1 for inflation). The maximum that a state can permit the community spouse to retain in 2006 was $99,540 (adjusted annually for inflation). While a few states have adopted the maximum figure as what the community spouse can own, most states permit the community spouse to own up to one-half of the couple's resources up to a maximum of $99,540 (in 2006). The resource allowance can exceed the maximum dollar figure if increased by court order, or if the community spouse can demonstrate the need for additional assets to produce income required to meet the spouse's minimum monthly maintenance needs allowance.

For example, suppose Anita and Kevin are married. Kevin enters a nursing home. They own their house and other assets of a value of $120,000. Anita will be permitted to keep the house, since it is an excluded asset. If the state allows her to keep ½ of the assets she will be permitted to retain $60,000 (½ of $120,000). The other $60,000 will have to be spent before Kevin can qualify for Medicaid.

The community spouse resource allowance does not include exempt assets described in the discussion on SSI (see § 12.1(b)), the most important of which is the home. The community spouse can retain, therefore, the home if the equity value is $500,000 (or $750,000) or less, its contents and the family car, plus up to the maximum resource allowance permitted by the state.

The calculation of the community spouse resource allowance depends upon the value of the couple's assets on the first day of the institutionalized spouse's continuous institutionalization for at least 30 days regardless of when the application for Medicaid occurs. A "snapshot" is taken of the value of the couples assets without regard for title or community property rights. The right of the community spouse to resources has no relation to how the resources are titled. The total value of any assets owned by one or the other or jointly is determined.

Based upon the value of all of their assets, the amount of the community spouse resource allowance is then calculated. When the institutionalized spouse eventually applies for Medicaid, the community spouse is granted the spousal resource allowance amount. All additional nonexempt assets must be spent until they are exhausted. At that point, Medicaid will take over the institutionalized costs if the income eligibility test is met.

When one spouse enters an institution, the state Medicaid agency can be requested to determine the amount of the potential community spousal allowance. The state agency is permitted to charge for this determination if it is not made as part of a Medicaid application. Nonetheless, a request for a determination should be made at the time of institutionalization, since to calculate it later when applying for Medicaid will make the calculation very difficult to reconstruct. Because the amount of the couple's assets that can be retained by the community spouse is determined by what they owned at the date of the commencement of the institutionalization, it is critical to calculate accurately what the couple owned at that date.

If the community spouse acquires additional assets after the "snapshot" date, i.e. the first date of institutionalization, such assets are not counted against the resource allowance and may be retained by the community spouse. If assets are acquired jointly or solely by the institutionalized spouse, it is not clear what happens. Several commentators have argued that the community spouse should be allowed to keep half of such assets, while others believe that all after-acquired assets must be spent-down for the cost of institutionalization. To date, there is no definitive answer.

An institutionalized individual's income can also be diverted from payment of the costs of institutionalization to support certain dependent family members. These can include minor children, dependent children, parents, or siblings of either spouse who reside with the community spouse.

§ 5.6   Transfer of Resources

Individuals who expect to enter a nursing home often contemplate giving away assets in order to create Medicaid eligibility. However, Federal Medicaid law imposes a period of ineligibility for individuals who transfer assets for less than fair market value if they subsequently seek Medicaid reimbursement for long-term, institutionalized care or home-based or community-based services. (At the option of the state asset transfers may or may not affect eligibility for noninstitutionalized Medicaid care.) Gifts made before February 8, 2006 (the effective date of the Deficit Reduction Act of 2005 (DRA)) and within 36 months of making application for Medicaid create a period of Medicaid ineligibility. The 36 month period is called the "look-back" period. For gifts made on or after February 8, 2006, the look-back period is 60 months. If gifts were made during the look-back period, the applicant is ineligible for as many months as determined by dividing the total value of the transfer by the average monthly cost of nursing home services (as determined by the state) in the state or community where the applicant resides. There is no limit on the number of months of ineligibility. If there was more than one transfer, the total value of all transfers is aggregated to determine the number of months of ineligibility.

For example, on February 1, 2005, Sylvia gave $150,000 to her daughter. On March 1, 2007, she entered a nursing home and applied for Medicaid. Because the transfer for Medicaid came within 36 months of the date of the application for Medicaid, it is within the look-back period. If the average monthly nursing home cost in her state is $5,000, Sylvia will be ineligible for Medicaid for 30 months ($150,000 divided by $5,000). For gifts made before the DRA, the penalty begins to run on the first day of the month of the transfer.

Suppose Tom gives his son $80,000 on June 1, 2006 (post-DRA). On June 1, 2010, Tom enters a nursing home. Because the post-DRA look-back is 60 months, the gift creates a period of ineligibility. For post-DRA gifts (on or after February 8, 2006), the period of ineligibility begins in the month the individual enters a nursing home or is medically eligible for nursing home care and would otherwise be eligible for Medicaid, except for the penalty period caused by the gift. In Tom's case, if upon entering the nursing home, he met the income and resource eligibility tests, the penalty period would begin on June 1, 2010. If the average cost of a nursing home in Tom's state is $5,000, the penalty period would be 16 months ($80,000 ÷ $5,000 = 16). Tom would become eligible for Medicaid on October 1, 2011, or 16 months after he entered the nursing home.

Regardless of the date of the gift, the period of ineligibility is not affected by when the applicant enters a nursing home. The period of ineligibility for Medicaid reimbursement of nursing home expenses is the same whether the applicant lives in the community or is institutionalized at the time of the transfer.

Transfers of assets by the community spouse to a third party create the same period of ineligibility as transfers by the institutionalized spouse. If the applicant held assets jointly or as tenants in common, any action by the joint owner or any other person that reduces or eliminates the applicant's ownership or control of the asset is a transfer and triggers the period of ineligibility if it occurred within 36 or 60 months of making application for Medicaid.

Transfers of assets will not affect Medicaid eligibility if the assets were transferred for fair value or were transferred for a purpose other than creating Medicaid eligibility. Transfers to or for the sole benefit of the institutionalized person's spouse (the community spouse) do not create a period of ineligibility, nor do transfers to blind or permanently and totally disabled children.

§ 5.7   Treatment of the Home

An applicant's home, the principal place of residence is not counted as a resource in determining

Medicaid eligibility so long as the individual's equity in the home does not exceed $500,000 ($750,000 if the state so elects). If the individual's equity exceeds $500,000 (or $750,000), the individual is not eligible for Medicaid. Note that the home is an excluded resource even if the individual does not live in it so long as there is an intent to return.

The intent to return is a subjective standard. Usually an expression to return by the applicant is sufficient no matter how implausible that may be from a medical standpoint. Even if the applicant lives in an institution and does not intend to return home, it still will not count as a resource as long as a spouse or dependent relative continues to live there.

If the home is sold the proceeds become countable assets unless they are used to purchase another home within three months of the date of receipt. Any proceeds not used to purchase a new home become countable resources unless spent within the month received. If, rather than selling the home, the applicant rents it, the rental proceeds are countable income and the home is a countable resource.

Jointly owned property that is not the applicant's principal residence will not count as resource if the sale of the property would cause the other owner undue hardship due to the loss of a place to live. If the joint property is the principal residence of the other owner, the sale of that property will be considered a hardship and so the property is not a countable resource and will not affect Medicaid eligibility.

Applicants who transfer their homes trigger the period of ineligibility unless the transfer is to a spouse; a child under age 21, blind or disabled; a sibling who has an equity interest in the home and who lived in it for at least one year before the date of the applicant's institutionalization; or a child who lived in the home for at least two years before the date of institutionalization and who provided care to the individual that permitted them to live at home rather than in an institution.

§ 5.8   Transfers, Trusts and Medicaid Eligibility

In the case of revocable trusts, the trust principal is considered a resource available to the applicant. Transfers *from* a trust (revocable or irrevocable) created or funded by the Medicaid applicant to a third party invoke the 60 month look-back period.

The applicant is considered to have established a trust if assets of the individual were used to form all or part of the corpus of the trust by the individual or by the individual's spouse, any person empowered to act on the individual's or spouse's behalf (e.g., a holder of a power of attorney) or anyone acting at the request of the individual or the spouse. Acts by a court on behalf of the individual using the individual's assets are also attributed to the individual.

In the case of an irrevocable trust established by the applicant, if any of the trust principal can be paid to or applied for the benefit of the applicant, it will be considered a resource of the applicant. Any distributions made to the applicant will be considered income in the month received. Any amount not spent before the end of the month becomes a resource and is counted as such in determining continued eligibility. Any distributions to a third party trigger the 60 month look-back period.

If the trust distributes income to or for the benefit of the applicant, such distributions are considered income. Any income (and principal) that can be paid to the applicant is considered available to the applicant and counted as a resource. The principal of the trust, however, if not otherwise distributable for or to the benefit of the applicant, is not considered a resource even if the trust can pay income to the applicant.

For example, Polly establishes an irrevocable trust that pays all the income to her, but cannot distribute principal to anyone. At Polly's death, the trust terminates and all the principal will be paid to her children. The trust is not considered a resource of Polly's, though the income paid to her will affect her eligibility for Medicaid.

By statute, certain trusts are not considered resources of the applicant. A trust for the benefit of a disabled individual under age 65 is exempt if at the death of the individual the state receives the principal of the trust up to the value of the Medicaid paid on behalf of the individual during his or her life. To qualify, the trust must have been established by a parent, grandparent or legal guardian of the person or a court and be funded with assets that belonged to the disabled individual.

Trusts are also exempt if created for the benefit of the individual if composed only of pension, Social Security or other income of the individual, if at the individual's death the state is reimbursed by the trust for all Medicaid assistance paid on behalf of the individual.

Finally, a trust for a disabled individual created by a nonprofit organization that maintains a separate account for each beneficiary (though the funds may be pooled for investment and management purposes) is exempt. The trust account must have been established by an individual, or a parent, grandparent, legal guardian, or court. At the death of the individual, to the extent that the trust has remaining assets, the state must be reimbursed for the value of the Medicaid that it provided to the individual.

§ 5.9   Recovery from the Estate

States are required to recoup payments for any Medicaid payments from any individual's estate for whom Medicaid paid the cost of institutionalization. If the Medicaid recipient was 55 years or older when he or she received Medicaid, the state must recover amounts spent on nursing home facilities, community-based services and related hospital and prescription drug services. States have the option of attempting to recover any other services that they provided. No recovery from the individual's estate can occur until after the death of the individual's spouse and if there is no child under the age of 21, blind, or permanently disabled.

The state must seek recoupment against the individual's estate as defined by state probate law, and, at the option of the state, may include in the estate any other assets in which the individual had any legal title or interest at the time of death. This could include nonprobate assets, for example, such as joint property or assets in a living trust.

§ 5.10 Applications and Appeals

Applications for Medicaid are made at the local office of the state Medicaid agency. Individuals who receive SSI generally do not have to apply separately for Medicaid. They are just issued an eligibility card. Anyone can file an application for individuals who are incapacitated or physically unable to visit the office. An applicant will need proof of citizenship, proof of age, a Social Security number, resources, income and other government benefits.

An individual is eligible for Medicaid reimbursement of covered benefits for any costs incurred (but not paid) for three months before the date of the application. A few states, e.g., New York, reimburse previously paid bills incurred during the three month period.

States must determine an individual's eligibility within 45 days of the application (60 days after an application based upon disability). The state must provide written notice of its decision and provide the reasons if it rejects an application. If rejected, the applicant has 90 days to request a "fair hearing" to appeal the rejection. Similarly, any denial or rejection of benefits entitles the recipient to notice and a right to appeal, although the recipient has only 10 days to appeal from the date of the mailing of the decision. The state must take final administrative action within 90 days of the request for a fair hearing. At the hearing, before a hearing officer who did not make the original decision, the individual has a right to representation, to present witnesses and documentary evidence and to make arguments.

After the hearing officer has issued a written opinion, the individual has 15 days from the date of the mailing of the decision to appeal for a new hearing. If still unsatisfied, the individual has a right to judicial review in the state or Federal courts.

CHAPTER 6

LONG-TERM CARE INSURANCE

As discussed in Chapter 4, Medicare and private Medicare "supplements" cover the cost of long-term care in very limited circumstances. These programs have numerous restrictions that result in their covering relatively few nursing home patient days. How, then, are the costs of such care covered? The answer is basically threefold: one, the joint state-Federal program covering medical costs for the financially needy, Medicaid, described in Chapter 5; two, personal resources of the individual patient and/or his or her "guarantor," collectively referred to as "private pay"; and three, private insurance policies specifically covering long-term care. This last possibility is considered in this Chapter.

§ 6.1 Nature of the Product

The phrase "long-term care insurance" describes a wide variety of private contracts between insurance companies and policyholders. Most such policies are sold by insurance agents to individuals, although access to long-term care insurance is increasingly provided on a group basis. Membership organizations like the American Bar Association or the American Association of Retired Persons, large employers, and health maintenance organizations are among the groups that make such insurance available. Typically, these groups provide no direct financial subsidy toward the cost of this insurance, but certain benefits such as guaranteed acceptability do accrue to participants in these programs.

The contract itself varies with the particular issuer. In general, the policy covers the cost of long-term care for the insured individual in certain settings, after an "elimination period" has expired, for a specified length of time. The major features of such contracts are considered later in this Chapter, but a few generalities might be helpful at the outset.

Long-term care insurance is primarily a product of state regulation. As a result, there is no general standardization of these policies, other than the minimum requirements for "tax-qualified" policies. See § 6.6 regarding such policies. The National Association of Insurance Commissioners has devised a model statute and model regulation for long-term care insurance, but state adoption of these models is inconsistent. Consequently, comparing policies is quite complicated due to the myriad of options and variations that exist. Nevertheless, because the alternatives of private pay and Medicaid are often unappealing, elder law practitioners increasingly look to long-term care insurance for their clients' needs.

§ 6.2 Coverage

Long-term care insurance covers skilled care in a skilled nursing facility (SNF), and usually intermediate care as well. Such care is characterized by the provision of medical assistance.

But many individuals do not require medical assistance as such. Rather, they need "custodial care," which is usually defined as providing assistance with the so-called Activities of Daily Living, or ADL's: eating, bathing, dressing, toileting, transferring from bed to chair, and maintaining continence. In the context of custodial care, medical care is usually limited to providing assistance with medications. It has been estimated that 19 out of 20 "nursing home" residents receive custodial care. Accordingly, most persons want a long-term care insurance policy that specifically covers custodial care.

Custodial care need not necessarily be provided in a skilled nursing facility. There are degrees of assistance that an older person may require, and some of the less intense requirements can be provided in that older person's home. Such care is often called "home health care" and may involve different services provided by home health aides, nurses, social service agencies, physical therapists, and other sources. This avenue of assistance may or may not be covered by long-term care insurance. If it is included, there are usually some restrictions tied to the cost of care or the length of time covered. Often, these cost restrictions are related to the policy's coverage of nursing home care. For example, a policy covering $100 per day of nursing home costs might also cover appropriate home health care, but only up to $50 per day in this setting.

Similar, although somewhat less common, is coverage for respite care. This coverage refers to costs incurred when an older person's regular caregiver—usually a spouse, relative, or close friend—needs a break, or respite, from the ongoing burdens of providing such care. For example, an adult child might bring his or her parent into the adult child's home on a more or less permanent basis. But when that adult child wants to take a vacation, costs will be incurred in securing substitute care. A respite care provision covers these costs.

Still another option that may be covered is hospice care. These facilities are devoted to the terminally ill and specialize in comfort care with minimal medical assistance being provided.

Finally, many newer policies provide coverage for the cost of an assisted living facility. See generally § 7.17 regarding such facilities.

§ 6.3   Financial Limits on Covered Costs

The coverage provided by private long-term care insurance is usually subject to several financial limitations.

a.   *Daily Dollar Maximum*

First, there may be a daily dollar maximum or a range of daily maximum coverages from which a policyholder can choose when initially securing the policy. Some maximums are designed to cover most if not all relevant expenses, while lower limits introduce a greater "co-insurance" element. In other words, the policyholder will pay the difference between the SNF's charges and the policy's limits. In general, the lower the limit, the greater the policyholder's remaining exposure to costs, but the lower the policy premium itself should be. This is an important interaction, because affordability of long-term care insurance is a significant obstacle for many older persons. Moreover, there is usually no certainty that any particular policyholder will *ever* need the policy's benefits. Thus, policyholders must balance their current ability to pay a policy's premiums against their possible—though by no means certain—exposure to future costs beyond that policy's limits.

Although daily maximums are the most common financial limit, some policies limit coverage to a stated percentage of the SNF's charges. This approach leaves the policyholder exposed to the remainder of those charges in a proportion that is constant, regardless of future cost inflation. Stipulated daily maximums, in contrast, are subject to erosion by cost inflation, since the policy limit is a fixed number of dollars. Because such policies must be purchased before the need for long-term care arises, and because the cost of such care typically increases over time, daily maximums create the possibility that a policy's benefits will become less comprehensive than when the policy was first obtained. For that reason, younger policyholders in particular often seek some sort of inflation protection "rider."

Inflation protection riders may be expressed as additional costs per day or as a percentage of the daily maximum. Additional variations include annual percentage increases that are simply added on or are compounded annually. Over a period of ten years or more, the compounding method yields a much higher benefit level and one more in accord with nursing home cost trends. Some inflation protectors, in turn, limit their effect to a specified number of years, commonly twenty years. In any case, inflation protection riders usually increase the premium cost of a policy considerably, especially for younger policyholders.

b. *Duration of Coverage*

A second major financial limit on covered costs is the duration of a policy's coverage. That is, the length of time that an insurance company will pay the designated benefits is also variable. Once again, the standard insurance trade-off applies: the longer the period of coverage, the lower a policyholder's exposure, but the higher that policy's premiums are likely to be. Duration periods typically start at one year and go up to five years or more. Less common is a benefit period equal to the policyholder's remaining life. Alternatively, the maximum coverage of a long-term care policy might be stated in terms of dollars consumed rather than time covered, a variation often described as a "pooling" of benefits. In any case, the effect is the same: limit the coverage of the policy and thereby moderate its premium cost.

c. *Waiting Period*

A final financial limit on covered costs is the waiting or elimination period. The period used is selected by the policyholder when the policy is first obtained and functions like a deductible in more familiar insurance contexts: no insurance benefits are paid during the first 30–120 days of an otherwise covered long-term care situation. Once again, the classic insurance trade-off applies: the longer the elimination period, the greater the out-of-pocket exposure the policyholder might face, but the lower the cost of the insurance policy itself should be.

§ 6.4 **Medical Limits on Coverage**

In addition to the financial limitations described in § 6.3, many policies have medical limits as well.

a. *Pre–Existing Conditions*

The most significant of the medical limitations deals with so-called "pre-existing conditions," medical conditions of a policyholder that existed when the policy was first obtained. Since many older policyholders have some sort of medical profile or history before they apply for long-term care insurance, this limitation can have considerable impact. Depending upon the particular insurance company's operating procedures, some pre-existing conditions may be judged so severe that a policy will not be issued at all. Denial of insurance or lack of access to long-term care insurance is not unusual for persons with certain medical conditions. Indeed, after attaining age 85, most people cannot obtain long-term care insurance, regardless of their health.

Other conditions do not preclude issuance of a policy but are simply excluded from its coverage. Common examples include alcoholism, drug addiction, illnesses caused by an act of war, attempted suicide or other intentionally self-inflicted injuries, or nervous disorders other than Alzheimer's disease.

In some circumstances, a company will issue a long-term care policy, but will charge a higher premium or will limit the amount of coverage that can be obtained, because of an applicant's medical history. More typically, a policy will be issued with the stipulation that coverage will not be provided for "pre-existing conditions." The phrase, "pre-existing condition," is usually defined in the policy itself, subject to state law or regulation. A typical definition might include any medical condition for which the insured sought treatment—or should have sought treatment—within some period preceding the policy's effective date, usually six months.

If long-term care becomes necessary after the policy takes effect but is attributable to a pre-existing condition, the company may deny coverage for a certain period of time beyond the customary elimination period. This denial period is usually specified in the policy and is generally no more than six months. In some cases, however, particularly group policies where acceptance by the insurance company is automatic for group members, the denial period may be much longer—even indefinite. In effect, such policies provide no coverage ever for long-term care that is attributable to a pre-existing condition.

b. Case Management

A second medical limit on covered costs is a case manager provision, or gatekeeper of sorts. Under this provision, an insured person needing long-term care will be examined by a caseworker, who is frequently an employee of the insurance company. This person will assess the policyholder's condition and determine whether that person's needs can best be satisfied in a SNF situation or in some less intensive setting. This assessment process occurs when long-term care is first required and may be redone regularly thereafter to monitor the policyholder's progress and ongoing needs. Any plan of treatment at variance with the caseworker's assessment will typically be denied coverage.

c. Prior Hospitalization Requirement

A third but less common medical limit on covered costs is a requirement of prior hospitalization, or use of a higher level of nursing care before a lower level will be covered. The prior hospitalization requirement typically mimics Medicare's rule that a minimum of three days in a hospital must precede the SNF admission. See generally § 4.3(b). Inasmuch as many patients with degenerative conditions, particularly Alzheimer's disease, go to a nursing facility directly from home without first going to a hospital, a prior hospitalization requirement is a major limitation on a policy's usefulness. Presently, three out of four states prohibit such clauses in policies sold to their residents. A somewhat smaller percentage also prohibit requirements that an intermediate care patient must have first received skilled nursing care.

d. Eligible Facilities

Another limitation that purports to be medically based is a restriction on eligible facilities. The policy may dictate that care must be provided in a skilled nursing facility, even if only custodial care is required. Other versions may limit coverage to "licensed" facilities or may exclude specific institutions or categories of institutions. All such restrictions place limits on the policyholder's choice of facility—presumably one of the benefits that private long-term care insurance is intended to provide.

§ 6.5 Other Key Policy Provisions and Options

a. Guaranteed Renewability

An important safeguard in long-term care insurance is that a policy be guaranteed renewable. Most policies are for a stated term of one year, but if a person requires long-term care before the next renewal date, it would be virtually impossible for that person to secure a policy from some other insurer. That is why many policies may not be canceled by the insurance company except for nonpayment of premiums. While an insurance company may raise its rates, it must do so for an entire "class" of policyholders, not just those policyholders who have filed claims for benefits. State law may also dictate under what circumstances policies may be canceled, other than for nonpayment of premiums, of course.

b. Waiver of Premium

Nonpayment of premiums can be a real problem once long-term care commences. At that point, finding the funds to cover a policy's renewal may be quite problematic. One response to this dilemma is a waiver of premium provision. Under this clause, a policyholder is not required to pay premiums to keep a policy in force once benefits become payable under the policy, or after some period—often ninety days—beyond that point.

c. Premium Refund Provisions

Another provision that appeals to some policyholders is a money-back or return of premium provision. Most long-term care insurance policies build up no cash-back or surrender value. They are akin to automobile or homeowner's insurance, or term life insurance for that matter. But some policies provide a certain amount of investment accumulation, which may be returned to the policyholder (or his or her heirs) if benefits are never obtained under the policy, or only minimally so. These provisions purport to act as incentives for family members to provide care to older relatives and to thereby forestall use of the insurance policy's benefits.

They may make some policyholders more comfortable with the large premiums often associated with long-term care insurance, in the sense that they stand to recover these sums if they never need long-term care. These provisions, however, typically raise the cost of the policy itself.

d. Nonforfeiture of Benefits

A somewhat related provision is called nonforfeiture of benefits. This provision provides some degree of coverage under a policy that has lapsed due to nonpayment of premiums. The amount of coverage depends upon how long the policy was in force, and many such policies require a minimum of ten years before any benefits are designated as nonforfeitable. Even then, only a specified portion of the policy benefit otherwise due, such as 30%, is payable. Alternatively, the full benefit may be payable, but only for a reduced period.

A related provision allows a policy to be "paid up" after a number of years, usually ten or more. After that time, no additional premiums are required, and the policy remains effective. Further rate increases, therefore, are irrelevant. Typically, these policies are structured to be "paid up" before a policyholder retires.

e. State Law Protections

State law may provide some policyholder protections beyond the parameters already described for certain key variables. Requirements for disclosure of coverage in readable typesize and in understandable language are common, as are mandatory free lookover periods after a policy has been presented. In addition, some state insurance guaranty funds may protect policyholders if their insurance company becomes insolvent. Not all states have such funds, those that do typically protect only policyholders who reside within their jurisdiction, and even then, the guarantee is usually limited to $100,000 of benefits payable. Because long-term care insurance is a long-term commitment that can impose significant costs on an insurer, the financial stability of the insurance company is another major consideration that prospective policyholders must fathom. State guaranty funds are only a partial response to this problem.

§ 6.6   Tax–Qualified Policies

So-called "tax-qualified" long-term care insurance policies first became available in 1997. These policies are eligible for various tax benefits, but must satisfy specific standards imposed by Federal law. I.R.C. § 7702B(b). No insurance company is required to offer tax-qualified policies, and many do not. The standard for determining when benefits are payable may be more restrictive in tax-qualified policies than in some nonqualified policies, so tax-qualified policies are not necessarily the superior product.

a.   Policy Requirements

To be "tax-qualified," a policy must be guaranteed renewable and must make available some nonforfeiture of benefits. See § 6.5(a) and (d). In addition, the policy may not condition long-term care benefits upon a patient's prior hospitalization or use of a higher level of nursing care. See § 6.4(c). The policy must also comply with particular provisions of the National Association of Insurance Commissioners' model act and model regulation. These provisions mandate certain disclosures, require that inflation protection be offered, and limit restrictions on home health care coverage. Other consumer protections are included as well.

A tax-qualified policy must also protect against "unintentional lapse," i.e., inadvertent termination of a policy due to nonpayment of premiums. To that end, an insured must be given the opportunity to designate someone to receive any notice of termination at least 30 days prior to its effective date. Furthermore, the company must reinstate the policy within five months of its termination if the insured is "cognitively impaired" or has lost "functional capacity." The insured must pay any past due premiums, however.

b.   *Tax Treatment*

Tax-qualified policies receive favorable tax treatment in several forms. First, tax-qualified policies may be offered by employers as a tax-free fringe benefit to their employees, just like health insurance plans. I.R.C. § 106(a), § 7702B(a)(1). Second, benefits paid by such policies are tax-free to the recipient, up to a daily benefit that is adjusted annually. In 2006, this limit was $250. Even this amount can be exceeded, moreover, if a person's cost of long-term care is higher. I.R.C. § 7702B(d)(2)(A), (4). So, if a policy provides a daily benefit of $300, this entire amount is tax-free if the actual cost of the long-term care received was at least $300 per day.

A third tax benefit is that the premiums are deductible as medical expenses. I.R.C. § 213(d)(10). This deduction, however, is limited according to an insured's age when the premiums are paid. These limits are adjusted annually for inflation. In 2006, the annual limits were as follows:

Age	Maximum
Under 41	$ 280
41–50	530
51–60	1,060
61–70	2,830
Over 70	3,530

Premiums in excess of these limits are not deductible. These limits are applied *per insured*, so a married couple can deduct the premium paid for the husband's policy and the wife's policy, subject to the applicable age limitation for each person.

In any case, these premiums are classified as medical expenses, so the deduction is further limited to the excess of such expenses over 7.5% of a person's "adjusted gross income" (AGI). I.R.C. § 213(a). To be sure, this threshold is applied to *all* of a person's medical expenses, but the usual result is that some portion of the premiums are rendered nondeductible.

For example, assume that Ian is 66 years old with an AGI of $60,000 from pension payments, interest income, dividends and a part-time job. He purchases a long-term care insurance policy with an annual premium of $3,300. He also pays $1,062 per year for Medicare Part B (see § 4.1(b)), $900 for a Medigap policy (see § 4.8), and $600 on prescription drugs. His 2006 medical expense deduction is calculated as follows:

Long-term care insurance premium, limited for a 66–year old to:	$2,830
Medicare Part B	1,062
Medigap	900
Prescription drugs	600
Total medical costs	$5,392
7.5% of AGI ($60,000)	(4,500)
Deduction	$892

Furthermore, medical expense deductions are "itemized" deductions, so they produce a tax benefit only if such deductions exceed a person's standard deduction. For Ian, the total of his interest expenses (less likely for a retiree), state income and real estate taxes, charitable contributions, and deductible medical expenses ($892 in this example) must exceed $6,400 (in 2006) before he derives any tax benefit from these expenditures. Clearly, the deductibility of premiums on "tax-qualified" long-term care insurance policies should not dictate their purchase, in most cases.

§ 6.7   State Partnership Policies

States have been authorized since 2006 to coordinate their Medicaid long-term programs with certain long-term care insurance policies. These so-called "partnership" policies allow policyholders to qualify for Medicaid coverage of their long-term care costs while retaining financial resources equal to the insurance benefits that those policies paid. See § 5.3(b) regarding Medicaid eligibility criteria regarding financial resources. The details vary by state but such programs all require a policyholder to have long-term care insurance that meets specified requirements.

In general, the policy must be a "tax-qualified" long-term care insurance policy as defined in I.R.C. § 7702B(b). As such, it must include various consumer protections established by the National Association of Insurance Commissioners (NAIC) regarding guaranteed renewability, unintentional lapse, prior hospitalization, mandatory disclosures, and the like. See § 6.6(a) regarding those protections. And if the NAIC revises any of the referenced provisions of its model act and model regulations relating to long-term care insurance, the Federal government must decide whether those changes should be required for "partnership" policies.

"Partnership" policies differ from "tax-qualified" policies, however, in one important respect—namely, inflation protection. "Tax-qualified" policies must make such protection available, but "partnership" policies must include inflation protection if the policyholder is under age 76 when the policy is first obtained. If the insured is under age 61 when he or she purchases the policy, that policy must include "compound annual inflation protection." And if the insured is 61 to 75 years old when the policy is purchased, the policy must include "some level of inflation protection" but not necessarily compound annual protection. See § 6.3(a) regarding inflation protection.

Finally, "partnership" policies must be portable among the states that have "partnership" programs. That is, long-term care insurance policies that satisfy "partnership" requirements in the state of the policy's issuance must be recognized as satisfying the requirements in the other "partnership" states.

§ 6.8   Accelerated Benefits on Life Insurance

An alternative to long-term care insurance is a rider on a person's life insurance policy that pays a percentage of that policy's death benefit before the policyholder dies. These funds are available for any purpose, including payment of long-term care costs. Such provisions are called "accelerated benefits" or "living benefits" riders and vary with the particular insurer. Most such riders, however, provide that payment will be made only to persons who are expected to die within six months or a year. They may also vary in terms of the percentage of the policy's death benefit that may be received in this manner. Accordingly, their usefulness in financing long-term care costs is somewhat limited.

From a Federal income tax standpoint, these benefits are excluded from taxable income if the insured person is either "terminally ill" or "chronically ill." I.R.C. § 101(g)(1). A person is "terminally ill" for this purpose if a physician certifies that the person has "an illness or physical condition which can reasonably be expected to result in death" within 24 months. I.R.C. § 101(g)(4)(A). A person is "chronically ill" for this purpose if the person requires "substantial assistance" in performing at least two of the following activities of daily living: eating, toileting, transferring, bathing, dressing, and continence. I.R.C. § 101(g)(4)(B), § 7702B(c)(2). For such persons, tax-free treatment applies up to a daily amount that is adjusted annually ($250 per day in 2006), or the actual cost of long-term care, if higher. I.R.C. § 101(g)(3)(C), § 7702B(d). This per-day limitation does not apply to "terminally ill" persons.

If an insurance policy does not have an "accelerated benefits" rider, the policyholder might sell the policy and then use the proceeds to pay for long-term care. Such sales, often called "viatical settlements," enable a policyholder to obtain a *portion* of the policy's death benefit prior to death. The amount received varies with a person's life expectancy: the shorter one's life expectancy, the greater the amount received. And if the insured's life expectancy is two years or less when the sale is made, the proceeds may be received free of Federal income tax. I.R.C. § 101(g)(2)(A).

A different consideration involves state law protections for life insurance proceeds. Many states provide that death benefits paid under life insurance policies cannot be attached by an insured's creditors, including that insured's medical care providers. Funds received under an "accelerated benefits" rider are almost never covered by this special treatment. Older persons with dependent relatives, therefore, might not want to access their "accelerated benefits" in order to preserve more funds for the support of such relatives.

CHAPTER 7

NURSING HOMES, BOARD AND CARE HOMES AND ASSISTED LIVING FACILITIES

§ 7.1 Introduction

As America's elderly population continues to grow, the number of those elderly who will live in nursing homes and other residential care facilities will increase as well. Currently, there are over 1.7 million elderly nursing home residents, 90 percent of whom are age 65 or older, residing in over 18,000 nursing homes, the majority of which are private profit-making facilities, often owned by a chain. The term "nursing home" can apply to a variety of facilities, but under Federal law a nursing home means an institution that provides skilled nursing care or rehabilitation services for injured, disabled or sick persons. The Federal definitions of "nursing facility" are found in the Medicare and Medicaid laws, both of which pay for nursing home coverage. (For a discussion of Medicare payment of nursing home expenses see §§ 4.3(b), 4.7(c). For a discussion of Medicaid coverage, see § 5.2.) Though similar, Medicare and Medicaid provide coverage for different levels of care. While both limit coverage to nursing home care, Medicare is more restrictive in what it defines as nursing care. Medicare will reimburse only care provided in a "skilled nursing facility", which is defined as an institution which is primarily engaged in providing skilled nursing care and rehabilitation services for injured, sick or disabled persons and is not providing primarily for the care and treatment of mental diseases.

Medicaid limits reimbursement to a "nursing facility", which it defines similarly to Medicare with an additional definition that greatly enlarges the number eligible for reimbursement. Medicaid includes in its definition of a "nursing facility" institutions that provide "on a regular basis, health-related care and services to individuals who because of their mental or physical condition require care and services (above the level of room and board) . . ." (42 U.S.C. § 1396r(a)(1)(C).) As a result of this "health-related care" clause, Medicaid is much more liberal in its coverage.

By definition, nursing homes provide medical care, though they also necessarily provide room and board to their residents as well as other custodial care. The term "custodial care" has no formal definition, but it is used to refer to the provision of room and board and of assistance in the activities of daily living which include eating, bathing and other personal care needs. Individuals who require custodial care do not necessarily need to live in a nursing home, for their needs can often be met at their home with help from spouses, family, friends or other relatives. If they can afford to, they can hire practical nurses (personal aides who lack formal training as nurses) to assist them.

Nursing homes were originally conceived as a financially efficient alternative to more costly hospitalization or individually provided home nursing care. The latter, though often promoted as a less costly alternative to nursing home care, is in reality more expensive if it provides the same type of care. Nursing homes insure a level of available medical services that is impossible to duplicate in the home setting at a reasonable cost. Nursing homes were developed because it is more efficient to bring patients to a central location where physicians, nurses, and other health care providers are available as needed. Nursing homes can also offer specialized care such as dieticians, rehabilitation specialists and social service providers that are not feasible to provide in isolated home settings.

Home care may be less expensive, however, if the medical needs are limited, and the individual does not require full-time custodial care. Proponents of in-home care generally assume that much of it will be provided by volunteer labor. In particular, the cost advantages of home health care depend upon a spouse, friend or relative providing cost-free care such as cooking meals, bathing or dressing the individual, and even assisting in routine medical care such as insuring that the individual takes prescription drugs. Without volunteer labor, custodial home care can be very expensive. If the individual also needs daily medical assistance or supervision, home care is often prohibitively expensive or simply not feasible.

Although often criticized, nursing homes are an essential part of the health care delivery system. They increasingly are used as cost-effective alternatives to hospitals. While many nursing home residents enter them directly from a home setting, others are discharged from hospitals to a nursing home because they continue to need skilled nursing care, which can be provided at much less cost than in a hospital. Though nursing homes can cost anywhere from $4,000 to $7,000 a month, they are a relative bargain compared to hospitals. By providing group medical care in an institutional setting, the nursing home provides relatively cost efficient means of providing supervisory medical care for the chronically ill.

Though almost no one wants to move into a nursing home, sometimes it is the only reasonable course of action. Admittedly, living in a nursing home means the loss of privacy, autonomy and personal freedom. The frail elderly, however, often can remain at home only because spouses or relatives provide volunteer labor and financial support. Some states provide custodial care in the home for a limited number of elderly. For most elderly, however, if they lack family support or if the family can no longer provide enough support, and they require medical assistance there is little choice but to move into a nursing home. Though often a necessity, nursing homes are not always comfortable places to live. As a resident, the individual must rise at the appointed time, eat at the specified meal times, dine with others, and accept what the home provides.

Many nursing home residents share a room, and even those with private rooms have little space to place a lifetime of furnishings that are rich with memories. Life in an institutional setting can be isolating and lonely. Yet a nursing home with its economies of scale in terms of personnel and special facilities is a practical solution to the extreme cost of providing round the clock custodial or nursing care to frail persons. In response to complaints about the institutional nature of nursing homes, many are trying to reinvent themselves as more humanistic, home-like settings. Residents are given more choice, the long hospital-like corridors are replaced by clusters of rooms, and patients with cognitive impairments are housed separately from residents who suffer only from physical ailments, but whose minds are clear.

Nursing homes are often thought of as long-term facilities for the elderly because many older individuals do spend a great many months, if not years, in them. However, many individuals who enter a nursing home are not old and depart within six months. For many, nursing homes are halfway houses for recovery by acute care patients after they leave the hospital. For these patients, a nursing home can be a place to regain health, not to die.

Of course, many older individuals do enter nursing homes because of chronic conditions such as strokes, cancer, heart conditions or other debilitating illnesses that prevent them from caring for themselves on a daily basis and give rise to a continuing need for medical attention. These individuals do not expect to leave the nursing home, unless it is to die at home or in a hospice.

§ 7.2   Paying for Nursing Homes

Though very necessary and relatively cost effective, nursing homes are still expensive. Costs vary greatly depending on where the facility is located, whether urban or rural or in a high-cost or low-cost labor area, the quality of the physical facility, the quality of the staff, the quality and extent of the programming, and the degree of luxury afforded to the residents. The cost can vary from $4,000 to over $7,000 a month. Paying for such care is a heavy financial burden for most residents. A few have sufficient income to pay for the annual costs of nursing home care for as long as they require it. Many more, however, lack enough income and pay the bills by drawing down on their savings. For some, relatives, particularly children, help pay the costs. A few have long-term care insurance that meets some or all of the costs. (See Long–Term Care Insurance Coverage § 6.2.) Many older residents of nursing homes rely upon Medicaid and to a limited extent, Medicare, to pay for their nursing home costs.

The cost of the nursing home is deductible under Section 213(d)(1)(C) of the Internal Revenue Code if the provision of medical care is the principal reason for residence in the facility, and if the resident's need for long-term care services is certified annually by a qualified health practitioner. The entire cost is deductible including amounts paid for food, lodging and non-medical services. However, if the individual is not there principally because of medical care, then only the portion of the monthly fee that is allocable to medical care may be deducted. Although a few persons enter nursing homes primarily for custodial care, rather than medical, in most instances the motive for living in the nursing home is the need for on-going medical care. (See deductibility of long-term care insurance premiums, § 6.6(b).)

§ 7.3   Nursing Home Regulation

Whether having entered a nursing home to recover or to die, nursing home residents are very vulnerable and in need of protection. As a result, specific Federal and state laws and regulations offer statutory protection to nursing home residents. Federal and state civil rights laws, consumer protection statutes, and state common-law remedies, such as tort and contract law provide additional protection for the nursing home resident.

The fundamental source of public regulation of nursing homes arises from the requirement of state licensure. Without a license, the facility cannot operate. Thus, states have great power to affect the policies and practices of nursing homes, and do so under various laws, regulations, and licensing requirements. The Federal government, in turn, imposes requirements upon nursing homes as well as mandating state responsibilities. Facilities that do not meet Federal requirements are barred from receiving Medicaid or Medicare reimbursement for their residents. Because almost half of all residents receive Medicaid reimbursement, the loss of Federal approval is not taken lightly. At present, the most important protection can be found in the Federal Nursing Home Reform Act (NHRA), enacted as part of the Omnibus Budget Reconciliation Act of 1987. The NHRA represented a major change in nursing home laws, as significant and pervasive as the emergence of Medicare and Medicaid in the 1960s. Although Federal regulations have championed residents' rights for a number of years, the NHRA marked the first time that explicit, specific statutory protections were enumerated. Administered by the Department of Health and Human Services, NHRA requires that nursing homes maintain and enhance the quality of life of their residents. Moreover, the Act provides explicit protections for nursing home residents, and mandatory annual reviews of nursing home compliance with those protections.

§ 7.4 Preadmission Screening of Residents

Nursing homes are not required to admit mentally ill or mentally retarded individuals. Nursing facilities that are Medicaid certified must have a program of Pre–Admission Screening and Annual Resident Review (PASARR) for individuals prior to admission and for those who are current residents. The purpose of the review is to identify individuals who are mentally ill or mentally retarded and to determine whether the facility is an appropriate residence for the individual. Mental illness does not, however, include dementia, such as Alzheimer's disease.

Mental illness is defined by the Secretary of Health and Human Services in consultation with the National Institute of Mental Health. Individuals are considered mentally retarded if they have significantly sub-average general intellectual functioning. Of course, if the facility is capable of dealing with such individuals, it may admit them. Individuals who resided in a facility as April, 1987 (prior to NHRA), must be reviewed annually. If they are found to be mentally ill or mentally retarded and do not require a nursing facility for services, the state must arrange their discharge if they have lived in the facility for less than 30 months and transfer them to an appropriate facility. Individuals who have lived in a facility for longer than 30 months have the option to remain there or to be transferred to a more appropriate institution. Individuals who have been targeted for transfer have a right to a fair hearing to resist it, as well as the right to object to the classification of mentally ill or mentally retarded.

§ 7.5 Enforceability of Admissions Agreements

Many nursing home facilities prefer private pay patients as opposed to those who are paid for by Medicare or Medicaid because the facility can charge more for a private pay patient. Whether a nursing home can refuse a Medicaid patient, or one who is likely to become a Medicaid patient, depends upon state law. Nursing homes have the right to be totally private pay and accept no Medicaid patients.

Most facilities, however, find it financially necessary to accept both private pay and Medicaid patients. State law may prevent the nursing home from giving preference to private pay patients in its admissions policy. Some states require that a certain percentage of the patients admitted be Medicaid patients.

Federal law prohibits nursing homes that accept Medicaid from requiring residents to waive Medicaid benefits or to forego applying for them, and bars advance deposits that cover more than two months of care. Federal law also prohibits a nursing home from requiring a third party to guarantee payment as a condition of admission. (42 U.S.C. § 1396r(c)(5)(A).) Whether the Federal law provides sufficient protection against third-party "financial responsibility" agreements is unclear. Despite Federal law, some facilities require the responsible party to agree to be personally liable if the patient is unable to provide payment from his or her income or resources. The legality of such contracts is in dispute.

Nursing home facilities have a right to require future residents to pay a deposit as a condition of their admission unless it is clear that the stay will be covered by Medicare. If so, no deposit can be required. Even if covered by Medicare, the resident may have to provide a deposit to pay for individual items not covered by Medicare, although the facility cannot force the patient to purchase these additional items as a condition of their admission. State law also addresses this problem and should be examined whenever a nursing home requires a deposit either as a mandatory requirement or as a "request."

§ 7.6 NHRA—Quality of Life

The basic thrust of the Federal Nursing Home Reform Act (NHRA) is to assure the quality of life of nursing home residents. Under the Act, nursing homes are required to have a quality assessment and assurance committee that meets at least quarterly to identify and implement plans to assure the highest practicable physical, mental and psychosocial well-being of each resident.

The facility must assess each resident's functional needs and must prepare a written plan of care. The plan must describe the resident's ability to perform basic functions and list all significant impairments. The assessment must be conducted within 14 days after admission to the facility, and thereafter once a year or after a significant change in the resident's physical or mental condition. In addition, the facility must examine each resident at least once every three months and, if necessary, modify the assessment plan. The facility must provide or arrange for the provision of whatever services are needed to fulfill the resident's plan of care, including rehabilitative, social, pharmaceutical, dietary, dental and social activities. All patients must be under the supervision of a physician unless the state permits the substitution of another professional, such as a nurse-practitioner. If the facility has more than 120 beds, it must employ at least one full-time social worker.

A nursing facility must provide licensed nursing services 24 hours a day and, unless waived by the state, must have a registered professional nurse for at least eight consecutive hours a day, seven days a week. The facility must inquire whether any potential aides are listed on a state registry that names individuals guilty of patient abuse or misappropriation of resident's property. All full-time nurse's aides employed for at least four months must have completed training and competency testing, and the facility must provide them regular in-service education.

§ 7.7 NHRA—General Rights

The NHRA has a list of requirements that are often referred to as the resident's bill of rights. (42 U.S.C. § 1396r.) Taken together these rights attempt to protect the quality of life of nursing home patients.

a. Freedom of Choice

Under the NHRA residents have the right to choose their own doctors, to be fully informed about medical care and treatment and any proposed changes in that treatment, and, unless adjudicated incapacitated, to help plan their care and treatment decisions.

It is fairly common for the nursing home to provide a physician for the resident, even though the resident has the option to choose. The right to refuse treatment is not explicitly mentioned in the NHRA, but that right is an implied one, and certainly exists under the doctrine of informed consent.

b.   *Freedom from Abuse and Restraints*

Absent medical necessity, residents have a fundamental right to be free of both chemical and physical restraints, as well as physical or mental abuse.

Residents may be restrained only if necessary to insure their physical safety or that of other patients, and then only pursuant to a physician's written order. The order must specify the circumstances and duration of the restraint's use. Restraints may never be used as discipline or for the convenience of the facility.

The resident must not be subject to physical or mental abuse, corporal punishment or involuntary seclusion. The facility must have written procedures and policies that prohibit mistreatment, negligence, and abuse of residents by the staff. Residents must be free from verbal, mental, sexual, or physical abuse. The facility must ensure that any incidents of abuse are reported immediately to the administrator of the facility, investigate all alleged abuse violations and file proper reports with the appropriate state agency.

c.   *Privacy*

Because autonomy and dignity are integral to a resident's personal well-being, privacy rights are broad and complete. A resident has a right to privacy with respect to accommodations, medical treatment, written and telephonic communications, visits, and meetings of family and resident groups.

d. Confidentiality

All personal and clinical records must be kept confidential. A resident, or a resident's legal representative, also has a right to access current records within 24 hours of making such a request.

e. Accommodation of Individual Needs

The facility must provide services that reasonably accommodate individual needs and preferences in a manner that maintains the dignity of the residents. The resident has a right to choose activities, schedules, and health care and to interact with other members of the facility and the outside community. The resident has the right to participate in social, religious and community activities that do not interfere with the rights of the other residents. The facility must design an activities program for the resident that is designed to meet the assessed needs of the resident. The activities program must be directed by a qualified professional specialist.

The facility must provide a safe, clean, comfortable, and home-like environment that is adequately maintained. Each resident's room must have private closet space, have proper lighting, and be kept at a comfortable temperature.

The resident must receive notice before being moved to a new room or before being assigned a new roommate. A resident can refuse a transfer to another room within the facility, if the transfer would be from a section of the facility that is a part of the skilled nursing home to a part of the facility that is not a skilled nursing home. A resident who refuses such a transfer cannot be denied Medicaid or Medicare benefits.

f. Grievances

Residents have the right to voice grievances about their treatment or care without fear of retaliation. The facility must make prompt efforts to resolve grievances, including those that relate to the behavior of other residents.

g. Participation in Groups and Other Activities

A resident has a right to organize and participate in resident groups, as well as social, religious, and community activities so long as they do not interfere with the rights of other facility residents. The families of residents have the right to meet together in the facility.

h. Examination of Survey Results

Upon a reasonable request, any resident may examine the most recent official survey results of a nursing home and any plan of correction that will be taken pursuant to such a survey. The facility must post a notice of the availability of the survey.

i. Access and Visitation Rights

Residents have the right of access to representatives of the state and Federal government, their individual physician, to the state's long-term care ombudsman, and any entity or individual that provides health, social, legal, or other services to the resident, and to their families or other visitors. The facility must provide reasonable access for residents to telephones from which private calls can be made. Married couples have the right to share a room, and all residents have the right to retain and use a reasonable amount of personal possessions.

j. *Services Included in Medicare or Medicaid Payment*

The Federal health care programs, Medicare and Medicaid, pay the costs for a high percentage of nursing home residents. Facilities are prohibited from charging residents for items that are paid for by these programs such as required nursing services; dietary services; activity programs; or medically-related social services; nor for routine personal hygiene items including soap, razors, toothbrushes, tissues, deodorants, incontinence care supplies, and over-the-counter drugs.

The facility may charge the resident's funds, if requested by the resident, for: telephone; television and radio for personal use; cosmetic and grooming items not paid for by Medicare or Medicaid; personal clothing; personal reading matter; flowers and plants; private room; and specially prepared or alternative food.

A facility can only charge a resident for items requested by the resident and cannot require a resident to request any item or service as a condition of admission or continued stay.

§ 7.8 NHRA—Notification of Rights

At the time of admission to the facility, a resident must be informed, both orally and in writing, of the resident's legal rights and of the requirements and procedures for establishing medical assistance. Upon request, a facility must also furnish a written statement of such rights to the resident.

§ 7.9 NHRA—Transfer and Discharge Rights

Many of the rights that are enumerated in the NHRA are identical to rights that have long been covered under other Federal regulations. In the area of transfers and discharges, however, the NHRA made substantial changes. It defines a transfer to include the movement of a resident to a bed outside of the certified facility whether or not the bed is in the physical facility. Prior to a transfer or discharge, the facility must notify the resident of the transfer or discharge. The facility must also note the reasons for the transfer or discharge and record those reasons in the resident's clinical record.

Under Federal law a resident may only be transferred or discharged under six specific conditions.

First, if the transfer or discharge is necessary to meet the resident's welfare and the resident's welfare cannot be met in the facility. Second, when it is appropriate because the resident's health has improved sufficiently enough so the resident no longer needs the facility's services. Third, when the safety of other individuals in the facility is endangered.

Fourth, if the health of individuals in the facility would otherwise be endangered. Fifth, if a resident has failed, after reasonable notice, to pay for the stay at the facility. Sixth, transfers or discharges, of course, are allowed when the facility ceases to operate.

For the first four reasons, the basis for the transfer or discharge must be documented in the resident's clinical record. In the first two cases, the resident's physician must provide the documentation, and in the fourth case, any physician can document the reason.

The resident must be given 30 days notice of the transfer or discharge. Shorter notice is permitted if required for safety reasons or if the resident's health has improved sufficiently to allow a more immediate discharge or transfer.

Nursing homes are also required to ensure that all residents receive safe and orderly transfers or discharges. This is a broad and significant protection for residents, as it extends a facility's liability for the health and welfare of its patients.

§ 7.10   NHRA—Equal Access to Quality Care

A nursing facility must establish and maintain identical policies and practices regarding transfer, discharge, and the provision of services required under the state plan for all individuals regardless of source of payment. No matter what method of payment is used, under the NHRA a nursing facility is required to provide equal access to care, which includes equal access to activities, as well as nursing, rehabilitative, social, pharmaceutical, dietary, and dental services.

§ 7.11   NHRA—Quality of Life

The facility must care for its residents in a manner that promotes each resident's quality of life. The dignity and individuality of each resident must be respected and enhanced. Residents must have the right to self-determination by being able to choose their activities, schedule their health care, and other significant life choices, and interact with others including nonresidents of the facility. Residents have the right to organize and participate in resident groups, and residents' families have the right to meet in the facility with other resident families. Such groups must be accorded a private meeting space, and be allowed to make requests or submit grievances to which the facility must respond.

§ 7.12   NHRA—Admissions Policy

Under the NHRA, a nursing facility (1) cannot require the waiver of an individual's right to benefits under the Medicare or Medicaid program; (2) nor can it require oral or written assurance that such individuals are not eligible for, or will not apply for, benefits under Medicare or Medicaid; (3) it must prominently display written information, and provide oral and written information, about such benefits; (4) cannot require a third-party guarantee of payment to the facility as a condition of admission to, or continued stay in, the facility; and (5) cannot accept any gifts or money from Medicaid recipients as a precondition of admission to, or continued stay in, the facility. Prior to passage of the NHRA, nursing facilities frequently restricted admission of Medicaid and Medicare patients. NHRA still does not require a "first come, first served" admission policy for nursing home residents, nor does it require all facilities to accept Medicaid paid residents.

§ 7.13   NHRA—Protection   of   Residents' Funds

Requiring residents to deposit personal funds with the nursing facility is forbidden. In addition, a nursing home, upon a resident's written authorization, must hold, safeguard, and account for personal funds under a specific system. The facility must assure a full and complete separate accounting of each resident's personal funds, maintain a written record of all financial transactions involving the personal funds of a resident deposited with the facility, and afford the resident access to such a record through quarterly statements or on request by the resident or his or her legal representative. The facility must deposit any amount of personal funds in excess of $50 into an interest-bearing account that is separate from the operating accounts of the facility, with all interest must be credited to the resident's account. Resident accounts of less than $50 may be maintained in a noninterest bearing account or a petty cash fund.

Each resident receiving Medicaid must be notified when the amount in the resident's account reaches $200 less than the applicable resource limit. The resident must also be notified that if the resource limit is reached, Medicaid or SSI eligibility may be lost.

Upon the death of a resident, the facility must convey the remainder of the resident's personal funds to the administrator of the estate within 30 days and provide a final accounting.

§ 7.14   State Long–Term Care Ombudsman

As a condition of receiving Federal funds for the protection of the vulnerable elderly, each state is required to establish and operate a Long–Term Ombudsman Office. The individual selected as Ombudsman (or the office) has the obligation to identify, investigate, and resolve complaints made by nursing home residents or complaints on their behalf. The Ombudsman is expected to investigate actions or decisions that may adversely affect the health, safety, welfare or rights of the residents. In addition to its oversight over nursing homes, the Ombudsman can investigate any other providers of long-term care services, and public agencies and other health and social service agencies. Under the Federal law, the Ombudsman must assist residents in protecting their health, safety, welfare, and inform them of their rights. If necessary, the Ombudsman can represent residents before governmental agencies. It must also analyze, comment on and monitor the development and implementation of laws, regulations and policies that affect residents. Finally, the office is expected to assist in the development of citizen organizations that promote the rights of residents and provide technical support for the development of resident and family councils.

§ 7.15 Common Law Rights

a. Tort

Although the NHRA, supplemented by other Federal regulations, accords extensive protections to the elderly nursing home resident, common law tort and contract remedies are also available. Nursing facilities are liable for both intentional and unintentional torts, although unintentional torts, i.e. negligence, are more common than cases involving intentional torts, such as assault, battery, and false imprisonment. Of course, merely because a resident suffers an injury does not necessarily mean that the nursing home is liable. Unless guilty of an intentional tort, the nursing home must be shown to have acted in a negligent manner.

Those patients wishing to sue a nursing home based on negligence must prove the traditional elements: duty of care, breach of duty, causation, and injury. In several cases, however, the existence of the injury may be sufficient to prove negligence. For example, the presence of multiple infected bed sores or thermal burns may be enough to establish a prima facie case of negligence and liability. Usually, however, the resident will have to provide evidence that the practices of the nursing home were substandard and responsible for the injury.

The standard of care can be described as both subjective and objective. The degree of care and skill that a particular nursing facility uses should be measured by the care and skill used by other facilities in the community. This "community" standard may prove itself meaningless, however, in a community where substandard practices are the norm. In those cases, a resident may look to the various Federal and state certification standards to provide a proper standard of care. Subjectively, the standard of a care is based on the nursing home's awareness of the particular resident's needs and habits. The nursing home's duty of care is assessed in light of the resident's physical and mental condition. For example, if the resident regularly wanders from the facility, the nursing home will be expected to provide appropriate care. If, because of a lack of supervision, that resident was allowed to wander and was subsequently injured, the facility would be liable.

A few states have enacted statutes that create the legal basis for a resident to sue a nursing home for substandard care. The NHRA, however, does not create a private right of action for nursing home residents or their families.

In recent years, juries have become more liberal in the amount of damages they are willing to award to residents who have been harmed by negligent or abusive care in a nursing home. As a result, residents and their families are more likely to sue for improper care than in the past. The problem of substandard care is apparently so prevalent, that at least one class action lawsuit has been filed alleging negligent care against a corporation that owns a chain of nursing homes.

In response, nursing homes increasingly insert provisions in the contract of admission that require any dispute between the resident and the facility to be submitted to binding arbitration. The validity of these provisions has generally been upheld by courts.

b. *Contract*

Nursing home residents may also recover under contract law. Residents enter a nursing home after signing a contract in which they accept the obligation to pay in return for the services provided. Because the nursing home is a party to the contract, it can be sued if it fails to fulfill its obligations. Breach of contract, misrepresentation, fraud, and breach of implied warranties are all legitimate grounds for a lawsuit. By incorporating statutory and regulatory provisions into the contract, residents are able to enforce contracts as third party beneficiaries. The resident may also attack portions of a contract as being in violation of state or Federal laws and, thus, not enforceable. In general, however, contract suits against nursing homes have not proven very fruitful, because the language of contracts favors the facility since residents have little bargaining power.

§ 7.16 Board and Care Homes

A great number of the elderly need assistance in their activities of daily living, but do not require skilled nursing home care or even basic health care. They, therefore, do not need to live in a nursing home or a nursing facility, but unfortunately they still cannot live alone given their mental or physical infirmities. Many of these individuals, of course, live with their relatives, but thousands of others live in what are known as "board and care homes." These nonmedical residential facilities are also known as group homes, foster homes, personal care homes, rest homes or even old age homes. While there is no official category of board and care homes, generally these facilities provide room, meals and assistance with daily activities such as bathing and dressing. While not providing health care, it is common for these facilities to assist residents in taking their medication. Often the residence director will hold the medicine and see that the resident takes it at the appropriate time.

Most of these homes are relatively small, averaging less than 25 beds and almost all are privately operated. In many cases, the owners live in the facility. These homes cater to older, particularly frail or mentally impaired individuals, usually with limited incomes. Many residents of these homes are Supplemental Security Income recipients. (See § 12.1, Supplemental Security Income General Eligibility.) Some are previous residents of state mental health care facilities who find they cannot live in the community by themselves and need to live in a group setting. Other board and care homes are more expensive and attract older, middle class individuals who can no longer live alone.

The most fundamental problem with board and care homes is the low quality of the care, which is often a result of the lack of financial well-being of the residents. Many of these homes have the resident turn over almost all of their SSI or Social Security funds, but still receive amounts are so low that the resulting care is minimal. A few states supplement SSI or even provide special supplements for board and care homes, but again, the amounts provided are so small that the room and board and supervision must necessarily be of the most modest sort. When combined with the physical disability of the individuals, and sometimes mental disabilities, many board and care operators face situations well beyond their competence or financial ability.

While there are over 40,000 such licensed homes (licensed by the state) with over a half million beds, there is no Federal law governing them. State law varies greatly. Although state licensing requirements are often minimal, they are not necessarily enforced. In addition, it is estimated that there are yet again more unlicensed homes than licensed homes. The quality of care in these unlicensed homes must be considered very doubtful.

The lack of Federal control over board and care homes is a result of the lack of Federal funding. Neither Medicare nor Medicaid programs pays for such homes since there is no skilled nursing care or other health care involved. Consequently, the Federal government has very little ability to control the quality of these facilities.

State licensing should offer some help, but in reality it is not very effective. The governing regulations vary widely from state to state with most requirements and subsequent inspections concentrating on the physical plant with little emphasis on the quality of life of the residents. There is nothing comparable to the Federal bill of rights for nursing home patients for board and care residents.

Even gathering information on the quality of life in board and care homes is difficult. There is no standard reporting system, and states are not required to make periodic reports to the Federal government. As a result, much of the information about board and care homes is anecdotal. Although board and care homes are often thought of as being suboptimal providers of care, in fact, they are an important source of housing for the elderly, particularly for the elderly who lack support of family or friends and who have limited financial resources. To the extent that the board and care homes provide some sort of group assisted housing, they meet an important need. The fact that they meet it at rather low levels is a result of a failure to provide adequate financial support for these elderly residents.

Individuals who live in board and care homes often suffer from mental disabilities to the extent that they might be considered incompetent if a guardianship was sought. However, often no guardianship is sought, rather the board and care home operator functions as a de facto guardian monitoring the individual's financial resources, helping them with their health care and in general taking care of the individual. Of course, for every honest board and care home operator who faithfully carries out these unofficial duties, there are undoubtedly others who take advantage of the situation to abuse their residents, financially, physically or psychologically. In effect, a resident at a board and care home can be almost a prisoner since the cost of the home usually takes all of the resident's income leaving no cash or resources and nowhere to turn.

Because board and care residents generally have low incomes they rarely seek attorneys. Any legal help they would get is usually provided pro bono, by a legal services program, or a law school clinic that provides free assistance to the elderly poor. As a result, the legal problems of these residents are met only sporadically.

§ 7.17   Assisted Living Facilities

Assisted living provides supportive housing for the elderly who need daily assistance, but not the level of medical care provided in a nursing home. Some describe assisted living as the up-scale version of board and care homes, and in truth assisted living in many ways replicates the older board and care home model. Assisted living, however, usually describes larger, more modern, and more expensive facilities that offer more services to the residents, most of whom are women over age 80. It attracts older persons who either cannot or choose not to live alone and who desire the privacy and personal autonomy provided in an assisted living facility as opposed to the more regimented lifestyle common to nursing homes. Many residents suffer from mild dementia or other mental impairments, but if they become too demented, the facility may not have the resources to care for them.

Assisted living facilities feature small apartments (usually singles, sometimes shared with another), which may share a bathroom with an adjoining unit. Some provide limited kitchen appliances, but most do not. The facility will have a dining room, which will serve three meals a day. A requirement for continued residence is usually that the individual be able to take meals in the dining room. Residents who become bed bound are usually required to move out of the facility.

The facility will provide in-unit assistance as needed for help with dressing, bathing and other personal care needs. Assisted living facilities, while limited in the amount of medical care that they can provide (if they provide too much, they will come under the state regulation of nursing homes), usually have nurses on duty 24 hours a day who monitor the residents' health, insure that they take their prescription drugs and injections, and treat minor health problems. In addition to providing room and board, the facility typically has common rooms, organizes recreation such as bingo or craft clubs, may have a small convenience store on site, and often provides van service to places of worship, stores, doctors, hospitals and such.

Upon entering the facility, the resident will sign an admission contract that will detail the unit to be occupied, the services to be provided, the monthly fee (and the right of the facility to raise it), the amount of the security deposit and the rights of the resident such as the right of privacy and the right to have visitors. The contract will also detail the right of the facility to evict the resident in the event the resident's health fails, he or she becomes too demented or becomes a problem for the staff or other residents.

The monthly fee for assisted living is usually 60 percent to 80 percent of the cost of a nursing home in the area. At present, there is no governmental subsidy of assisted living costs, nor is there likely to be given the relative affluence of the residents. The portion of the assisted living fee that is attributable to medical care is deductible under Section 213(d)(1)(C) of the Internal Revenue Code if the resident is certified annually by a qualified health practitioner as requiring long-term care. The facility normally will provide residents with an allocation of the monthly bill between deductible medical expenses and nondeductible costs of room and board and non-medical services. A resident with a long-term care insurance policy may be able to collect the benefits because of residence in the assisted living facility. Most policies pay benefits if the policy holder is institutionalized (such as a nursing home or assisted living facility), has need for daily custodial care such as bathing or dressing, or is suffering cognitive impairment such as dementia. Many residents of assisted living facilities qualify under these standards. Per diem amounts paid under a long-term care insurance policy are not taxable unless they exceed the actual cost of the long-term care and $210 per day (in 2002). I.R.C. § 7702B(d). (See § 6.6(b) for a discussion of the deductibility of long-term care insurance premiums.)

CHAPTER 8

HOUSING ALTERNATIVES AND OPTIONS

One of the most critical decisions facing older people is determining where to live. Typical housing choices range from houses to apartments to condominiums to cooperatives, most of which are available to, and suitable for, persons of all ages. But advancing age often entails new needs and restrictions based upon declining capabilities. As a result, different choices and options become relevant, often involving some version of congregate or group living arrangements. This Chapter addresses the housing alternatives that are oriented to older persons and the planning considerations that they typically involve.

§ 8.1 Changing Housing Patterns of Older Persons

According to survey data from the American Association of Retired Persons, 86% of older adults want to stay in their current residence as long as possible, preferably the rest of their lives. Their residences, however, are not always suitable for persons who may be less capable of maintaining independent households. Sometimes, the home can be made more accommodating to an older person's needs by installing safety bars in bathrooms, alert systems in strategic locations, and elevators in staircases.

In other circumstances, periodic visits from relatives, friends, home care aides, church members, and others can help an older person "age in place" by cooking meals, shopping, doing housekeeping, performing home maintenance, and making repairs. Some services meeting the standard of medical necessity may be covered by the Federal government's health care program for older Americans, Medicare. See § 4.3(c) regarding Medicare coverage of home health care services; see also § 5.2 concerning Medicaid coverage of such services. Most home-oriented services, however, are not covered by government programs, or by private long-term care insurance policies in many cases. See generally § 6.2 regarding such insurance policies.

On the other hand, state agencies acting under the Older Americans Act of 1965 work with community groups and similar organizations to provide homemaking services for older persons. These services might include "meals on wheels," light housekeeping, minor home repairs, and the like. Some agencies restrict their target audience according to various criteria, and others charge for the services provided, typically on a sliding scale that is based on an older person's ability to pay. See generally § 16.7. For other people, private care management agencies can arrange and monitor these services, with charges based upon the level of assistance that they provide. But whatever the arrangement might be, home-oriented services often enable an older person to stay in his or her present residence without further ado.

Another housing alternative involves taking in younger tenants, siblings, or adult children on a permanent basis. These persons might undertake various household tasks in exchange for direct compensation, an interest in the home itself, in lieu of rent, or as part of some other financial arrangement. Sometimes, physical modifications to the home may be necessary to create certain areas of privacy, such as bathrooms and home entrances. Local zoning laws may also determine whether nonrelatives can share a home in this manner. But "home sharing," as this arrangement is sometimes called, or "accessory apartments," can provide an older person with needed homemaking and home maintenance services, plus a sense of personal security and companionship. In so doing, the older person may be able to remain in his or her home indefinitely. To be sure, such arrangements necessarily require trustworthy and cooperative partners, because the possibility of abuse and overreaching in this most intimate of caregiving settings cannot be dismissed lightly. See generally § 16.4. Nevertheless, home sharing can often be the best possible solution for all parties involved.

In other situations, an older person will need to leave his or her home and move to some other setting. A common pattern in the past involved moving into the home of one's adult son, daughter, or other close relative. While this arrangement remains viable, various competing societal trends have combined to make this option less typical today. Some of these trends include the increased likelihood that one's children no longer live close by, the increasingly intense career requirements of these adult children and their spouses, and the presence of young children at a later stage in their lives.

Consequently, some older people find that they must relocate to settings that are oriented primarily, if not exclusively, to them. Such settings often provide social stimulation and transportation for persons who are unable to access public transportation easily and safely. They may also provide nursing care at varying levels ranging from minimal to intensive. Residential facilities that provide medical care as their primary mission are often called nursing homes; see generally Chapter 7. All of these choices have major social and psychological implications for the older people involved, as well as for their families and friends.

These choices also have major financial implications, because a home is a financial asset for the vast majority of older Americans. It is an asset, to be sure, that is qualitatively different than stocks, bonds, and annuities, most of which are rarely imbued with a lifetime of memories spanning the spectrum of human emotions. Nor do these other assets become the center of an older person's day-to-day activities as physical mobility diminishes. But the home is a financial asset nonetheless. In fact, four out of five older Americans own their home or apartment unit, and more than three-quarters of those older homeowners have no mortgage debt outstanding. For most of these people, moreover, a debt-free home represents the bulk of their accumulated net worth. How they will access this store of financial value will determine, in large part, the range of living arrangements that they can consider.

Accordingly, this Chapter begins by considering the Federal tax consequences of disposing of one's principal residence, whether by sale, gift, or will. Alternative options for utilizing an older homeowner's investment in his or her residence, sometimes called home equity conversion, are then analyzed. Finally, some residential options that are specifically geared to older persons, primarily continuing care retirement communities, are then examined.

§ 8.2   Computing Gain or Loss on a Home

Older people often change residences by selling their homes following the death of a spouse or the departure of grown children. Either circumstance may make their current home seem too costly to heat and cool, too burdensome to maintain and repair, or simply too big for a single person or a couple without children. The problems are intensified if the home in question also has a yard that demands care, attention, and money. In other circumstances, older people simply decide to move to some other region of the country or to some other part of the state—perhaps to follow friends or families, perhaps to find a milder climate or more varied recreational opportunities, or perhaps to reduce their homemaking responsibilities. As a result, older persons may sell their present residences and acquire new residences. The tax consequences of such transactions will depend, as a threshold matter, upon whether they yield a gain or a loss.

When an older person sells his or her home, gain or loss is computed as the difference between the home's "amount realized" and its "adjusted basis." The "amount realized" is generally the sales price received minus selling expenses, primarily the commission paid to the real estate agent and related legal fees. So, if Martha sells her home for $300,000 and pays a 6% sales commission and $2,000 of legal fees, the commission is $18,000 ($300,000 x 6%), and the "amount realized" is $280,000 ($300,000 − $18,000 commission − $2,000 legal fees).

Her "adjusted basis" in the home is her original cost plus amounts that have been expended over the years for permanent improvements—fencing, landscaping, swimming pool, deck, additional rooms, and the like. Repairs of the home pertaining to its operating systems and maintenance, like painting and roof shingle replacement, are not permanent additions to a home's "basis." The distinction between maintenance-type of expenditures and permanent improvements is not always easy to make, however. More difficult still for most people is the burden of retaining documentation of permanent improvements, especially if those improvements were made decades earlier.

The "adjusted basis" of a home also includes closing costs that were not previously deducted. Such costs typically relate back to the original acquisition of the home and include the cost of title insurance, legal fees for the home purchase and closing, recording costs of the deed and related mortgage, if any, inspection fees, and other costs required by local practice or custom. Interest prepaid on a home's mortgage is usually *not* part of the home's "basis," because this expense was either deducted at the time of closing where permitted, generally on the original acquisition loan, or deducted over the life of the loan, which is typically the case for a refinancing loan or a home equity loan. If unamortized interest costs remain at the time the home is sold, those costs are usually deducted as interest expense, rather than being included as part of a home's "adjusted basis." In any case, once these various costs are accumulated, the homeowner has his or her "basis" in the home.

Sometimes, there is a negative or downward adjustment to a home's basis to account for depreciation claimed on the business or rental portion of the home. Most of the details pertaining to depreciation can be relegated to the plethora of books that deal with Federal income taxation generally or with real estate taxation particularly, since they are not of specific significance to older homeowners as such. But a few points are appropriate here.

First, if an older person used part of the home as the principal place of business in preceding years, depreciation expense might have been allowable on the portion so used. The depreciation expense actually deducted, however, may have been much less than the full amount one might calculate, due to the various "office-in-the-home" limitations of I.R.C. § 280A. These limitations restrict the applicable depreciation deduction to the amount that the home-based business' gross income exceeds its business-related expenses, the allocated portion of the mortgage interest expense and property taxes (which are deductible even without a home-based business), and the allocated portion of repairs, maintenance, utilities, and insurance. So limited, only a portion of the depreciable amount would actually have been deducted, and only that portion would now reduce the home's "basis."

Similarly, as noted in § 8.1, an older person might rent out part of his or her home—either for additional income or for companionship and/or assistance in maintaining the home. Converting part of a home into a rental unit entitles the homeowner to deduct part of the home's cost as depreciation. Once again, however, there are various restrictions and limitations relating to how much depreciation pertains to the rental portion of the home and how much can actually be deducted, after considering other pertinent expenses. In any case, to the extent that a homeowner did deduct the cost of his or her home via depreciation deductions, those deductions reduce a home's "adjusted basis" in computing gain or loss upon its disposition.

In addition to these adjustments for depreciation, a homeowner's basis may be adjusted downward due to prior home sales. Under the tax law that applied *prior* to May 7, 1997, gains from the sale of a principal residence were not taxed if the homeowner purchased a new residence that cost as much as the sale proceeds from the former residence. Instead, the *basis* of the new residence was lowered by the amount of the untaxed gain. Although this provision (so-called I.R.C. § 1034 "rollover") has been repealed, this basis adjustment will be part of the gain computation process for many—if not most—of the residences being sold by older homeowners.

For example, assume that Allison and Billy sold a home in 1989 before they bought their current residence. They realized a gain of $87,000 on the 1989 sale, but they paid no tax on that gain, because their new home cost more than the sale proceeds from their former residence. Accordingly, if their new home cost, say, $200,000, their basis is $113,000 ($200,000 cost − $87,000 untaxed gain)— not $200,000. This adjustment is a trap for the unwary, since many people—regardless of age— presume that their gain is measured from their home's purchase price ($200,000 in this example), rather than from some special "adjusted basis" figure.

In any case, once a home's "amount realized" and "adjusted basis" are determined, gain or loss is found by subtracting the two figures. If the "amount realized" exceeds "adjusted basis," the homeowner has achieved a gain, and the opposite situation produces a loss. But this loss is not recognized for tax purposes and provides no tax benefit. The tax code states that "no deduction shall be allowed for personal, living, or family expenses," and a loss from the sale of a personal residence is considered such an "expense." I.R.C. § 262(a); Treas. Reg. § 1.165–9(a) (1964).

This restriction on deducting losses is important, because homes do not inevitably appreciate in value. Changes in a neighborhood's attractiveness due to environmental factors, rezoning, construction of nearby businesses, or simply the whims of local real estate markets may combine with a home's own history of neglect, disrepair, dilapidated condition, or outmoded features to produce an economic loss upon its disposition. But the point remains that longevity of ownership does not by itself guarantee a profit and that taxable gain is not a foregone conclusion on any specific real estate investment, including the home of an older person.

§ 8.3   Tax Treatment of Gains on Residences

If a gain has been realized, it is generally taxable in the year of sale. In almost all cases, this gain is treated as long-term capital gain, because the home is a capital asset that has been held more than 12 months. But virtually all such gains are *exempt* from taxation due to a special provision that applies to the sale of a principal residence. Under this provision, gain is taxed only to the extent that it exceeds $250,000, or $500,000 for a married couple. I.R.C. § 121(b)(1). So, if Amanda and Peter are married and they sell their home for a $400,000 gain, none of their gain is taxable.

This special exclusion is available to *all* home-owners, not just older homeowners, as long as the home being sold was the owner's principal residence during two of the preceding five years. Older home-owners are particular beneficiaries of this provision, however, because they are more likely to be sellers of homes that have gone up in value over many years. And since the median *sale price* of a used home in this country is under $210,000, the $250,000/$500,000 exclusion of *gain*—which is roughly a home's sale price minus its cost—covers most gains from the sale of a residence.

a. Eligibility Requirements

The principal eligibility requirement is that the seller owned *and* used the home as his or her "principal residence" for at least two years during the five-year period immediately preceding the home's disposition. I.R.C. § 121(a). For married couples, the exclusion applies as long as both spouses satisfy the "use" test, even if only one spouse owns the home. I.R.C. § 121(b)(2)(A). So, if Amanda in the preceding example owns the home in her name alone, the exclusion can apply as long as she and her husband, Peter, used the home as *their* principal residence. Second homes, vacation homes, and the like, however, do not qualify. On the other hand, a houseboat or trailer can qualify, if that is where a person lives most of the time.

Of particular significance to older people is a rule that treats time in a nursing home as time in a person's residence for purposes of the two-year test. I.R.C. § 121(d)(7). This rule applies only if the homeowner lived in the residence at least one year during the five-year period preceding the home's disposition and continued to own the residence while in the nursing facility. Thus, if Jennifer bought a new residence and lived there one year before moving into a nursing home, she can apply the $250,000 exclusion after being in the nursing home one year.

Even if the nursing home rule does not apply, a person who has not satisfied the two-year test can obtain a *prorated* exclusion if he or she sells the home because of a change in health. I.R.C. § 121(c). Assume that Byron moved into a new residence and suffered a stroke six months later, which required him to move in with his sister. The six-month period during which Byron occupied his home is one-fourth of the two-year testing period. Therefore, one-fourth of the $250,000 exclusion, or $62,500, would be available.

Once the two-year ownership and use tests are met, the exclusion applies without regard to how the sale proceeds are used. So, if Suzanne sells her home to move into an "assisted living facility" (see § 7.17) or a "continuing care retirement community" (see § 8.7), the exclusion can apply. Similarly, the exclusion can apply if Suzanne moves in with her daughter or simply rents an apartment on her own.

There is one exception, however, that applies to a homeowner who claimed depreciation deductions *after* May 6, 1997. To the extent of such deductions, gain from the sale of a principal residence is taxable, even if the total gain realized is less than the general exclusion amount. I.R.C. § 121(d)(6). For example, assume that Matt sold his home for $220,000 net of selling expenses. Assume further that this home's basis (say, $78,000) reflects $2,000 of depreciation deductions claimed after May 6, 1997 for an office he maintained in his home. His gain of $142,000 ($220,000 amount realized − $78,000 adjusted basis) is less than the $250,000 that is generally excludible. Nevertheless, the $2,000 of gain representing depreciation deductions claimed after May 6, 1997 is taxable.

b. *The Effect of Ownership Arrangements*

As indicated above, the residential gain exclusion is generally $250,000, but married taxpayers can exclude up to $500,000 of gain, even if only one spouse owns the home. I.R.C. § 121(b)(2)(A). The specific ownership arrangement is important, however, if either the husband or the wife dies before the home is sold. In that case, the surviving spouse is treated as any other unmarried person and can exclude only $250,000 of gain. Thus, in the preceding example of Amanda and Peter, where Amanda owned the home in her name alone, assume that Peter died and that Amanda sold the home a year later. As an unmarried taxpayer, Amanda may exclude only $250,000 of gain—not $500,000.

Amanda can avoid this result by selling the home during the year in which Peter died, because she would still be able to file a joint tax return, and the $500,000 exclusion would apply. I.R.C. § 6013(a)(3). So, if Peter died in July and Amanda sold the home in November of that same year, she can exclude $500,000 of gain.

The tax consequences described above apply when the nonowner-spouse (here, Peter) dies first. But if the owner-spouse (here, Amanda) dies first, the residential gain exclusion interacts with the tax code's basis rule for property received from a decedent. Under this provision, the property's basis is generally its *fair market value* when the owner died. I.R.C. § 1014(a)(1). As a consequence, *all* of the gain that has accrued to that point is excluded from tax, without limitation.

For example, assume that Amanda's cost basis in her home is $100,000 and that the home is worth $650,000. If Amanda is the sole owner and she dies, Peter's basis in the home is its fair market value on the day that Amanda died—namely $650,000. Thus, none of the $550,000 gain ($650,000 value – $100,000 Amanda's basis) is taxable.

In any case, the overwhelming majority of married couples own their homes in joint tenancy. The date-of-death basis rule generally applies in these circumstances to half of the home that is owned by each joint tenant. Continuing with the preceding example, assume that Amanda and Peter own their home as joint tenants. If either of them dies, the survivor's basis consists of that person's basis in his or her half of the property ($100,000 cost basis × 50% = $50,000), plus the fair market value of the decedent's half on the day that person died ($650,-000 date-of-death value × 50% = $325,000)—a total of $375,000 ($50,000 + $325,000). And if this home is later sold for, say, $700,000, the realized gain is $325,000 ($700,000 sale proceeds – $375,000 surviving spouse's basis). Of this amount, $250,000 can be excluded by the residential gain exclusion, so only $75,000 is taxable—or none at all if a joint tax return, with its $500,000 exclusion, can be filed. This result obtains, moreover, regardless of which spouse dies first.

The split basis rule just explained is subject to two general exceptions. First, if the home being sold was acquired before 1977 and the deceased spouse provided the entire consideration, the surviving spouse's basis is the property's fair market value when the deceased spouse died. *Gallenstein v. United States*, (6th Cir.1992); *Hahn v. Commissioner* (Tax Ct.1998). Second, this treatment also applies to homes that are held as community property, regardless of when the home was acquired or which spouse provided the consideration. I.R.C. § 1014(b)(6).

In any case, joint tenancy is extremely important to unmarried couples, because they may never file a joint tax return and thereby obtain the $500,000 exclusion. But if an unmarried couple, Jerry and Elaine, own their home as joint tenants, each may exclude $250,000 of gain on his or her half of the residence—effectively excluding $500,000 of gain. Similar considerations apply to a couple whose marriage is not recognized for Federal purposes; e.g., a marriage of Jerry and George. See 1 U.S.C. § 7.

§ 8.4 Gratuitous Transfers of a Residence

Not all dispositions of an older person's residence are sales. As part of a realignment of housing arrangements, an older person might want to give his or her home to a favored relative or friend, perhaps in gratitude for assistance previously received, or because the older person plans to join the donee's household indefinitely. As long as there is no *quid pro quo* in this transaction, it will be treated as a gift for income tax purposes.

If the transfer, however, has elements of a commercial exchange for value, it will be treated like any other sale. In such circumstances, the "amount realized" will be the fair market value of the consideration received at the time of the transaction. And if that value is difficult to determine, the fair market value of the home will be determined instead, and then imputed to the consideration received. Thus, if Linda transfers her home to Travis as consideration for Travis' promise to take care of Linda, the transfer will be treated as a sale of the home for a promise equal in value to the home that Linda transferred. As such, this transfer is not a gift for income tax purposes.

a. *Inter Vivos Gifts*

Lifetime transfers of a residence are basically the same as lifetime transfers of any other property.

They may lower the amount of assets in a person's taxable estate for estate tax purposes, and they avoid the probate process because the older person does not own the property at his or her death. On the other hand, lifetime transfers of a residence are often undertaken to assure retention of the home within the family—a nonfinancial objective that is usually not compelling for other, less sentimentally regarded assets.

As long as a home's value does not trigger any gift tax, lifetime transfers generate no immediate tax consequences. A donor may give up to $12,000 (in 2006; adjusted periodically) per year per donee before tapping into a cumulative lifetime gift tax exemption of $1 million. For example, in 2006, Norma could give a residence valued at $1,024,000 to her two adult children, or to an adult child and that child's spouse, without incurring any gift tax liability ($12,000 per donee × 2 donees = $24,000 + $1,000,000 lifetime exemption = $1,024,000).

In general, the donor's basis carries over to the donee, effectively shifting the tax to the donee. I.R.C. § 1015(a). As a result, any increase in the home's value since its acquisition is not recognized for income tax purposes until the donee sells the residence—an event that might be years, or even decades, in the future. And if the donee uses the home as his or her principal residence, the gain exclusion described in § 8.3 would apply to the first $250,000 of gain ($500,000 on a joint return).

For example, if Norma gives her son Andy a home worth $300,000, on which her "adjusted basis" is $35,000, there will be no immediate income tax due on the $265,000 increase in the home's value that accrued while Norma owned the home. When Andy sells this home, his basis in the home will generally be Norma's basis—namely, $35,000. And if Andy uses this home as his "principal residence" for at least two years before selling it, only $15,000 of the $265,000 gain will be taxable. On the other hand, if Andy has his own home and does *not* use Norma's former home as his "principal residence," the residential gain exclusion will not apply. In that case, Andy will be taxed on the entire $265,000 gain—but not until he chooses to sell the home.

An alternative arrangement that Norma might consider is a "bargain sale" to Andy at less than full fair market value. For example, she could sell her home to Andy for $285,000, thereby making him a gift of $15,000 ($300,000 current value − $285,000 sale price). The sale for $285,000 would generate a gain to Norma of $250,000 (amount realized of $285,000 − Norma's basis of $35,000), all of which would be shielded from taxation by Norma's residential gain exclusion. Andy would then take the home at a basis equal to his cost—namely, $285,000. The $15,000 of additional gain is effectively deferred until Andy disposes of the home sometime in the future, at which time, Andy might be eligible for the residential gain exclusion himself. Financing and other aspects of the transaction would, of course, need to be bona fide.

In any case, there is a so-called "bouncing basis" rule that applies if (a) the home's market value at the date of gift was less than the donor's basis, *and* (b) the donee later sells the home at a loss. Both conditions must apply for this rule to apply, in which case the donee's basis is the home's market value at the date of the gift, rather than the donor's basis. I.R.C. § 1015(a).

To illustrate this curiosity, assume that Paula's home cost $150,000 when she bought it, but it is worth only $110,000 when she gives it to her son, Bill. If Bill later sells the home for $100,000, his loss is measured from the home's value at the date of gift—namely, $110,000—so his loss is only $10,000. Such a loss is still nondeductible, of course, because it derived from the sale of a personal residence, as noted in § 8.2. If Bill sells the home for more than Paula's basis of $150,000, however, his gain is measured from that amount in the usual fashion, since he is not selling the home at a loss— the second condition of the "bouncing basis" rule. As a final possibility, if Bill sells the home for some amount between Paula's basis of $150,000 and the home's value at the date of the gift, $110,000, Bill has neither a gain nor a loss for Federal income tax purposes. See Treas. Reg. § 1.1015–1(a)(2) (1971).

b. *Testamentary Transfers*

In other circumstances, an older person may stay in his or her residence even if he or she can no longer live there alone. For example, an older person might have an adult son or daughter move into the home and help with daily chores and with the home's upkeep. As long as there is no contractual agreement—written or oral—to bequeath the home in exchange for these services, the adult child can receive the home tax-free as an inheritance.

From the older person's perspective, the home will be treated like any other asset with no special deference given its status as a former residence. The home will be included in the probate process, and it will be part of the decedent's taxable estate for estate tax purposes if that person's total assets make such a consideration relevant.

On the other hand, the new owner will take as his or her basis in the home its *market value* at the date of the donor's death, rather than the donor's basis. I.R.C. § 1014(a)(1). A home that has appreciated before the owner's death, in other words, will never have that appreciation subjected to income tax.

Returning to the example of Norma, with a home that is worth $300,000 but cost only $35,000, assume that Norma retains the home until she dies. Assume further that Andy then gets the home, either as a beneficiary under Norma's will or via intestate succession. Andy's basis in the home is now $300,000, rather than $35,000. None of the $265,000 of gain that accrued on the home up to that point is subjected to Federal income tax. Instead, Andy will owe tax only on the home's appreciation in value that occurs *after* that date. On the other hand, if the home has declined in value, its market value at the date of death becomes the new owner's basis. So if Norma's home was worth $27,000 when she died, that figure would be Andy's basis, not Norma's cost of $35,000. The so-called "step up in basis" rule, therefore, can actually produce a step *down* in basis, depending upon the home's value when the owner dies.

Be that as it may, the step-up feature of this rule has no dollar limit. Unlike the residential gain exclusion that would have shielded $250,000 from tax if Norma had sold the home before she died, this provision exempted the *entire* $265,000 of gain from income taxation. On very large amounts, to be sure, the estate might be liable for Federal estate tax, which is based on the assets' market value on the date the decedent died. But the estate tax affects very few older Americans, and in any case, the "step up in basis" rule is not limited to properties that were subjected to estate tax. Thus, very significant gains on residences can escape taxation entirely if the owner holds the property until he or she dies. Moreover, this "step up in basis" rule applies even if the home was no longer being used by the older person as his or her principal residence. The rule simply requires that the older person hold the property at his or her death.

§ 8.5 Reverse Mortgages

Older persons often find that physical infirmities or other diminished capabilities require that they leave their home of many years, necessitating the home's sale or other disposition. Many other older

people are quite capable of staying in their home
but for a different type of disability, one that is
financial in nature. More specifically, the various
costs of maintaining a home, such as repairs, utilities, insurance, and property taxes, seemingly increase each year. At the same time, most private
pensions are not indexed for inflation, and individual investments may yield wildly varying amounts,
especially in a volatile interest rate environment. As
a result, older people find that their incomes may be
fixed or even declining, while the costs of staying in
their home go up. Hence, the ability to meet these
ongoing financial obligations becomes an impedi-
ment to their "aging in place."

As already noted, a home is the principal financial
asset for many older Americans. And in most cases,
that home no longer bears a mortgage; i.e., it is
owned free of debt. In many cases, although certainly not in all, the home's value has increased since it
was first acquired, sometimes significantly so. The
product of these forces is the phenomenon of older
people owning an appreciated asset that is free of
debt, but produces no income, while generating
costs that seem to rise inexorably. This phenomenon is often described as being "house rich but cash
poor." The question then becomes how can older
homeowners tap into the equity value of their
homes to pay for the ongoing expenses of home-
ownership, as well as for other costs of day-to-day
living.

Selling the home frustrates the strongly held desire of most older people to stay in their home as

long as possible. It might also generate undesirable tax consequences if the potential taxable gain upon the home's disposition exceeds the $250,000 that is generally excludible on the sale of a principal residence. See generally § 8.3.

Accordingly, a financial instrument called a "reverse mortgage" has been developed that pays the older homeowner a fixed sum each month, the total of such payments—with interest—being collected when the home is sold. This arrangement allows the homeowner to remain in his or her residence while receiving a current financial return based on the home's value. The monthly payments received supplement retirement income, help meet the home's ongoing expenses, and pay for such costs as in-home health care, long-term care insurance, and other medical needs. Generally, there are no restrictions on how these payments may be spent.

Reverse mortgages had been available for several decades, but with considerable variation from one region of the country to another. In 1991, the Federal government expanded its insurance of reverse mortgages, thereby increasing the availability of such mortgages, although localized shortages often remain. The Federal program, moreover, is limited to mortgages of a specified size, so state programs and private financial arrangements remain important for applicants seeking amounts in excess of these limits.

The features of any specific reverse mortgage depend in significant measure upon the program under which that mortgage is made—whether it is a state or local program, the Federal government's insured mortgage program, or a private contract between the originating financial institution and the older homeowning borrower. The more salient features concern loan duration and payback schedules, borrower eligibility, loan size, and disclosure requirements.

a. *Duration of Loan*

Some reverse mortgages are simply lines of credit secured by a home's equity that allow the borrower to draw down funds as desired. Other reverse mortgages are fixed-term agreements that provide a series of monthly payments for a specified period, the total—including interest—being repayable at the end of that period, unless the mortgage is extended or refinanced. For example, Bruce borrows $500 per month for ten years, at the end of which time, he must pay the $60,000 of accumulated principal, plus the interest that has accrued on that amount.

Another version of the reverse mortgage provides monthly payments as long as a homeowner occupies the home as his or her principal residence. Repayment is not required until the homeowner moves or dies, said repayment coming, presumably, out of the sales proceeds of the home. If desired, a homeowner's heirs, usually his or her children, can choose to keep the home in the family by paying off the reverse mortgage, or by refinancing it themselves. If a home is jointly owned, repayment is not required until both co-owners have ceased using the home as their principal residence. But the point remains that an older homeowner need not pay off the loan as long as he or she lives in the home. This feature addresses the single greatest obstacle to older persons' tapping their home equity—namely, a fear of "outliving" that equity and being forced to leave their home prematurely. The so-called "life tenure" reverse mortgage eliminates that risk.

This feature, however, comes at a very real financial cost. Borrowers under "life tenure" reverse mortgages receive smaller monthly payments than those with fixed-term reverse mortgages, because payments continue until the homeowner dies or leaves the home, which may be many years away for any given homeowner. For example, a 75–year old homeowner applying $100,000 of home value to a reverse mortgage at an interest rate of 5% would receive approximately $610 per month on a ten-year reverse mortgage, but only $380 per month if a life tenure reverse mortgage is selected instead.

In either version of a reverse mortgage, the older a borrower is when the loan is obtained, the higher the monthly payment will be, because of the likely shorter term of the loan. Even fixed term reverse mortgages, after all, are due before the end of the fixed term if the homeowner leaves the home, either because of death or because that person moves to a nursing home, for example. Considering the same home value and the same interest rate used above, an 85–year old homeowner would receive approximately $780 per month on a ten-year reverse mortgage, and $610 per month on a "life tenure" version. A 65–year old homeowner, by contrast, would receive approximately $450 per month on a ten-year reverse mortgage, but only $260 per month on a "life tenure" payout, using the same interest rate and home value.

Incidentally, for these purposes, the Federal reverse mortgage program assumes a life expectancy of 100 years. For that reason, the monthly payout amounts on a ten-year reverse mortgage and on a "life tenure" reverse mortgage would be exactly the same if the borrower is 90 years old when the loan is obtained.

Be that as it may, a borrower under a "life tenure" reverse mortgage never needs to fear being forced out of his or her home to pay off a loan. Moreover, a borrower under such a mortgage never owes more than the home brings when it is sold. So, even if the sum of the monthly payments received and the accumulated interest thereon exceeds a home's realizable value, the borrower's liability is limited to that realizable value. Under the Federal government's reverse mortgage program, the government makes up the deficiency, if any, to the lending institution, thereby encouraging such institutions to make these loans without fear of financial loss.

b. *Borrower Eligibility*

The age of a borrower is a common eligibility requirement, but certain types of residences are also restricted. In the Federal government's program, for example, a homeowner must be at least

62 years old and reside in a single-family dwelling. Condominiums are also eligible, but shareholder-owned cooperatives are not. State-authorized programs necessarily vary; in some states, the minimum age is only 60 years old, while other states use 65 years. In Florida, it is 70 years.

c. *Interest Rates and Loan Size*

Some states have caps on the interest rates that may be charged on reverse mortgages. Others, like California, compensate a lender for this limitation by authorizing "shared appreciation;" i.e., equity kickers that give the lender a portion of the price appreciation that accrues on the underlying residence. Even in areas of escalating real estate prices, however, many older homeowners are not completely comfortable with such arrangements.

The permitted size of a loan is a very important limitation. Some states simply apply a percentage of a home's appraised value, typically 80%. The Federal program has a limited loan range of $200,160 to $362,790 (2006 limits), with the exact limit depending upon the county in which the home is located. A similar program run by Fannie Mae has a limit of $417,000 (in 2006). Persons requiring larger sums need to consider other loan programs. Federal program loans, however, are generally easier to find, and can be sold by lenders on the secondary market—increasing their availability still further.

d. *Disclosure Requirements*

Reverse mortgages usually have special disclosure requirements, because most homeowners are not familiar with an arrangement that pays *them* every month to stay in their own home, while deferring repayment until some unspecified future date. Special disclosure formats are authorized, with boilerplate language in capital letters, and so forth. In addition, the Federally insured reverse mortgage program requires prospective borrowers to receive financial counseling before obtaining a reverse mortgage. Such counseling typically covers budgeting and general financial planning, and often tax implications and Medicaid/public assistance ramifications as well. Moreover, this counseling is usually provided by various state-authorized agencies that regularly deal with older Americans, rather than the loan-originating institutions themselves.

e. *Income Tax Considerations*

In general, reverse mortgages generate few income tax considerations. The proceeds of a loan are not taxable, regardless of the payout schedule of those proceeds. Nor is the interest deductible to most older homeowners, who typically report on the cash basis, and accordingly have no deduction until the entire loan is paid off. Even then, interest expenses on a reverse mortgage would be deductible only as "home equity indebtedness," which is limited to loan principal amounts of no more than $100,000. See I.R.C. § 163(h)(3)(C)(ii). Many reverse mortgages exceed that threshold.

But a reverse mortgage can affect the taxation of the home's appreciation in value. When a reverse mortgage becomes due—either because its fixed term has expired or because the borrower has moved out of the home—the home is usually sold to provide the necessary repayment funds. In most cases, the gain realized at that time will be shielded from tax by the $250,000 residential gain exclusion explained in § 8.3. Any gain in excess of this amount, however, would be taxable. And if the homeowner had intended to avoid this tax by retaining the home until his or her death, a reverse mortgage might upset this strategy.

For example, assume that Eric's home has an unrealized gain of nearly $300,000. If he holds the home until he dies, none of that gain will be subject to income tax, even if he lived in a nursing home his final years. (See generally § 8.4(b) regarding the income tax implications of property transferred at death.) But if Eric obtained a reverse mortgage before he moved into the nursing home, that mortgage would be payable upon his departure from his home. Although he could pay off that mortgage by selling assets other than his home, people with reverse mortgages usually have few significant financial resources other than their home. Accordingly, Eric will probably sell his home upon moving to the nursing home. As a result, Eric will be taxed on $50,000 of gain, after applying the $250,000 residential gain exclusion explained in § 8.3. In effect, the reverse mortgage prevented him from obtaining the unlimited gain exclusion that applies when property is held until death.

On the other hand, if Eric stays in his home until he dies, the reverse mortgage will be paid off at that time. The entire gain will be exempt from Federal income taxation, without regard to the stream of monthly payments that Eric received during his lifetime. Nevertheless, a reverse mortgage has the possibility of upsetting one's tax planning, because it might become payable upon the borrower's medically necessitated departure from his or her home— an event that is often sudden and unanticipated.

f. Public Assistance Implications

Many older persons who might be candidates for reverse mortgages find that their cash flow absent a reverse mortgage entitles them to various public assistance benefits that are means-tested. Supplemental Security Income and Medicaid are the most prominent of such programs, but food stamps might also be included, as well as other, more limited programs. See generally Chapter 5 (Medicaid) and Chapter 12 (Supplemental Security Income). In any case, the Federal government, and many states as well, has determined that payments received from a reverse mortgage are not income for purposes of determining eligibility under these public assistance programs. But if these payments remain unspent by month's end, they become possibly disqualifying "resources." Thus, it becomes extremely important for persons in these situations to monitor their cash flows and to ensure that reverse mortgage payments are completely spent before month's end.

A related aspect of reverse mortgages pertains to the unique status of a person's principal residence under means-tested public assistance programs, particularly Medicaid. As explained more fully in § 5.7, the residence is often an "exempt resource," meaning an asset that is ignored when determining an older person's eligibility for the program's benefits. Many factors determine whether a residence is in fact so treated, including an older person's marital status and his or her continuing ability to use that home as a personal residence. But if a home is regarded as an "exempt resource," a reverse mortgage has the effect of reducing the value of this largely protected asset while possibly increasing the person's available cash on hand, which is not so protected. This result may be acceptable to the older person who needs public assistance, but it remains a noteworthy feature of reverse mortgages nonetheless.

§ 8.6 Other Home Equity Conversion Mechanisms

The desire of older persons to utilize the value of their home equity while continuing to live in their home has spawned various mechanisms in addition to reverse mortgages. One of the most direct of these mechanisms is a home equity loan. Such loans are not uniquely developed for older homeowners, and in fact are usually not helpful. Most home equity loans provide either a line of credit to be drawn upon as the homeowner determines or a single lump sum—neither of which necessarily produces a dependable income stream. Worse, home equity loans typically require that the borrower demonstrate a dependable source of income that can support monthly repayment obligations. Most older homeowners do not want the obligation to make monthly repayments, and those homeowners most in need of additional income are not likely to have the income that is necessary to obtain a home equity loan. In some circumstances, however, a home equity loan might be suitable; e.g., to finance structural home improvements that will enable an older homeowner to remain in the home. But such circumstances are relatively limited.

a.   Sale–Leasebacks

Another mechanism that taps an older person's home equity is the sale-leaseback. In this transaction, the home is sold and then simultaneously leased back to the older person, generally for the rest of that person's life. The sale side of this transaction provides the older homeowner with a downpayment that represents part of his or her equity in the residence, plus a stream of monthly payments that represent the balance of the purchase price. This series of monthly payments is sometimes correlated to the older person's remaining life expectancy. The leaseback side of the transaction assures the older person of continued occupancy of his or her residence, but at the cost of making monthly rental payments.

Ideally, the gain on the sale of the home will largely be shielded from income taxation by the older person's $250,000 residential gain exclusion explained in § 8.3. Furthermore, the monthly sale payments to the older person should exceed that person's rent obligations, thereby providing the older person with an additional source of income while he or she lives in the home. Of course, rental payments tend to increase over time, thereby creating a source of financial uncertainty for the older person/tenant. But if the lease agreement limits these rental increases, the validity of the purported sale—or at least the purported sales *price*—may be questioned by the Internal Revenue Service (IRS). And if the sale is not valid, the older person will not be able to apply the residential gain exclusion. Moreover, even if the sale is valid, any gain in excess of $250,000 will be taxable to the older homeowner.

This question of rent increase limitations highlights one of the major hurdles of a sale-leaseback—namely, the conversion of the older homeowner into a tenant. In this new role, the older person necessarily gives up significant control of his or her property and may well resent the attending restrictions and resulting financial insecurity. Indeed, many older homeowners, having been free of the burden of monthly housing payments for some time, find this aspect of the transaction simply unacceptable.

A second major hurdle is finding a suitable purchaser of the home, one who is willing to buy the home subject to the sort of leasehold restrictions that the older homeowner requires. In most cases, only a family member will agree to these terms. Of course, that family member must have sufficient financial wherewithal—either in cash or via borrowed funds—to consummate the transaction. A related problem is determining an appropriate sales price for the home, as well as an appropriate rental value therefor, given the accompanying leasehold restrictions. Because most sale-leasebacks involve family members, the IRS applies strict scrutiny to all aspects of the transaction before accepting its characterization.

A sale-leaseback is clearly not a simple undertaking. Sales documents, lease agreements, and financing arrangements must be prepared, although some transaction costs can be avoided if the older homeowner finances the sale directly, rather than through a third-party financial institution. That arrangement, however, raises its own set of financial considerations concerning the possibility of buyer default and other such matters.

Nevertheless, in certain circumstances, the numbers can work out well. The older homeowner may be able to shelter most of the gain from the sale of the home due to the residential gain exclusion explained in § 8.3. The purchaser/landlord may be in a higher tax bracket than the older homeowner, so that deductions for property taxes are worth more to the new owner. In addition, the new owner will be holding the residence as rental property, thereby entitling that person to claim tax deductions for home repairs, insurance, and depreciation, all of which are usually nondeductible to a person who lives in the home that he or she owns. These deductions would, of course, be offset by the rental payments received, but in most cases, a net loss will result.

On the other hand, the tax law now limits the amount of net losses that an owner of residential rental property can deduct in any one year. That statute also limits the amount of depreciation that can be deducted in the early years of property ownership, with the result that sale-leasebacks have lost some of their tax-based appeal to the purchaser/landlord. Moreover, many sale-leasebacks are premised on rates of appreciation in the home's value that may not be completely realistic. Of course, such appreciation in the home's value represents a foregone benefit from the perspective of the older person who sold the home as part of the transaction. In any case, it is impossible to formulate rules of thumb for determining when a sale-leaseback will be beneficial to all the parties concerned.

A sale-leaseback can also affect an older person's eligibility for certain means-tested public assistance. As noted in § 8.5(f), funds on hand at the end of a month constitute a "countable resource" for purposes of assessing a person's eligibility for Supplemental Security Income (SSI), Medicaid, and certain other programs as well. Therefore, the downpayment received when a home is sold, and the excess of the sales payments received over the monthly rent paid, will be considered a "resource" if these funds remain unspent at month's end. In addition, if the monthly sales price payments are documented in an installment note or some similar obligation, that note is a "resource" to the extent that it can be negotiated. For example, assume that a note calling for twenty years of monthly payments of $500 each can be sold for $83,000 "in the open market," as the SSI regulations stipulate. It is, therefore, a "countable resource" valued at $83,000, notwithstanding the fact that it originated from the sale of an "exempt" resource—namely, the principal residence. Finally, any interest received would constitute "countable income," which decreases a person's SSI benefits dollar for dollar. See generally § 12.1, dealing with eligibility for SSI benefits.

b. *Sale of a Remainder Interest in the Home*

Another mechanism to tap an older person's equity in his or her home is retaining a life estate in the home while selling the remainder interest. In essence, the older homeowner continues to live in the residence the rest of his or her life—the retained life estate. And the actuarially determined value of the residence after that time, i.e., the remainder interest, is sold for a specified sum, typically paid over a series of years.

For example, if Beth is 75 years old, the IRS actuarial tables show that the remainder interest in her home is 48% of its total value. So if Beth's home is worth $150,000, she would sell the remainder interest for $72,000 ($150,000 × 48%). Had Beth been younger, say 60 years old, she would be expected to live longer, and her remainder interest would accordingly be worth less—in this case, 25%, according to IRS tables.

In any case, it is often quite difficult to find a buyer for a remainder interest outside of one's family, no doubt because the real economic value of such an interest is so intimately tied to the life estate owner's actual longevity.

Once a remainder interest is sold, the gain is usually taxable in full. Although a sale of a remainder interest is eligible for the $250,000 residential gain exclusion, this provision does not apply if the buyer and the seller are "related" to one another— which is usually the case in these transactions. I.R.C. § 121(d)(8)(B), § 267(b)(1), (c)(4).

Moreover, the treatment of such sales proceeds for public assistance purposes largely parallels that of payments received under a sale-leaseback. That is, any portion of a payment that represents interest is unearned income, which reduces a person's SSI benefits dollar for dollar. In addition, any proceeds from such a sale that are not consumed before the end of the month in which they are received become "resources" for purposes of the SSI and Medicaid resource eligibility tests. See generally Chapter 5 (Medicaid) and Chapter 12 (SSI).

§ 8.7 Congregate Housing for Older Residents

Older persons often find that at some point in their lives, living in a congregate or group setting is quite appealing. Such a setting may include some degree of regular meal service, social activities designed to foster continued interaction with one's age peers, transportation to cultural, religious, and recreational outings, readily accessible services such as beauty and barber shops, and handy pharmaceutical outlets. Congregate care units designed for older persons typically have grab bars and other safety features in the bathrooms, pullcords or similar alert/alarm systems, as well as other arrangements to ensure that older residents can obtain assistance when they need it. Some complexes are quite elaborate and provide a great variety of optional services. Others are more modest but still respond to the needs of older persons.

The Federal government subsidizes construction of congregate housing for the "elderly" under various statutory provisions. Oftentimes, these units are sponsored by nonprofit organizations, especially church-affiliated or other religious groups. In exchange for the Federal subsidy, the project must be supervised by the local public housing authority and must charge a below-market rental rate. This rental rate, moreover, can be reduced still further depending upon an individual tenant's financial situation. Such so-called "Section 8" rent subsidies are calculated as a percentage of a tenant's income, with certain modifications. See generally 42 U.S.C. § 1437f. The Federal government then pays the difference between the actual rent charged and the market rental rate for that unit. From the perspective of the older tenant, these rental subsidies are the most important statutory feature of the Federal government's various housing programs.

For purposes of this special subsidy, an "elderly" person must be at least 62 years old and must satisfy certain limitations on that person's income. Generally, a person's income may not exceed 80% of the median income in the local area, as adjusted for family size. In measuring income, virtually all sources of income are counted, including Social Security benefits, pensions, alimony, and even regular contributions from other persons. Inheritances and food stamps, however, are not considered in computing a person's income for this purpose. On the other hand, if a person's assets yield less than the current passbook savings rate, as determined by the Housing and Urban Development agency, those assets are included in a person's income to the extent of the difference. For example, if Shirley owns stock in a biotechnology company that pays no dividends, the stock's market value (say, $10,000) will be multiplied by the passbook savings rate (say, 1.5%), and Shirley will be deemed to have $150 of income pertaining to this asset.

These facilities, it should be emphasized, are for older persons who are basically self-sufficient. The housing units typically are individual apartments with their own kitchen areas. Some complexes provide a medication reminder service, but not all do so. In any case, nursing care of any consequence is usually not provided, although a nurse may be on call to assist in emergency situations. Persons needing regular nursing care, even at the relatively low level of "custodial care," must look elsewhere—usually, a traditional "nursing home" setting. See generally Chapter 7.

Another housing alternative that combines the features of congregate care with the provision of nursing care when needed is the continuing care retirement community, or CCRC. Sometimes called "life care" communities, CCRC's provide individual apartments with kitchens, a communal dining room serving one to three meals daily, a wide range of special services and conveniences, and some type of nursing facility to which CCRC residents have guaranteed admission when they require such care. The level of care provided generally spans the spectrum from "independent living" and "assisted living" through "skilled care." (See generally Chapter 7 regarding the levels of nursing care.) The basic thrust of the CCRC is convenience: nursing care is available when needed on the premises, but separate residences are maintained since residents are generally expected to provide most of their own care. Almost all facilities accept Medicare reimbursement for covered services, but most do not accept Medicaid. Regulation of CCRC's is largely a product of state law, so requirements vary from virtually none in some states to extensive disclosure requirements and contractual restrictions in other states.

The financial aspects of CCRC's vary considerably among the nearly 1,000 CCRC's presently in operation. Most do, however, charge entrance fees that range from $150,000 to $500,000 per unit, or more.

Although such fees may seem high, most CCRC residents move into a CCRC after they have sold their home, so the entrance fee comes largely from that sale transaction.

In addition to the entrance fee, most CCRC's charge a monthly service fee that covers utilities, maintenance, insurance on common areas, meals, and other incidental services. These fees can be $3,000 per month or more and can usually be raised upon the CCRC's providing notice as required in the admission agreement. Note that nursing care is generally not included in these monthly charges. If such care is provided, it is billed according to the CCRC's nursing room rates, although some CCRC's allow a certain number of nursing care days at no additional charge, depending upon the particular CCRC's contractual arrangement. In some cases, moreover, the resident must continue to pay the monthly charge on his or her CCRC unit while also paying the billed amounts for care in the nursing facility.

As this brief overview suggests, CCRC's can be fairly expensive and complicated. Some CCRC's refund part of the entrance fee if a resident no longer occupies a CCRC unit within a specified number of years—typically, five—after entering the CCRC. But that practice is not universally followed. Most CCRC's do, however, provide that a resident need not leave the facility simply because his or her financial resources have been exhausted. It is this feature that gives rise to the label, "life care community," and that accounts for much of the CCRC's appeal to older persons—the promise that they will be cared for, *even* if they can no longer pay for such care. That feature, moreover, creates the most significant risk for prospective CCRC residents—namely, that a CCRC's open-ended promise of care will drive it into bankruptcy, effectively vitiating the CCRC's guarantee of lifetime care.

Responding to this risk, state regulations mandate that extensive financial disclosures, including a facility's financial statements, be made available to prospective CCRC residents. Most states require further that CCRC's must provide a detailed description of the services that are included in the monthly fee, the services for which extra charge is made, and a schedule of such extra charges. Many states also require that admission contracts be written in "plain English," that cancellation/rescission periods be stipulated, and that the conditions under which refunds of the entrance fee are available be clearly set forth. CCRC's must also indicate whether residents are required to maintain certain types of health insurance, whether they must designate someone to handle their financial affairs or health care decisions if they become unable to do so, and similar such matters.

In addition, many states impose various requirements on the operator of a CCRC. These requirements are intended to benefit the CCRC's residents, even though they do not apply directly to such residents. For example, some states mandate certain levels of financial reserves, require escrow accounts to preserve the residents' entrance fees for a

specified period of time, impose bonding requirements, require periodic audits, demand that financial reports be filed with a regulatory agency, and
even set advertising standards.

Entering a CCRC, however, is not just a financial
decision. Many of the considerations that apply to
nursing home and assisted living facility admissions
apply equally to CCRC admissions; e.g., quality of
care provided, condition of the facility, attitude of
the staff, rights of the residents, how the appropriate care level is determined, and so forth. See
generally Chapter 7 regarding nursing homes and
assisted living facilities.

And yet, the relatively looser state regulation of
CCRC's—as well as the lack of any Federal level
oversight—makes scrutiny of CCRC admission documentation even more critical. For example, does a
CCRC resident's monthly fee decline if his or her
spouse dies? Upon such occurrence, moreover, is the
resident required to move to a different unit in the
"singles" wing of the CCRC? The period after a
spouse's death is traumatic at any age, no less so
for long-married spouses. A forced change of units,
even within the CCRC, at this time might be particularly stressful. Similarly, what provision is made
for a CCRC resident who needs a nursing facility
bed when the CCRC's nursing area is full? Since the
convenience and guarantee of such a bed are major
selling points of a CCRC, the contract should clarify
this possibility.

There are also income tax considerations. Since the entrance fee, and possibly the monthly charges, cover medical care, a corresponding portion of these expenditures might be deductible as medical expenses. The value of this deduction will vary with the particular CCRC resident's tax situation, due to the various limitations that pertain to medical expense deductions. See § 6.6(b) concerning such deductions generally.

Furthermore, if the CCRC offers a refundable entrance fee, that fee is treated for tax purposes as a no-interest loan from the resident to the CCRC. Accordingly, the CCRC resident must recognize imputed interest income based upon current interest rates. This provision does not apply, however, if the CCRC resident/lender is at least 65 years old, the CCRC provides long-term skilled nursing care without "additional substantial payment," and the entrance fee does not exceed an annually adjusted figure, which for 2006 was $163,300. I.R.C. § 7872(g). For entrance fees in excess of this threshold, interest income is imputed, but only on that excess.

Finally, there are social considerations. As in any group living situation that caters exclusively to older persons, some people find the companionship of others of similar vintage appealing. Shared memories, similar outlooks on current events, the absence of noisy children, and social activities planned with their interests and abilities in mind, may make the congregate setting ideal. Others will prefer the exposure to persons of different ages, the continuing involvement in wider community matters, and the correspondingly lower incidence of death as a defining feature of one's day-to-day environment. The reason there are so many housing options for older persons, after all, is that no one option is best for everyone.

CHAPTER 9

GUARDIANSHIP

§ 9.1 What is Guardianship?

Our legal, social and economic worlds operate on the assumption that adult individuals are capable of making decisions on their own behalf. If, because of a mental disability, an individual is unable to make responsible decisions, society must appoint someone to make decisions for that individual. The process of providing a substitute decision maker for a mentally disabled person is referred to as guardianship or conservatorship. In some states, the term "guardianship" refers to making decisions about the disabled person's person, while "conservatorship" refers to decisions about that person's property. In other states, the term guardianship is used to describe a substitute decision maker for both person and property. (In Louisiana, guardianship is referred to as interdiction.) The person appointed to serve as the substitute decision maker is generally referred to as a guardian or conservator while the disabled person is most often referred to as a ward, an incapacitated person or an incompetent. For purposes of this Chapter we will use the terms guardianship, guardian and incapacitated or incompetent person though the reader should bear in mind that the proper terminology differs from state to state.

The appointment of a guardian results from a state judicial proceeding, and each state law of guardianship is unique. Even states that have adopted the Uniform Probate Code have often modified its guardianship provisions. Given the variance in state guardianship laws, the discussion that follows is necessarily general in nature, and not always applicable to any particular state. Even though state laws do differ, however, in general they subscribe to similar principles so that this Chapter is an accurate guide to the broader outlines of guardianship.

In almost all cases, guardianship is an involuntary procedure imposed by the state upon the incapacitated persons for the protection of their person and property. Voluntary, private alternatives to guardianship exist and are discussed in Chapter 10, Alternatives to Guardianship. Unfortunately, due to lack of foresight or lack of advice, many individuals fail to make any provision as to how they or their property should be managed in the event they should lose their mental capacity. Thus the need for guardianship.

§ 9.2   Who Requires a Guardian?

All adult individuals are presumed legally competent unless adjudicated incompetent by a court with appropriate jurisdiction. Each state has a law that declares under what conditions an individual can be found to be incompetent, or as is now the preferred term, incapacitated, and for whom a guardian can be appointed. There is no federal law of guardianship except for the guardianship statute in effect in the District of Columbia. Although the laws of the various states differ, a common formulation of an incapacitated person is one who lacks the capacity to make responsible decisions.

Note that the test is whether the person has the *capacity* to make responsible decisions, not whether the person's decisions are in fact responsible. Everyone, including older persons, has the right to behave foolishly or make irrational decisions without fear that he or she will be declared incapacitated and fall under the control of a guardian. Persons who cannot make responsible decisions, however, need protection. They must not be left in limbo, unable to act for themselves and prey to victimization by others.

Increasingly, state statutes use a functional definition of incapacity; that is, the statutes look to the behavior of the individual to determine whether he or she lacks capacity. In the past, definitions of incompetency often classed individuals as incompetent if they suffered from a mental disability, such as mental retardation, a particular status such as "old age," or required that the court specifically find the existence of a particular problem such as mental illness or chronic intoxication before the individual could be declared incompetent.

The current theory is that an individual should never be considered incapacitated merely because of his or her physical or mental status. For example, just because an individual is very old, frail and chronically ill does not in itself mean that the individual is incapacitated and in need of a guardian. Instead, the need for a guardian depends upon a showing that the individual has suffered a loss of mental capacity. Today, the accepted view is that individuals have a variety of mental capacities, and if the individual suffers the loss of some or all of these capacities, regardless of the cause of the loss, the individual may need a guardian.

Although just because an individual is old does not mean that he or she needs a guardian, it is estimated that over 80 percent of incapacitated persons who have a guardian are age 60 or older. The relatively high number of elder persons is due to the prevalence of dementia among older persons, the after-effects of strokes, and the onset of mental illness, particularly depression. Unfortunately the high number of older, incapacitated persons also reflects ageist attitudes that equate being old with being incompetent. All too often some older persons are thought of as being mentally incapacitated though a younger person who behaved in the same manner would not be considered incapacitated.

All persons are presumed to be competent. Only a court can make a determination of legal incapacity. The appointment of a guardian, though a judicial determination, is distinct from other determinations about mental functioning. Individuals are not legally incapacitated merely because they have been found insane for criminal law purposes or because

they have been involuntarily committed to a treatment facility on account of mental illness or mental
retardation. Physical incapacity alone should never
be sufficient grounds for the appointment of a
guardian. Though some guardianship statutes define an incapacitated person as one unable to communicate, given recent advances in technology, everyone, no matter what their physical limitations,
should be able to communicate in some manner or
means.

§ 9.3 Types of Guardianships

Guardianships are generally one of three types.
First, guardianship of the estate, or as it is also
known, conservatorship, which is limited to substitute decision making for matters concerning the
incapacitated person's property (assets). Second,
guardianship of the person, which gives the guardian control over decisions affecting the person of the
incapacitated person, such as where to live or
whether to consent to medical treatment. Third,
plenary guardianship, which grants the guardian
power to make decisions over both the incapacitated
person's property and person. The three types of
guardianship reflect the fact that courts frequently
find an individual to be incapacitated only in respect to his or her person or property, but not both.
For example, the court might find that an individual has the capacity to make decisions as to his or
her personal life, but lacks the capacity to handle
financial affairs. In some cases courts prefer to
appoint different guardians of the property and the

person. They often appoint a bank as guardian of the property and a family member as guardian of the person. Frequently, courts appoint a family member or spouse as plenary guardian with the authority to make decisions about both the person and the property of the incapacitated person.

In the past, guardianship was thought of as an either/or proposition: the individual either did or did not have the required competency. Courts had to make a decision, was the individual competent or not? In the past few years, however, the idea that someone is either "competent" or "incompetent" has come into disrepute. Increasingly, individuals are thought of as having varying degrees or types of capacity which can create a need for substitute decision making for part, but not necessarily all aspects of their lives. For example, an elderly individual may be able to handle small amounts of money, but may have lost the capacity to handle investments. In the past, the only alternative would have been to appoint a guardian of the estate even though it would have been overly restrictive of the individual's autonomy. Today in almost every state, the court has the option of appointing a "limited" guardian.

Under most state statutes, a limited guardian can be appointed whenever the loss of capacity is less than complete. The power granted to the limited guardian should be no more than is required to meet the needs of the incapacitated person. The person retains control of all other aspects of their life. If the individual's capacity declines further, the power of the limited guardian can be increased. The goal of limited guardianship is to retain the maximum autonomy and independence of the incapacitated person consistent with the loss of capacity and the need for a substitute decision maker. Limited guardianship, with the goal to avoid intruding into the individual's life anymore than is necessary reflects the doctrine of the least restrictive alternative that originated in mental health law.

The concept of limited guardianship recognizes that guardianship, though ultimately helpful to the incapacitated person, also represents a severe loss of personal liberty and autonomy. To lose the right to make decisions for oneself is a serious loss of independence. Limited guardianship attempts to minimize that loss of autonomy while still providing substitute decision making for those areas of life that the incapacitated person can no longer handle. Limited guardianship makes guardianship more palatable in situations where traditional, plenary guardianship would result in excessive intrusion into the incapacitated person's life, and permits an incapacitated person to get help without undergoing a demeaning finding of total incompetency.

Yet for all its apparent advantages, limited guardianship is not often used. Many object to it on the basis that it is too complicated to employ. They argue that it is not feasible to detail the contours of the incapacity and create an appropriate, individualized guardianship. Others claim that limited guardianship is too time consuming and too expensive to be of much practical significance. Those concerned with management of the property of incapacitated persons particularly object to limited guardianship because they believe it denies them the necessary authority to effectively handle the ward's assets. Despite these objections, reformers believe strongly in limited guardianship and continue to press for its statutory adoption and implementation by the courts.

§ 9.4   Procedural Issues

a.   The Petition

The first step towards the appointment of a guardian is the filing of a guardianship petition. Courts are reactive in that they have no power to initiate guardianship proceedings or to appoint a guardian unless a proper petition has been filed. In almost all states any interested person may file a petition requesting that the court find that the respondent (the alleged incapacitated person) is legally incapacitated and to appoint a guardian. (A handful of states limit who may file a guardianship petition.) Most guardianship petitions for older persons are filed by spouses, children, relatives, friends or concerned neighbors. Institutions such as social service agencies and hospitals also frequently file petitions if no family member is available or willing to do so.

State law and local court rules determine the contents of a guardianship petition. In general, the petition must name the alleged incapacitated person, the cause, nature and extent of the incapacity, the type of guardianship sought (person or property, limited or plenary) and the name of the proposed guardian. Most courts will not accept a petition unless it identifies a proposed guardian or guardians. (A petition could seek the appointment of two guardians, one for the person and another for the estate.) Sometimes the lack of an available potential guardian will delay or even prevent the filing of a guardianship petition.

The petition often is required to list the nature and value of the alleged incapacitated person's property and the source of income or support including any governmental assistance. The petition should also state the alleged incapacitated person's address and living arrangements. Some states require the petition to explain why no less restrictive arrangement is appropriate. Some also require a statement as to how guardianship will meet the needs or solve the problems of the alleged incapacitated person. If a guardian of the person or plenary guardian is sought, the petition may have to describe what actions the guardian expects to take. If a limited guardianship is sought, the petition will have to state what particular powers should be granted to the guardian.

State law usually provides that guardianship petitions be filed in the court with jurisdiction over probate matters. The petition must be filed in the county in which the alleged incapacitated person lives or in which he or she is "present." For example, Mrs. Samuelson owns a home in Smallville, Small County, but after a recent stroke she has been living with her daughter in Bigville, Big County. Most states would permit a guardianship petition to be filed in either county, that is, either in the county of her domicile or the county where she is physically present. If Mrs. Samuelson owned a summer home in another state, X, a petition could be filed in state X for purposes of appointing a guardian who would have power only to act concerning her property located in that state.

Timely notice of the filing of the petition and of the guardianship hearing must be provided to the alleged incapacitated person. Practically every state requires notice be given regardless of the individual's mental state. Procedural fairness requires need for adequate notice. As a result, many state statutes now contain specific requirements such as the kind of language to be used in the notice and the size of print. Notice must be given in time to permit the alleged incapacitated person to defend against the petition, but the number of days required between the filing of the petition and the hearing varies greatly from state to state. Anywhere from three to ten days is common. Most states require notice of the petition to be given to all appropriate parties, such as family members, creditors and persons with whom the alleged incapacitated person lives.

b. The Hearing

State law usually permits, but does not compel, the presence of the alleged incapacitated person at the guardianship hearing. Alleged incapacitated persons can waive the right to be present, or the court can permit them not to appear. If they are absent it is usually because of concerns for their health or because their presence would serve no purpose, such as in the case of a comatose individual. Some states grant the court wide discretion as to whether to require the presence of alleged incapacitated persons by permitting their absence if their presence would not be in their best interest. In these states, the presence of the alleged incapacitated person often depends upon local court practices. Some courts will want the incapacitated person present, while others routinely hold the hearing without them.

To permit the presence of the alleged incapacitated person, some courts hold the hearing at the individual's residence. For example, if the individual is infirm, but communicative, and living in a nursing home, the court may hold the guardianship hearing at the nursing home to observe the individual while protecting him or her from the physical burden of traveling to the court house.

Although not constitutionally required, many states permit the alleged incapacitated person to request a jury trial. Even if the state requires a jury trial, in most states it can be waived by the alleged incapacitated person. Most incapacitated persons do not elect a jury trial, preferring a judge, who has more experience in these matters, to rule on the issue of incapacity.

To assist the courts in understanding the circumstances that gave rise to the filing of the petition, several states require or permit the use of a court visitor. Even when state law does not require their use, many courts routinely send a representative to visit alleged incapacitated persons in their place of residence. The court visitor reports to the court as to the alleged incapacitated person's physical and mental condition, his or her reaction to the possibility of having a guardian, and whether his or her physical or mental condition permits a personal appearance at the hearing. The visitor also often interviews the petitioner and the individual nominated to act as guardian to understand why the petition was filed, and whether the proposed guardian is capable of carrying out the responsibilities of the position. The visitor's report does not determine whether the individual is incapacitated, but it often plays a significant role in determining whether the court appoints a guardian, who will be named guardian, what powers will be granted to the guardian, and what the guardian will be expected to do with the incapacitated person or his or her property.

Many states require that the alleged incapacitated person be represented by counsel. If the individual cannot afford a lawyer, the state will provide one. Some states use a guardian ad litem either to represent the alleged incapacitated person or to determine if a lawyer should be provided. (A court visitor may also be used to advise the court about the need for counsel for the alleged incapacitated person.) For example, a guardian ad litem who finds the individual to be comatose, might inform the court that a lawyer is unnecessary because the individual is clearly incapacitated. Conversely, the guardian ad litem might recommend appointment of counsel if the alleged incapacitated person strongly denied being incapacitated or if there is no apparent need for a guardian. A few states do not require the appointment of counsel, and many permit alleged incapacitated persons to waive the right and attempt to represent themselves.

c. Choice of Guardian

If the petition is granted, and the individual is found to be incapacitated, a guardian must be appointed. To insure that a guardian will be available, almost all states require that the petition nominate a potential guardian. The court will likely appoint the nominee as guardian unless there is some identifiable reason not to do so. For example, if the proposed guardian lacks the ability to assume the responsibilities of a guardian, or if in the past he or she behaved badly towards the incapacitated person, the court will appoint someone else. Many state statutes provide a preference list of who the court should appoint, usually giving the highest priority to spouses, followed by children, other relatives, friends and so forth. The court is always free, of course, regardless of the priority list or who was nominated in the petition, to select the person or institution that will best serve the interests of the incapacitated person.

Realistically, the court's choice of who to appoint as guardian is limited to those persons or entities who are willing to act as guardian, because the court has no power to compel anyone to accept appointment as guardian. An adult child, for example, can not be forced to act as guardian for an incapacitated parent. Because courts are effectively limited to selecting guardians from those who are willing to serve, more often than not the court will appoint the individual or entity nominated in the petition. If no one else is available, the court may have the power to appoint a guardian who will be paid by the state. Often such guardians are lawyers whom the court knows and respects.

Petitioners are thus the de facto selectors of guardians, and they must have a guardian available to serve before a petition for guardianship can be filed. There are probably many potential petitioners who do not file petitions because they are unable to locate a guardian, particularly if they want the court to appoint a guardian of the person. Many people do not want to serve as guardian because of the time it takes, or because they are reluctant to assume the role of making critical life choices for another individual. Guardians of the estate are somewhat easier to find since the duties, although time consuming, are more manageable. Protecting and investing the assets of the incapacitated person, collecting their income and paying their bills, requires careful record keeping, but does not have the same emotional burdens associated with being a guardian of the person. Also, entities such as banks are willing to serve as guardians of the estate because courts will approve the payment of fees to guardians from the estate of the incapacitated person.

In recent years, state laws have been liberalized to permit nonprofit entities to be appointed as guardian. As a result, some social service entities now provide guardianship services for which they are paid, either from the estate of the incapacitated person, or by the county or state. These agencies often serve as guardians for individuals who lack a willing or available family member to act as guardian when the size of the incapacitated person's estate is not sufficient to bear the cost of a bank trustee. Nonprofit guardianship entities are also appointed if the incapacitated person requires significant attention to their personal needs, a function which a bank might not be prepared to perform.

Several states have created public guardians to act as the guardian of last resort when no private individual or entity is available. Public guardians are agencies, offices or public officials whose job is to act as guardian of the estate or person. Some are employed by the state or the county, others are hired on an "as-needed" basis. A few states contract with nonprofit guardianship entities to provide guardianship services to incapacitated persons who need, but lack, guardians. Most states charge the cost of the public guardian to the estate of the incapacitated person if they can afford to pay; if not, the state bears the cost. Some states give the public guardian less power than private guardians and some restrict their ability to initiate guardianship petitions. Most states expect a public guardian to work closely with social service agencies in an attempt to meet the needs of the incapacitated person. In some states public guardians are actively involved in the day to day details of the incapacitated person's life. In other states, because of a large case load, the public guardian acts mainly to make major medical decisions and to decide where the incapacitated person should live.

d. Cost of Guardianship

The appointment of a guardian does not come cheap. Almost all guardianship petitions are filed by a lawyer, who is usually hired by the person seeking to be named the guardian or by some other interested person. Typically, the lawyer's fees will run anywhere from $500 to $3,000; even higher if the petition is resisted by opposing counsel. In addition to court fees (usually fairly modest), a physician or other qualified professional will have to be paid for preparing an affidavit that affirms the potential ward's incapacity. If the physician or other professional must testify in person, the cost will be even greater, perhaps $500 to $1,500 a day. Other possible costs include hiring a social worker to prepare a plan of how the alleged incapacitated person will be cared for, investigatory expenses and witness fees. If the court uses a visitor or guardian ad litem, he or she will also be paid a fee. If the case is appealed, additional legal costs will be incurred.

If the guardianship petition is successful, most courts will order that all costs be borne by the estate of the incapacitated person. The guardian may also charge a fee for his or her services, subject to court approval. Naturally banks who act as guardian expect to be paid for their efforts, usually receiving an hourly fee. A bank that acts as guardian of the estate may be paid an annual fee equal to a percentage of the value of the incapacitated person's assets. Nonprofit entities that serve as guardian are usually paid a flat sum, often several hundred dollars, for each guardianship, or else an hourly fee. Family members or friends who serve as guardians are not normally paid for their time. As with all guardians, however, any out-of-pocket expenses that they incur will be reimbursed from the assets of the incapacitated person. As previously stated, public guardians are usually paid by the state, which may in turn seek reimbursement from the estate of the incapacitated person.

§ 9.5   Supervision of the Guardian

Once appointed, a guardian is accountable to the court. Soon after appointment, the guardian of the estate typically is required to inventory the incapacitated person's assets. Thereafter, the frequency of financial accounting varies greatly from state to state. The current tendency is to require more frequent accountings than in the past when accountings took place only upon the termination of the guardianship or upon the resignation or death of the guardian. Today, many states require annual or periodic accounting by the guardian of the estate. All states require a final accounting at the end of the guardianship whether on account of the termination of the guardianship, resignation of the guardian, or death of the incapacitated person. In particular, the guardian must account for all income received and for all expenditures during the period of the guardianship. The guardian of the estate must maintain accurate financial records. Any mistakes or malfeasance may give rise to liability to the incapacitated person, or may result in penalties being assessed by the supervising court. As a result of the need for financial management acumen, some jurisdictions favor the appointment of banks as guardians of larger estates while preferring individuals to act as the guardian of the person.

Guardians of the person must also report to the court, although the frequency of their reports varies greatly from state to state. In the past, guardians of the person made few, if any, reports to court and usually contacted the court only if they required special instructions or were faced with a decision for which they wanted judicial guidance. If the guardian of the person approached the court for guidance, the court would naturally request a description of the incapacitated person's circumstances. In the normal course of affairs, however, the guardian would not have any formal reporting duties. Even the death or resignation of the guardian often would not trigger a formal report, though the court would be expected to review the incapacitated person's circumstances and needs before it selected a successor guardian. If the guardianship ended because of the death of the incapacitated person, the lack of any formal reporting requirements often meant that the court was never informed. The guardian would merely cease its efforts, while the guardianship remained an open file in the court records.

The informality of the past is giving way to more formal reporting requirements. In part as a reaction to cases where the guardian abused his or her discretion and mistreated or neglected the incapacitated person, many state laws now mandate regular judicial review of all guardianships. Court supervision can take many forms, from requiring regular written reports by the guardian to using court visitors to visit the incapacitated person and to make findings to the court. Many jurisdictions require a guardian of the person, after their appointment, to make a preliminary report to the court, and thereafter make annual reports. In the initial report, the guardian will be required to describe the living conditions of the incapacitated person, prepare a plan on how the guardian intends to promote the welfare of the incapacitated person, and explain how he or she expects to deal with the problems that gave rise to the guardianship. In an annual report, the guardian describes any changes in the mental and physical condition and any unmet needs of the incapacitated person and advises the court whether the guardianship should be continued or whether the powers of the guardian should be modified.

In carrying out their responsibilities guardians are expected to act in the best interests of the incapacitated person, which is defined as making decisions in a manner consistent with the values, aspirations and life style of the incapacitated person. To that end, the guardian must either ask the incapacitated person what he or she might like, or if such communication is not possible, attempt to carry out the preferences expressed before the onset of the incapacity. If the incapacitated person never expressed a preference or has none, the guardian can rely on a reasonable person standard and act in a way that a reasonable person would have under the circumstances. Guardians who fail to carry out their fiduciary obligations may be removed by the supervising court or ordered to act in a more appropriate manner. Generally, state law permits any interested person (including the incapacitated person) to petition the court and make it aware of any guardian who transgresses his or her obligations or in any way acts against the best interests of the incapacitated person.

§ 9.6   Powers of the Guardian

The nature and the extent of a guardian's powers depend upon the nature of the guardianship, whether of the person, property or plenary, the type of guardianship, limited or general, the applicable state law, local court rules and customs, and any specific orders given by the court. For the most part, guardians are given a general grant of authority and thereafter carry out their duties without ongoing court supervision. Of course, the guardian will periodically report to the court (see discussion above in § 9.5, Supervision of the Guardian), but on a day-to-day basis the guardian is free to act within the limits of his or her delegated power.

In most states guardians of the person or plenary guardians generally have the power to dictate where the incapacitated person will live. For example, the guardian may decide that the incapacitated person can no longer live alone and help the individual to move into some type of assisted living arrangement. In many cases the incapacitated person needs to move into a nursing home, but lacks the capacity to sign the admission agreement with the facility. Often, the guardianship is sought to permit the guardian to consent to the move and to sign the agreement. Whether a guardian may move the incapacitated person into a nursing home without prior court approval depends on state law. In many cases, when seeking approval of the guardianship petition, the petitioner will inform the court of the intent to move the incapacitated person into a nursing home and thereby obtain the court's approval at the same time that the guardianship is approved.

A guardian of the property of the incapacitated person has extensive powers over the person's assets. The guardian must take charge of the assets of the incapacitated person, collect the income and pay for the support and maintenance of the incapacitated person. Unless specifically ordered by the court, the guardian of the property is governed by the state statute that is often fairly specific as to how the guardian can invest the assets of the incapacitated person. Still, the powers of a guardian of the property are greater than they might appear. For example, if the property guardian objects to placing the incapacitated person into a particular facility, it may be able to prevent the placement by refusing to pay the cost of the facility. If the guardian of the property and the guardian of the person cannot agree as to the best course of action, it is not clear as to who should prevail. In the end the decision may have to be made by the court.

Although guardians of the person and plenary guardians have wide latitude to act, there are limits. Normally a guardian cannot vote for the incapacitated person, cannot consent to his or her marriage, in most states the guardian cannot consent to a divorce on behalf of the incapacitated person, and, in a few states, may not consent to termination of life-sustaining treatment without prior court approval. (See Health Care Decisionmaking § 3.6)

When appropriate, courts can appoint temporary or, as they are also known, emergency guardians. Almost every state guardianship statute permits the rapid appointment of a guardian if circumstances dictate. For example, if an individual's property is at risk, the court can quickly appoint a guardian of the property to take control of the incapacitated person's property to protect it from harm or loss. Courts often grant temporary guardians only limited powers, and so much as is needed to meet the emergency. If the incapacity and the need for a guardian persists, the court will hold a hearing as to the appointment of a permanent guardian. To expedite the appointment of a temporary guardian, many state statutes streamline procedural requirements. For example, formalities of notice may be relaxed and time limits compressed.

§ 9.7 Termination of the Guardianship

Guardianships automatically terminate upon the death of the incapacitated person. The death, incapacity or resignation of the guardian, however, does not terminate the guardianship. The supervising court will merely appoint a successor guardian. Normally, no guardian is permitted to resign unless there is an available successor guardian, since the incapacitated person cannot be left in the legal limbo of lacking legal capacity to make decisions, but also lacking a substitute decision maker.

If the incapacitated person regains capacity, the guardianship should be terminated. Generally, the incapacitated person must petition the court to terminate the guardianship. Traditionally, the burden of proof was on the petitioner, the incapacitated person, to prove the restoration of capacity. In some instances, the guardian will agree that guardianship is no longer needed. In those cases, the petition for termination is essentially noncontested. If, however, the guardian opposes the termination, the incapacitated person faces the burden of marshaling evidence to support the contention that he or she is no longer legally incapacitated. Sometimes this can be difficult because the incapacitated person often lacks the financial resources to pay for a medical opinion or to otherwise produce evidence of restored capacity. As a result, many states have reformed their guardianship statutes to reverse the burden of proof in guardianship termination proceedings and put the burden on those who would continue the guardianship. States commonly permit the incapacitated person to request termination of guardianship by an informal request to the court rather than necessitating a formal petition with accompanying requirements of notice. Irrespective of the formal requirements, no guardianship should be allowed to continue if the incapacitated person has regained legal capacity or if the guardianship is not promoting the best interests of the incapacitated person. If the court agrees, it can remove and replace the guardian, terminate the guardianship or limit the guardian's powers to reflect a partial restoration of capacity.

CHAPTER 10

ALTERNATIVES TO GUARDIANSHIP

The preceding Chapter focused on guardianship and its implications for both the guardian and the ward. Guardianship often involves a degree of public exposure, loss of control, cost, and procedural delay that many persons—old and young—find unappealing. Nevertheless, the institution of guardianship serves a very important function: the management of a person's financial affairs when that person is no longer willing or able to do so. This is a genuine need for many older persons, and guardianship can fill that need if no alternative arrangement has been made. It must be said, however, that guardianship represents a failure of planning, because almost every need for the substitute decision-making that guardianship provides can be accomplished through pre-need planning.

§ 10.1   The Nature of Pre–Need Planning

This Chapter focuses on alternatives to guardianship when the luxury of pre-need planning is still available. These alternatives can be as simple and direct as co-ownership of property or as involved as a revocable or so-called "living" trust. They have different implications regarding the probate process, and different tax consequences as well. But each alternative avoids, or reduces, the need for guardianship by authorizing someone or some institution to handle certain types of financial transactions on behalf of an older person. These alternatives might be thought of as do-it-yourself guardianship, in a manner of speaking. Attorneys are still usually involved, but courts generally are not, and the overall cost and burden pale by comparison to most guardianships.

Alternatives to guardianship, however, are not risk-free. Whatever the device may be—whether holding property in joint tenancy, giving a durable power of attorney, or creating a revocable trust—some person is being given significant power over an older person's financial resources. How this person uses that power will determine whether the guardianship alternative that was chosen was a good decision. Of course, it is the older person—and not some court—who is designating the person who will have this power, and that fact alone usually makes the older person more comfortable with the concept of substitute decisionmaking. It is not unusual, however, for the older person's expectations in this regard to be dashed, and disappointment on a personal level is then compounded by the resulting financial injury or even ruination. Nevertheless, if a person cannot manage his or her financial affairs, the only alternative to these arrangements is guardianship.

Another aspect common to the various guardianship alternatives is the requirement of legal capacity on the part of the older person. Property interests are being conveyed, and competence in a legal sense is absolutely necessary. See generally § 2.3. As a result, the older person faces a difficult dilemma. He or she may never need assistance in managing his or her financial affairs, but if that person waits until it is clear that such assistance is needed, it may then be too late. The older person might, at that point, lack sufficient capacity to execute an arrangement that would make guardianship unnecessary. In a very real sense, therefore, the older person must create whatever alternative that he or she prefers before that person really needs it. But the point remains that pre-need planning requires sufficient legal capacity.

§ 10.2 Joint Ownership

Probably the most common arrangement made to ensure financial management is joint ownership of property. The specific forms include joint tenancy, tenancy in common, and for married couples, tenancy by the entirety. They have many characteristics in common, but a major distinguishing feature involves the need for probate when one of the joint owners dies.

In a joint tenancy, the two (or more) co-owners have a right to "survivorship." When the first joint tenant dies, the other joint tenant(s) automatically succeeds to ownership of the property in question without going through probate. In effect, joint tenancy operates as a will substitute, since the jointly held property passes independently of the decedent's will. To be sure, a financial institution might put a hold on certain joint tenancy property for a month or so in some states, but the much longer delay that results from probate is avoided. A tenancy in common does not have this survivorship feature, and the share owned by a deceased tenant in common passes either by will or by intestate succession (when there is no valid will), like any other property that is owned by the decedent. As a result, joint tenancy is often the preferred arrangement, particularly among members of an immediate family.

Creating a joint tenancy is often quite simple. Adding a new signature card on a bank account, or changing a deed on real estate may be sufficient; no special forms are needed. As a result, older persons frequently add a younger relative—son, daughter, nephew, niece—or other trusted individual to their bank accounts to enable that person to cash checks, pay bills, deposit interest and dividend receipts, and the like. With respect to real estate, there may be some costs incurred in creating a joint tenancy, but most other assets can usually be put into joint tenancy without direct expense. Some wealthy individuals may face Federal gift taxes on such transfers, but the overwhelming majority of older persons face no such risk in this regard.

Another key feature of joint tenancy is its immediate vesting of unfettered control over the property involved in the other joint tenant. This feature can be both an advantage and a disadvantage. On the positive side, it enables the joint tenant to take charge right away and to manage the older person's affairs. Conversely, it subjects the property involved to any debts or claims that may be made against the new joint tenant. Business loans, spousal obligations like child support or alimony, gambling debts, investment losses, or the costs of substance abuse might require satisfaction from the joint tenant's assets, one of which is the older person's account that is now held in joint tenancy. Even when all of the assets are supplied by the older person, those assets might be used to pay the new joint tenant's obligations.

A related aspect is the ability of the new joint tenant to legally deplete the account and to thereby effectively disinherit the heirs. Usually, the creation of a joint account is not intended to be a testamentary transfer, but rather more of a "convenience account." In some states, in fact, such an account might be created, and it does not convey ownership rights as such. But even when such an account is not so created, most older persons view a joint account in this manner and expect that any proceeds remaining at their death will be shared with the other heirs. A joint tenant is a co-owner of the property, however, and can use the account as he or she sees fit. Some older persons choose, therefore, to place in joint ownership only some of their assets, or to use different joint tenants for different assets.

Creating a joint tenancy usually has Federal income tax consequences while the older person is alive. Typically, any income attributable to jointly held property is reported under only one joint tenant's Social Security number. Nevertheless, each joint tenant must report and pay tax on his or her share of the property's income. Thus, if Mom adds Son to her mutual fund account as a joint tenant, the dividend income earned on that account should be reported one-half by Mom and one-half by Son. If Son is in a higher tax bracket than Mom, joint tenancy has imposed a real cost in the form of higher income taxes owed.

On the other hand, when the older person dies, the joint tenancy usually has no Federal income tax consequences. Instead, the surviving joint tenant—generally the younger person in this context—takes as his or her "basis" in the property its fair market value when the other person dies. I.R.C. § 1014(b)(9), § 2040(a). So, if Mom in the preceding example died, Son's basis in her mutual fund account is its value on the day that Mom died. Any increase in value that accrued while Mom owned the account is effectively exempted from Federal income tax. Incidentally, this is the same result that would have obtained if Mom had not created the joint tenancy. I.R.C. § 1014(a).

The tax treatment just described does not apply, however, if the joint tenants are married to each other. In that circumstance, the property is treated as belonging one-half to each spouse. I.R.C. § 2040(b)(1). Accordingly, when one spouse dies, the market-value-at-death rule is applied only to the deceased spouse's half.

For example, assume that Husband and Wife purchased stock as joint tenants several years ago at a cost of $10,000 and that Husband died when the stock was worth $40,000. Wife's basis in the stock is the cost of her half ($10,000 cost divided by 2 = $5,000), plus the fair market value of Husband's half ($40,000 divided by 2 = $20,000)—a total of $25,000. If Husband had owned the stock in his name alone, Wife's basis at his death would have been $40,000, the stock's fair market value on that date. In other words, holding the property in joint tenancy had adverse tax consequences in this case.

But this treatment of married joint owners has two exceptions. First, if the joint tenancy was created before 1977 (and many elders still have such assets), the market-value-at-death rule applies to the *entire* property, not just half, as long as the deceased spouse provided all of the consideration. *Gallenstein v. United States* (6th Cir.1992); *Hahn v. Commissioner* (Tax Ct.1998). Second, the same result applies to assets held as community property, regardless of when the assets were acquired or which spouse provided the consideration. I.R.C. § 1014(b)(6). In effect, the surviving spouse in these two situations is treated as a nonspousal joint tenant.

§ 10.3   Durable Powers of Attorney

Another alternative to guardianship is a durable power of attorney, or DPOA. This document authorizes a named person or persons to handle certain specified types of transactions as agent or "attorney-in-fact" for the principal, the person conveying the power of attorney. Limited powers of attorney are, of course, commonplace in transactional practice, but a DPOA is usually intended to apply in a wider range of contexts. In addition, it is "durable" in the sense that it remains valid even *after* the principal no longer has legal capacity to convey property or handle similar transactions. Legal capacity must exist, however, when the DPOA is first executed.

Durable powers of attorney are almost exclusively governed by state law, and some state statutes even contain prescribed forms. But some generalities are possible and serve to distinguish a DPOA from co-ownership of property, as described in § 10.2.

First, a DPOA conveys much authority, but no property interest as such. Accordingly, there is no need to change how any particular asset is titled. Nor is there any effect on the probate process. The DPOA remains effective during a principal's incapacity, but it expires upon the death of the principal. Thus, it does not override a will or circumvent the need for probate with respect to the principal's assets. Similarly, a DPOA has no Federal income tax consequences, because it changes nothing concerning the ownership of the principal's property.

A second major distinction is the timing of its effectiveness. Many DPOA's take effect upon their execution, much like co-ownership of property, but that is not the only possibility. A so-called "springing" DPOA can be executed that will take effect only when the principal's legal capacity has diminished. This arrangement often appeals to some older persons who feel uncomfortable with the wideranging scope of power that a DPOA typically conveys. Of course, other arrangements—such as limiting the scope of the DPOA, naming co-agents, or having different agents control different assets—can also mollify this apprehension. But a springing power of attorney most directly acknowledges that there is no present need for the agent's services.

A major disadvantage, however, accompanies a springing DPOA—namely, when *does* it take effect? The whole purpose of a DPOA is to facilitate management of an incapacitated individual's income and assets, with a minimum of hassle. Third parties, particularly financial institutions, may be uncertain that a springing DPOA has become effective without some sort of documentation that the triggering event in question—usually the principal's incapacity—has occurred. Similarly, a disgruntled heir or other claimant might challenge an agent's actions by asserting that the springing DPOA has not yet taken effect. The result can be the very public exposure and humiliation of the principal that the DPOA was intended to avoid.

Clearly, the triggering mechanism in a springing DPOA is a major consideration. Specific procedures may vary with the creativity of the DPOA's drafter, but typical formulations often involve testimonials from one or more physicians, sometimes doctors who are named in the instrument itself. Compliance with the specified procedures can be complicated by the unavailability of the named testifiers or their inability to agree on the state of the principal's legal capacity. Cumbersome delays and related costs can ensue as well—all of which diminish the potential usefulness of the DPOA.

An alternative to the springing DPOA that still addresses a principal's hesitancy in granting this authority is delayed delivery of the DPOA. That is, a presently effective DPOA is prepared, but it is not delivered to the agent who is named therein until it is intended to be effective. Typically, the attorney who prepared the DPOA will hold it in safekeeping until such time as he or she determines that it is needed. This procedure is not completely free of pitfalls either, but it does at least obviate the need for third parties to satisfy themselves that the DPOA they see is in effect.

As to the form of the DPOA itself, the authorizing statute often includes a prescribed format, as already noted. Usually, this format is merely suggestive rather than mandatory, but the DPOA must be in recordable form if real estate transactions are contemplated. In any case, a principal might want to tailor the DPOA to his or her particular needs and specific assets. The cost to prepare a DPOA will depend, therefore, upon the degree of individualization desired and the scope of the alterations made. Moreover, such customization can make the very idea of a DPOA more palatable to an older principal, particularly if he or she is reluctant to grant the agent some specific power. It can also bolster the presumed validity of the instrument as an expression of the principal's intentions.

The scope of the DPOA itself is a matter of decision for the principal. It can cover bank accounts, certificates of deposit, securities, brokerage accounts, insurance policies, real estate holdings, trusts, retirement accounts, annuities, and similar assets. By executing this one document, in other words, a principal can confer control over a wide range of properties without the need for separate forms, signature cards, and the like. In addition, many important functions, like canceling credit cards, changing the postal address for someone moving to a nursing home, filing for reimbursement of medical expenses under private Medigap policies, and making prepaid funeral arrangements can be accomplished using a DPOA. Preparing and filing tax returns, making estimated tax payments, and negotiating refunds and audits may also be covered under a DPOA, although the Internal Revenue Service has more limited power of attorney forms to handle some of these tasks. Finally, many statutes permit a DPOA to designate the agent as guardian of the principal, should guardianship become necessary at some point.

Of course, a DPOA need not be quite this extensive. A principal may limit the scope of the DPOA or use different DPOA's for different assets. Assets of a more personal nature—like stamp collections, precious coins, or jewelry—might be excluded altogether. Some powers, in fact, cannot be included in a DPOA; e.g., the power to vote, prepare a will, get married, or seek a divorce. On the other hand, some powers can be added if desired, although they usually are not included as a matter of course; e.g., the power to make gifts. The power to make gifts is not standard practice, because allowing an agent to give away a principal's assets increases the risk that those assets will be unduly depleted. This risk already exists, of course, but sanctioning transactions in which a principal receives nothing in return for the assets being transferred exacerbates this exposure.

It should be noted, however, that the power to make gifts is often useful in implementing a principal's estate planning objectives. Times change, the applicable statutes get modified, property values rise and fall, and a well-designed estate plan can be severely buffeted by these forces. A so-called "gifting" power in a DPOA can enable an agent to accomplish the principal's wealth transfer goals with a second look, even when the principal's diminished legal capacity prevents him or her from making the necessary alterations directly. For similar reasons, a gifting power is also useful in facilitating Medicaid eligibility, if that becomes appropriate in light of changing circumstances and legal developments.

Nevertheless, the risk posed by granting a power to make gifts remains. That is why many courts, including Federal tax tribunals, require the explicit inclusion of a gifting power in a DPOA for gifts to be recognized. Furthermore, gifts by an agent to him-or herself must often be specifically permitted to avoid the taint of self-dealing. While some states apply fiduciary standards to agents under a DPOA, those standards can be quite problematic when the power to transfer property gratuitously has been authorized. A principal can, however, limit the gifting power by setting annual maximums, designating acceptable donees, or designating a special agent for this specific purpose.

A final protection, of course, lies in the DPOA's revocability. As long as the principal has legal capacity, he or she may revoke the DPOA, name a new agent, or designate a co-agent as a check on the actions of the first agent. In reality, however, it is often quite difficult to revoke the authority of the DPOA, since the document itself is usually in the possession of the agent and typically is not recorded in any official location. Although a DPOA requires notarization in most states and often witnesses as well, these initial formalities provide no real protection once the instrument becomes effective.

It must be remembered, however, that the need for a dependable and responsible agent is not unique to a DPOA. It is a major consideration when placing property in joint tenancy, or when naming a trustee under a revocable trust, for that matter. But it cannot be ignored. Depending upon the nature of the principal's financial affairs, an agent might need to monitor investments, pay bills, contest charges, arrange payment of medical costs, and generally take over another person's financial life. Selecting a person who feels comfortable with these responsibilities can be particularly difficult if there are no close friends or relatives living nearby, if there are several adult children or children from more than one marriage, and so forth. The person selected as agent may resent the responsibilities and the time commitment required—especially if the principal's financial records are in disarray. The persons not selected may envy the agent's power and the evident trust of the principal that designation as agent conveys. Incidentally, this problem also arises in connection with a health care proxy or a power of attorney for health care. See generally § 3.5.

§ 10.4   Revocable Trusts

Another alternative to guardianship involves a revocable, or so-called "living," trust to hold an older person's assets. The trustee of the trust might be a close friend or relative, perhaps in addition to a bank trust department or other financial institution. Alternatively, the older person setting up the trust, the "settlor," might serve as trustee, usually in conjunction with another trustee who will take over completely if the older person is no longer willing or able to handle financial matters. By its terms, a revocable trust can be changed, a trustee can be replaced, or the entire arrangement can be revoked—as long as the settlor has the requisite legal capacity. After that point, the trust becomes irrevocable and continues in place, even after a settlor's death. The trust's assets are then distributed according to the instructions in the trust's originating instrument, without passing through probate. A revocable trust, in other words, can serve two distinct but very significant purposes: an alternative to guardianship, and a will substitute. The advantages and disadvantages of such a trust, therefore, need to be considered from both of these perspectives.

As an alternative to guardianship, a revocable trust is the most expensive and complicated arrangement discussed thus far. Legal fees are incurred in creating a trust, and these fees will vary with the amount of customization and specificity that the trust instrument contains. This process of customization, to be sure, allows a settlor to delineate precisely how funds are to be handled during his or her lifetime and even thereafter. In other words, the trust instrument's details manifest the settlor's wishes and preserve that person's control over the assets in question. But such control does not come cheaply.

There are other costs as well. A trustee, especially an institutional trustee, will charge an annual fee that is usually determined as a percentage of the asset value of the trust. Accounting fees may be incurred depending upon the scope of a trust's activities, and tax return preparation fees may also be necessary. If the settlor serves as a co-trustee, however, the trust's income is reported on the settlor's tax return. In that case, a separate income tax return for the trust is not required, and the related preparation costs are not incurred. Finally, but by no means of least significance, costs will be incurred in transferring a settlor's assets to the trust, both for preparing the transfer documents and for any local taxes that might be imposed if real estate is conveyed into the trust.

For those willing and able to incur its costs, a revocable trust offers several advantages over other guardianship alternatives. First, a trust is a long-recognized form of holding property, so financial institutions are often more comfortable and more cooperative with the trustee of a revocable trust than with an agent acting under a DPOA. This is particularly the case if the settlor served for a while as co-trustee, thereby enabling the financial institution to become accustomed to the trust's role in that person's financial affairs. When the successor trustee then takes over from the older person, the transition can be quite smooth. This comfort level difference is also due to the fairly clear fiduciary standards that apply to trustees, particularly when the revocable trust instrument provides more explicit instructions than a typical DPOA—which is usually the case.

Those instructions, moreover, constitute a second major advantage of revocable trusts. A revocable trust document can specify how an older person wants his or her funds spent, regardless of how some reviewing court or general standard of reasonableness might view such expenditures. For example, a trust might authorize payment for expensive home care assistance or other help needed to keep the older person in his or her home—even if this arrangement is actually more expensive than a nursing home. Similar "frills" might include a private room in a hospital or nursing home, or care for a cherished pet. Such expenditures might ordinarily be considered imprudent, but if the trust instrument authorizes them, they are the settlor's wishes, and they will be permitted. In this fashion, a trust preserves an older person's sense of personal autonomy and control over his or her money—important aspects that might make an older person more comfortable with the entire concept of relinquishing day-to-day involvement in financial matters. For some people, this feature of a revocable trust might mean the difference between making the advance arrangements that can avoid guardianship and failing to do so.

A third advantage is that revocable trusts more easily attract professional financial assistance and asset management. Certainly, an agent under a DPOA can engage experts to provide assistance, particularly with respect to tax matters, but some professional asset managers provide their services primarily, if not exclusively, to trusts. This feature might be particularly attractive if an older person does not know anyone whom he or she would want to appoint as agent under a DPOA. For example, an older person might have faith in her nephew's general prudence and honesty, but not in his financial acumen or economic sophistication. If such qualities are deemed important, given the nature of that older person's assets, a bank, trust company, or certified public accountant might be named trustee under a revocable trust. The nephew could still be named co-trustee to provide a more "personal" dimension to the arrangement, but that is not mandatory.

In other circumstances, a revocable trust can be interposed to preserve family peace. The opposite situation of having no financially capable friend or relative is having several relatives who deem themselves to be worthy candidates. In this situation, giving any one person a DPOA might lead to resentment and family disputes. Splitting up the financial responsibilities among them might help the situation, but that approach could lead to communication problems, overlapping authority, lack of coordination of financial activities, and general confusion. A trust company, in contrast, can provide centralized management of financial affairs without alienating the family members in question.

There are disadvantages, however, to a revocable trust as an alternative to guardianship. In addition to the various fees described earlier, a trust creates a new legal entity, and disposition of assets held in a trust might be somewhat more cumbersome than when assets are held outright—at least while the owner has the required legal capacity. And if a settlor serves as co-trustee, this person must now act *like* a trustee. The assets, in other words, are no longer those of the settlor—a point many older persons fail to appreciate. Moreover, if real estate is held in a trust, it can be more difficult to obtain a mortgage on the property, because lenders have more difficulty selling a mortgage on trust-held property in the secondary mortgage market. In addition, vehicles held in a trust still face some difficulty obtaining appropriate insurance, although increasing familiarity with revocable trusts should diminish this problem over time.

Finally, a revocable trust provides no Federal income tax advantages. Revocability alone classifies a trust as a "grantor trust," the income of which is taxed to the settlor at his or her regular income tax rates. I.R.C. § 671, § 676(a). And if a trust is no longer revocable due to its settlor's legal incapacity, it is still a grantor trust, because its income may be used for the settlor's benefit. I.R.C. § 677(a)(1).

§ 10.5 Revocable Trusts as Testamentary Devices

As noted above, a revocable trust can serve as a will substitute as well as a guardianship alternative. Although the primary focus of this Chapter has been on the latter use of a revocable trust, some consideration of its testamentary implications is appropriate here as well.

A revocable trust owns the property that comprises its corpus, so when the settlor dies, the assets that are held by the trust are not part of the probate estate. Indeed, much of the appeal of a revocable trust for some people is precisely this feature: it avoids probate for the assets that it holds. Instead, those assets are distributed after the settlor's death according to the instructions that are provided in the trust instrument itself. Moreover, this distribution can take place without the time delays, public exposure, or court fees and other costs attendant to the probate process. To be sure, the revocable trust has its own set of costs, as detailed already, so the net cost savings might not be as great as was anticipated when the trust was first considered.

Avoidance of probate, in any case, applies only to the assets that are in the revocable trust. A will, or intestate succession in the absence of a will, is still necessary to dispose of the settlor's assets that were not transferred to the revocable trust. Such assets might include personal items like jewelry, clothing, automobiles, and sentimental objects that require no "management" as such and accordingly were never contemplated as part of the trust. Other omitted assets might include securities or similar financial holdings that were acquired after the trust was created and were never transferred to the trust. Perhaps, the failure to transfer those assets was due to neglect or forgetfulness on the part of the settlor. Alternatively, perhaps the assets were acquired after the settlor lost his or her legal capacity, so the settlor could not transfer them to the trust. But whatever the cause, executing a revocable trust instrument accomplishes very little unless the assets that were intended to be in the trust get there. Sometimes, an older person will establish a revocable trust and will also execute a DPOA, with the agent thereunder having authority to transfer assets to the trust as necessary.

Besides the usual benefits of probate avoidance, revocable trusts offer a particular advantage to the settlor who owns real estate in more than one state. Probate typically requires an additional proceeding in each state in which a decedent owned real estate, while a single revocable trust can handle real property holdings wherever they are located. On the other hand, those states that impose inheritance taxes usually exempt real estate that is located outside their jurisdiction. But if a resident owns a revocable trust, *all* of the trust's property—including any out-of-state real estate—is trust property, which in turn may be classified as personalty. As such, these real estate holdings become subject to that state's inheritance tax. And if that tax is imposed under a progressive rate schedule, these real estate holdings might bear a higher tax than the cost of the ancillary probate proceeding that was avoided.

Another advantage of a revocable trust over a will is the trust's lesser susceptibility to challenge by disgruntled heirs. With a trust, the settlor is still alive, and claims of legal incompetence and undue influence may be more difficult to prove if the settlor is supervising the trust's operations and is capable of testifying. Moreover, the assets of a trust can be used by a trustee to defend a trust's validity, thereby depleting the trust's corpus and further discouraging such challenges. Finally, trust assets can be distributed to the beneficiaries fairly quickly, requiring would-be challengers to seek relief against the beneficiaries themselves. And if, for some reason, a settlor wanted to leave a spouse less then the state's "statutory share," a trust would be more effective in this regard—if the state does not permit the spouse to elect against the trust assets. (The

Uniform Probate Code and many states, however, have eliminated this discrepancy.)

To be sure, using a revocable trust as a will substitute has its disadvantages. Creditors usually have a significantly longer period in which to file claims after the death of a settlor than the relatively brief period—often no more than six months— that applies to a probated estate. (One approach to this dilemma uses a revocable trust for most of a person's assets and a will governing much fewer assets to trigger the shorter filing deadline.) Another disadvantage is that a trust cannot file a joint Federal income tax return with a surviving spouse in the year of a settlor's death, while an estate can. Similarly, the prohibition on recognizing losses from related party transactions applies to trusts, but not to estates. I.R.C. § 267(b)(4)–(8).

Finally, a revocable trust has no effect on a decedent's Federal estate tax. The trust's assets are included in that person's gross estate, either because the trust is revocable, or because the income therefrom is being used for that person's benefit. I.R.C. § 2036(a)(1), § 2038(a)(1).

CHAPTER 11

SOCIAL SECURITY BENEFITS

The foundation of retirement income in the United States is a government program that is generally referred to as Social Security. More than 91% of current retirees receive monthly benefits from this program. In fact, nearly three out of five retirees receive at least half of their income from Social Security. Yet, this program was never intended to provide sufficient retirement income by itself. Retirement financing is often described as a three-legged stool, with Social Security comprising only one of those legs. The other two legs, incidentally, are personal investments and employer-based pension plans. See generally Chapter 14 regarding pension plans.

Of these three retirement financing mechanisms, Social Security has the broadest applicability. In exchange for payroll taxes collected from employees and their employers, Social Security provides a lifetime series of monthly payments that are based in rough measure upon an employee's earnings history. Social Security coverage also entitles its recipients to medical insurance once they are 65 years old through a related, although separately funded, government program called Medicare. See generally Chapter 4. These two programs enable older persons to obtain a basic level of retirement income and coverage of their most pressing medical needs.

But Social Security goes far beyond ensuring retirement income. Its official name is Old–Age, Survivors and Disability Insurance (OASDI). See 42 U.S.C. § 401 et seq. As this name suggests, Social Security provides benefits to a worker's surviving spouse and children under age 18, plus disability coverage if a worker is unable to work until his or her expected retirement age. Actually, Social Security goes still further and provides derivative benefits to a worker's spouse, even while the worker is still alive. Ex-spouses also receive benefits based upon a worker's employment history, if they were married to the worker in question at least ten years. Social Security, in other words, is very different from private retirement/disability plans.

Indeed, the scope of its beneficiaries is only one of the major ways in which Social Security differs from private programs. Social Security benefits are inflation-protected via Cost of Living Adjustments, or COLA's, that increase the amounts paid to whomever receives these benefits. Some private pension plans and disability arrangements have some version of inflation protection, but most do not.

Moreover, Social Security is completely portable. Most forms of employment are covered by Social Security, including self-employment. Self-employed persons pay the entire 12.4% payroll tax on their net earnings, rather than splitting this burden 6.2% from the employee and 6.2% from his or her employer. But the point remains that it does not matter where the employment is located, the nature of the work involved, or the industry in question. Work is work, an important consideration as Americans increasingly find themselves having a series of employers over their lifetime, rather than one employer for their entire working life.

A final major distinguishing feature of Social Security is its solvency. Because the Federal government collects the necessary taxes, Social Security's promised benefits are secured by the most reliable credit available. Programmatic changes may be made, to be sure, and the Social Security system has undergone major alterations of its tax rates, entitlement parameters, and other features periodically. But ultimately, it will pay what is to be paid, on time and in full. Thus, Social Security occupies a special role in the financial life of older Americans.

§ 11.1 Eligibility

To receive the various benefits of Social Security, a worker must have worked in "covered employment" for a specified number of calendar quarters. The required number of "quarters of coverage," as this element is generally described, varies with the specific benefit involved and the age of the worker. To receive retirement income, a worker born after 1928—which includes virtually all persons currently contemplating retirement—must have at least 40 "quarters of coverage" credited to his or her work history. 42 U.S.C. § 414(a)(2). Without at least 40 "quarters of coverage," *no* retirement benefits are paid by Social Security. This all-or-nothing feature makes the crediting of "quarters of coverage" a critical threshold issue.

a. Quarters of Coverage

A "quarter of coverage" generally refers to calendar year quarters, although income need not be earned strictly within the three months of the calendar quarter. For example, if Joseph works during the months of June and July and meets the other requirements, he will be credited for working a calendar quarter, even though his actual working time occurred during the second and third quarters of the calendar year.

To count as a "quarter of coverage," a worker's earnings must at least equal the required minimum, which is adjusted annually for inflation. 42 U.S.C. § 413(a)(2)(A). In 2006, this minimum was $970. Note that this minimum relates to *total* earnings. It is irrelevant how many hours the worker needed to work to earn this total or the wage rate that he or she received. The figure refers, moreover, to cash wages before Federal and state taxes, and before Social Security's payroll tax, as well. Fringe benefits are not part of this wage base, unless those benefits are treated as taxable income for purposes of the Federal income tax. Employer-provided health insurance, for example, is usually a very valuable fringe benefit, but it is specifically excluded from a person's taxable income by § 106 of the Internal Revenue Code. Accordingly, the value of such insurance does not count in Social Security's computation of earnings received in covered employment.

On the other hand, regardless of how high a person's income might be, he or she can receive credit for no more than four "quarters of coverage" in any one calendar year. So if Joseph from the earlier example earns $5,000 during his two months of work, he will receive credit for the annual maximum of four calendar quarters, and not the 5.15 ($5,000 divided by $970 = 5.15) that his wages would seem to "earn." Moreover, only whole quarters of coverage are credited. So if his wages had been $3,600 instead of $5,000, at the 2006 rate of $970 per quarter, he would receive credit for three calendar quarters, not 3.71 ($3,600 divided by $970 = 3.71). But if he takes another job during the week before Christmas and earns at least $280 that week, those earnings will be combined with the summer employment to produce total earnings of $3,880—enough to "complete" his fourth "quarter of coverage" ($970 × 4 = $3,880) for Social Security purposes.

Self-employed persons, on the other hand, must earn at least $400 in a given year for such earnings to count in determining "quarters of coverage." So if Joseph's $280 in pre-Christmas earnings were derived from his own business, they could not be used to "complete" his fourth "quarter of coverage." The flip side of this rule is that self-employment earnings of less than $400 per year are not subject to Social Security's payroll tax, while earnings of an employee are subject to this tax from the very first dollar earned. Nevertheless, once $400 of self-employment earnings—net of related expenses—is achieved, those earnings can be combined with other sources of wages and salaries to obtain "quarters of coverage."

b. *Covered Employment*

To count towards "quarters of coverage," all wages and salaries must be earned in "covered employment." This requirement is generally of little consequence, because Social Security covers almost all working environments, including part-time employment. Even babysitting and housecleaning are covered by Social Security, if the person performing these services received at least $1,500 per year (in 2006) from any one employer. Compliance by putative employers in these circumstances is often less than complete, but Social Security at least purports to reach even such episodic types of employment. In fact, almost all situations that give rise to the status of "independent contractor," as opposed to employer-employee, result in the independent contractor's being subject to Social Security tax as a self-employed person. The locus of tax collection is obviously critical in this determination, but the point remains that the work involved is "covered" by Social Security in either case—whether as earnings from employment, or as earnings from *self*-employment as an independent contractor.

On the other hand, there are some forms of employment that are not covered by Social Security. Federal government workers who were hired before

January 1, 1984 are generally not part of the Social
Security system, except for members of Congress
and Federal judges who are so covered without
regard to when they began their service. Similarly,
employees of state and local governments are not
covered by Social Security, unless their governments have elected to be so covered. Although all
states have elected at least partial coverage by Social Security, some of these coverage agreements
apply to only a few employees. Nevertheless, if an
employee does not participate in his or her state or
local government's retirement system, that person's
employment is covered by Social Security, even in
the absence of a coverage agreement. This provision
does not apply, however, to persons who are employed to relieve them from unemployment, or to
patients or inmates working in hospitals, prisons,
and other institutions. See I.R.C. § 3121(u).

Another category of excluded employment involves students who are enrolled and regularly at-
tend classes at a school or college. If the student
works for the educational institution that he or she
attends, that employment is not covered by Social
Security. This exclusion also covers domestic service
in the college's fraternities and sororities. Furthermore, this provision applies to students who work
at a school's "auxiliary organization" that operates
exclusively for the benefit of that school; e.g., food
service, dormitories, or bookstore. But if the school
is an instrumentality of a state or local government
that has a coverage agreement with Social Security,
and if that agreement applies to such services, the

coverage agreement takes precedence, and the employment in question *is* covered by Social Security.

Also excluded from Social Security coverage is employment by a parent of his or her child who is under age 18. Children aged 18–20 years who work for their parents are also excluded, as long as they do not work in the parent's trade or business. In any case, services performed for a corporation are covered employment, without regard to the identity of the corporation's shareholders. And services performed for a partnership are similarly covered, unless the requisite family relationship exists between the employee and each partner in the employer-partnership.

In addition, a person under age 18 who performs "domestic services" in an employer's private home is excluded from Social Security's coverage, unless performing such services constitutes that person's "principal occupation."

Finally, persons who object to insurance on religious grounds may file for exemption from Social Security. This exemption is limited in several ways: one, both the employee *and* the employer must belong to a "recognized religious sect" that has been in existence since December 31, 1950; two, this "sect" must have established tenets and teachings that oppose insurance; and, three, this "sect" must generally provide for its own dependent members.

Other special provisions stipulate that employees in certain situations are not "employees" for Social

Security purposes. Some examples include religious ministers, licensed real estate agents, and persons whose compensation is "directly related" to sales or other output. But in each case, the applicable provision designates these persons as self-employed for Social Security purposes, and their work is therefore considered "covered employment" by virtue of that status. In other words, they are still "covered" by Social Security.

Whether a worker has completed the necessary number of "quarters of coverage" can best be determined by requesting a "Personal Earnings and Benefit Estimate Statement" from the Social Security Administration. This Statement is sent annually to every person aged 25 years and older during the third month preceding that person's birthday. It can also be requested at any time via a fairly simple form. Among other features of this Statement is a report on the number of "quarters of coverage" that one has attained, as well as the earnings reported in each year. There is no charge for this information, and workers should make sure that any omissions of covered employment from this Statement are corrected. Generally, tax returns and wage reports on Form W–2 can be used to supply missing earnings figures. By so doing, a worker will receive credit for the appropriate number of "quarters of coverage."

§ 11.2 Worker's Retirement Benefits

If a worker has completed 40 "quarters of coverage," he or she is entitled to a monthly benefit at "full retirement age" equal to his or her "primary insurance amount." A person's "full retirement age" is based upon that person's year of birth. See 42 U.S.C. § 416(*l*)(1). Persons born before 1938 have a "full retirement age" of 65 years. Younger persons face an elongation of their "full retirement age" according to the following table:

Year of Birth	Full Retirement Age
1938	65 years and 2 months
1939	65 years and 4 months
1940	65 years and 6 months
1941	65 years and 8 months
1942	65 years and 10 months
1943–1954	66 years
1955	66 years and 2 months
1956	66 years and 4 months
1957	66 years and 6 months
1958	66 years and 8 months
1959	66 years and 10 months
After 1959	67 years

But whatever the "full retirement age" may be, that is the age at which a worker can receive his or her undiminished "primary insurance amount," or PIA.

a. Early Retirement Options

A worker can choose to begin receiving retirement benefits as early as age 62, but at the cost of reduced monthly benefits. This retiree would, of course, be receiving more monthly benefit payments, so the benefit amount itself must be reduced to take account of that longer payout period. Specifically, a worker can elect so-called "early" retirement by accepting payments that are reduced for each month before "full retirement age" that the worker starts receiving Social Security retirement benefits. The amount of this reduction is $\frac{5}{9}$ of 1% per month for the first 36 months + $\frac{5}{12}$ of 1% for each additional month thereafter. 42 U.S.C. § 402(q).

To illustrate this computation, assume that Hannah was born in 1944 and wants to begin receiving Social Security benefits at age 62 years. According to the year-of-birth chart shown above, Hannah's "full retirement age" is 66 years. By taking retirement benefits at age 62, she incurs an "early" retirement penalty of 48 months (4 years × 12 months). Accordingly, her benefit reduction is $\frac{5}{9}$ of 1% per month × 36 months (namely, 20%) + $\frac{5}{12}$ of 1% × 12 months (namely, 5%), a total reduction of 25% (20% + 5%). If her "primary insurance amount" (PIA) were, say $1,000, her monthly benefit would be reduced by 25%—namely, $250—to $750. In effect, Hannah receives 75% of what she would otherwise get at her "full retirement age" of 66 years. In similar fashion, she would have received 80% if she had waited until age 63 to begin receiving Social Security benefits, 86.67% if she had waited until age 64, or 93.33% if she had waited until age 65.

In any case, note that these reductions are permanent. Hannah will not "return" to her undiminished PIA upon reaching her "full retirement age." Instead, she will stay with a monthly benefit of $750—as calculated above—increased annually by the cost-of-living adjustments (COLA's) that apply to Social Security benefits generally. Even then, these percentage COLA's will be applied, effectively, to the reduced retirement benefit that Hannah received at age 62 (namely, $750), rather than to her PIA of $1,000.

On the other hand, Hannah receives her Social Security benefits now. She may need the money presently, she may have concerns about her health and her likely longevity, she may anticipate earning enough on her investments to offset the reduction in her benefits, or she may have other reasons to begin receipt of her Social Security "early." Historically, the majority of Social Security recipients start receiving benefits before reaching their "full retirement age"—usually at age 62.

b. Deferred Retirement Options

A person who delays receipt of Social Security benefits until his or her "full retirement age" receives his or her "primary insurance amount," or PIA, without any reduction for early retirement. A retiree might, however, want to go still further and defer receipt of Social Security benefits *beyond* "full retirement age." In such cases, the retiree gets a bonus in the form of "delayed retirement credits" that are added to that person's PIA to compensate for the shorter payout term that deferred retirement necessarily entails. 42 U.S.C. § 402(w).

The amount that delayed retirement increases a retiree's PIA is based upon the year in which the retiree was born, according to the following table:

Year of Birth	Annual Percentage
1935–1936	6
1937–1938	6.5
1939–1940	7
1941–1942	7.5
After 1942	8

These annual increases apply for each year that a retiree delays retirement, up until age 70. After that point, delayed retirement produces no further increase in one's benefit amount. In other words, there is no reason to defer receipt of Social Security benefits after reaching age 70. Moreover, these annual percentages are applied on a monthly basis for those persons who retire between birthday anniversary months; e.g., at age 66 years and 5 months.

To take a simple example, assume that Leah was born in 1943 and wants to retire at age 68. According to the preceding table, her annual percentage increase is 8%, and she is entitled to three years of "delayed retirement credit," because her "full retirement age" is 66 years. Thus, her "delayed" retirement bonus would be 16% (2 years × 8% per year). If her Social Security benefit—including intervening cost-of-living adjustments—would otherwise be, say $1,200, Leah would now receive an additional 16%, namely, $192 ($1,200 × 16%), producing a new monthly benefit of $1,392 ($1,200 + $192). Future cost-of-living adjustments would then be applied to this figure.

§ 11.3   The Primary Insurance Amount (PIA)

At the heart of the options for "early," "full," and "delayed" retirement is a worker's "primary insurance amount," or PIA. Various Social Security Act amendments have modified the PIA formula and its nuances over the years, but for persons born after 1921, the methodology involves applying a three-part formula to a worker's Average Indexed Monthly Earnings, or AIME. The three-part formula recovers 90%, 32%, and 15% of a worker's AIME, with the three percentages applying at two "bend points" that are adjusted annually for inflation. The "bend points" applied are those that are in effect during the year in which the worker became 62 years old. If a worker turned age 62 during 2006, for example, the applicable "bend points" were $656 and $3,955. Assuming that this worker's AIME was $4,000, this person's PIA would be calculated as follows:

90% of the first $656 = $590.40

32% of the next $3,299 ($3,955 − $656) = $1,055.68

15% of AIME over $3,955 = $6.75

The sum of these components—namely $1,652.83—is then rounded to the next lower multiple of ten cents, and the PIA becomes $1,652.80.

Note that this methodology is applied when a worker becomes 62 years old, because that is when he or she is first eligible to receive Social Security retirement benefits. Of course, those benefits will be reduced if the worker receives benefits at that age, as explained in § 11.2(a). But the point remains that a worker's PIA is first computed when he or she is 62 years old. If a worker does not elect "early retirement," but instead waits until reaching "full retirement age," the monthly benefit actually received will be that person's PIA, plus any cost-of-living adjustments that have occurred since the worker became 62 years old.

Any earnings received after a worker turns 62 might increase his or her PIA by raising the average earnings (AIME) on which a person's PIA is based. The Social Security Administration automatically "recomputes" a person's PIA whenever a higher benefit amount would result. The "bend points" of the year in which the worker turned 62 years old, however, remain in place when making this "recomputation." Only the person's earnings average changes. But the larger one's AIME, the larger one's PIA will be.

On the other hand, the PIA formula tends to minimize the impact of increases in a person's AIME. That is, the formula does produce a higher PIA as a worker's AIME rises, but not proportionately so. For example, if the worker's AIME in the preceding example had been one-fourth higher, say $5,000 instead of $4,000, that person's additional $1,000 of AIME would have increased his or her PIA by only $150, since those additional earnings would fall in the 15% bracket. The PIA in that case would be $1,803 ($1,653 + $150)—an improvement of only 9.1% over the $1,653 previously computed, despite an increase in the worker's AIME of 25%.

Similarly, an AIME of $2,000 (half of $4,000) produces a PIA of $1,020—clearly less than the $1,653 derived previously, but more than half of that amount (namely, $827). Social Security's bottom-weighted PIA formula, in other words, is intentionally redistributive in its impact—in contrast to an employer-provided defined benefit plan, which would base its payout more strictly on a worker's earnings history. See generally Chapter 14 regarding such plans.

a. Average Indexed Monthly Earnings (AIME)

AIME is a multi-step construct that basically tries to compute a worker's average monthly wage over his or her working life. For each year after 1950, a worker's wages are indexed by comparing the national average of wages for that year to the national average of wages for the year in which the worker became 60 years old. For example, if Samuel is 62 years in 2006, his earnings from 1977—say, $16,-000—would be indexed by multiplying that figure by a fraction that compares average wages of that year (1977) to average wages of 2004, the year in which Samuel turned 60. Accordingly to Social Security's figures, this process would look like the following:

$$\$16,000 \times \frac{\$35,648.55 \ (2004 \ \text{average})}{\$9,779.44 \ (1977 \ \text{average})} = \$58,324.08$$

Samuel's wage for 1977, therefore, would be $58,324.08 for this purpose. In similar fashion, each of Samuel's earning years would be indexed to 2004.

For his earnings after 2004, the actual numbers would be used without adjustment. From this array of adjusted and unadjusted earnings, the 35 largest figures would be selected and totaled, and then divided by 420 (35 years × 12 months) to derive the Average Indexed Monthly Earnings, AIME.

Two features of this process are particularly significant. First, in all of these computations, *only those wages that were subject to Social Security tax are considered*. Social Security tax is applied each year to a person's wages, subject to a cap. Wages above that cap bear no Social Security tax and accordingly are ignored in *all* of these computations. In 1977, for example, the year in which Samuel earned $16,000, the cap was $16,500, so all of his wages were subject to Social Security tax. But if his 1977 wages had been $18,000 instead of $16,000, only the first $16,500 would have been considered and indexed, because only that portion is relevant for Social Security's purposes. In 2006, the cap was $94,200. At this level, approximately 85% of all wages are subject to Social Security tax. But the point remains that higher income wage earners will find that only a portion of their wages are considered in deriving their AIME.

Second, AIME is derived from 35 years of data even if a person does not have 35 years of earnings. If Samuel had gone to graduate school or stayed at home caring for his children and, as a result, has only 28 years of earnings, their sum would still be divided by the equivalent of 35 years to derive his AIME. His AIME, in this case, will be significantly lower than his actual average wage. On the other hand, the bottom-weighted three-part formula of the PIA will mitigate somewhat the impact of this lowering of Samuel's AIME. In addition, he may qualify for spousal benefits that might compensate, to some extent, for his years of low or no earnings. See generally § 11.4(a) regarding such benefits. But the point remains that a person's earnings are divided over 35 years, whether the person worked that many years or not.

In any case, if a person has earned income for a given year, it is critical that his or her Social Security record reflect that fact. As was indicated in § 11.1, a person receives a "Personal Earnings and Benefit Estimate Statement" from the Social Security Administration every year. Among other items, this Statement lists a person's reported earnings subject to Social Security tax—whether as an employee or as a self-employed person—for each year. Particularly for persons who worked for more than one employer during a given year, this Statement should be checked carefully. It is, after all, the basis on which a person's AIME will be computed, which in turn produces that person's PIA and all the Social Security benefits and options that derive from that figure.

b. *Government Pension Offset*

Although the bottom-weighted feature of the PIA formula is intended to help persons who had lower wages throughout their careers, it could also benefit persons who were primarily employed outside the

Social Security system, but who had *some* "covered employment." Because the amount of their "covered employment" would be relatively small, the bottom-weighted PIA formula would provide disproportionately large benefits to persons who were not necessarily low-income earners overall. This "windfall," as it is called, is addressed by the governmental pension offset provision.

This provision applies to persons who worked at any level of government, if their employment was not part of the Social Security system. Federal government employees, however, are covered by Social Security if they were hired after 1983. Some hired before that date are also covered by Social Security. As a result, this pension offset provision applies primarily to persons who worked for state and local governments that have chosen to remain outside of Social Security's coverage. Such persons might have had covered employment before or after their governmental employment, or via a second job, or via side-line self-employment. In such circumstances, the usual PIA formula does not apply.

Instead, the governmental pension offset lowers the percentage that applies to the first tier of the PIA formula from 90% to 40% for persons who receive pensions from noncovered governmental employment. The same "bend points" are used, and the calculation of AIME is the same, but the three-part PIA formula becomes 40–32–15 instead of 90–32–15. In this manner, the first tier of benefits, using the 2006 "bend point" of $656, is only $262.40, rather than $590.40, as computed previously. This mechanism effectively mitigates the intentionally more generous PIA formula vis-a-vis lower-income employees who only appear to be lower-income employees because most of their earnings were in "noncovered employment."

On the other hand, some of these workers truly are lower-income employees. In recognition of that possibility, the law limits the possible reduction in a retiree's Social Security benefit to half of that person's pension benefit from the noncovered employment. For example, in the preceding computation, the monthly Social Security benefit was reduced by $328 ($590.40 − $262.40). If that person's pension from his or her noncovered employment were $400 per month, that person's Social Security benefit would be reduced by $200 (half of $400), instead of $328.

Moreover, for persons with more than 20 years of Social Security coverage, the 40% applied to the PIA's first tier is increased by 5% for each additional year of such coverage. So, a person with 21 years of Social Security coverage would use 45% instead of 40% in the adjusted PIA formula. A person with at least 30 years of Social Security coverage would, in effect, suffer no detriment from this offset provision, because that person would apply the same 90% (40% + 10 years × 5%) that the PIA formula generally utilizes.

Note that this relief mechanism is calibrated according to *years* of Social Security coverage, not quarters. A year of work for this purpose requires covered earnings of at least a specified amount, which is adjusted annually. In 2006, it was $17,475. Any lesser amount does not constitute a year for purposes of this mitigation provision.

A related provision applies to persons who receive a pension from "noncovered" governmental employment *and* who are also entitled to Social Security benefits because of their status as a spouse or former spouse. (See generally § 11.4 regarding such benefits.) A person in this situation has his or her Social Security benefit reduced by two-thirds of the governmental pension amount.

For example, assume that Elaine receives a state government pension from her own "noncovered" employment of $1,500 per month. Assume further that she would also be otherwise entitled to Social Security benefits of, say, $1,100 per month either as a spouse, divorced spouse, surviving spouse, or surviving divorced spouse of a "covered" worker. Because of this offset provision, two-thirds of her governmental pension of $1,500 (i.e., $1,000) will reduce her Social Security benefit to $100 per month ($1,100 − $1,000). Note that if her Social Security benefit had been less than two-thirds of her "noncovered" governmental pension, her *entire* Social Security benefit would have been lost.

§ 11.4   Derivative Benefits

One of the features that most distinguishes Social Security from a private pension plan is the range of benefits that can be paid to a retiree's family while the retiree is alive and collecting benefits in his or her own right. Unlike private plans that typically provide survivors' benefits only, Social Security benefits can be paid to a retiree, that retiree's current spouse, that retiree's ex-spouse if their marriage lasted at least ten years, and that retiree's children if they are still in high school, among others—all at the same time. Social Security benefits that *derive* from a worker's earnings record will now be considered, along with the options and limitations that they entail. In all such cases, these derivative benefits are based upon the worker's "primary insurance amount," as described in § 11.3, but their payment does not affect the worker's own retirement benefit.

a.   Spousal Benefits

The spouse of a retired worker is eligible for a benefit equal to one-half of the worker's "primary insurance amount," or PIA, plus Social Security's customary cost-of-living adjustments. 42 U.S.C. § 402(b)(2), (c)(2). For a spouse to receive such a benefit, the worker must also be receiving retirement benefits. So if Dick is 66 years old, but has chosen to defer receipt of Social Security benefits, no spousal benefit may be paid to his wife, Judy.

On the other hand, Judy might be eligible for a worker's retirement benefit in her own right. Recall that the bottom-weighted nature of the PIA formula yields disproportionately larger benefits for lower-income workers. Accordingly, Judy might find that she would get a larger benefit based upon her own work record than her spousal benefit based upon

Dick's earnings history, *even if* Dick had higher earnings overall. For example, if Dick's PIA were $1,200, Judy's spousal benefit would be half of this amount, or $600. If Judy's PIA based upon her own earnings exceeds this latter amount, her full share worker's benefit would be more advantageous. On the other hand, if Judy was out of the compensated workforce for a number of years, the averaging of her earnings over 35 years might produce a worker's benefit that is less than half of Dick's PIA, even with the bottom-weighted impact of the PIA formula. In any case, Social Security automatically provides a person with the larger benefit, whether it be the spousal benefit or the worker's retirement benefit.

To receive a spousal benefit, a person must be at least 62 years old, or have in his or her "care" a child of the worker who is not yet 16 years old. In addition, the spouse must have been married to the retired worker at least one year. 42 U.S.C. § 416(b)(2), (f)(2).

A spouse receives less than half of the worker's PIA if he or she starts receiving these benefits before reaching "full retirement age." A spouse who has not reached this age will receive actuarially reduced benefits computed similarly to the "early" retirement benefits that were described in § 11.2(a). This time, however, the "early" receipt penalty is $25\!/\!36$ of 1% per month for the first 36 months + $5\!/\!12$ of 1% for each additional month thereafter. The amount of the "early" receipt penalty will vary, therefore, depending upon the "full retirement age" of the spouse in question.

For example, a spouse who reached age 62 in 2006 has a "full retirement age" of 66 years, per the table in § 11.2. If she claims her spousal benefit at age 62, she incurs a reduction based on 48 months, the number of months between age 62 and her "full retirement age." Accordingly, her benefit reduction would be $^{25}\!\!/\!_{36}$ of 1% × 36 months (i.e., 25%) + $^{5}\!\!/\!_{12}$ of 1% × 12 months (i.e., 5%), a total reduction of 30% (25% + 5%). This reduction is then applied to the 50% of the worker's PIA to produce a spousal benefit of 35% (70% [after the 30% reduction] × 50%) of the worker's PIA. In similar fashion, she would receive 37.5% of the worker's PIA, if she began receiving benefits at age 63, 41.67% if she began at age 64, and 45.84% if she began at age 65.

Note that these percentages are applied to the worker's "full retirement age" PIA, not what the worker actually receives. So if Dick started receiving reduced Social Security benefits when he became 62 years old, that reduction would not affect Judy's benefits. Judy would receive reduced spousal benefits—i.e., less than 50% of Dick's PIA—only if she started receiving benefits before *she* reached her "full retirement age." In any case, spousal benefits are not reduced if a spouse has in his or her "care" a child of the worker who is under age 16.

When a worker dies, a person receiving a spousal benefit that is based upon that worker's account succeeds to that worker's *actual* benefits. In that circumstance, if the deceased worker spouse had elected to receive reduced Social Security benefits because of "early" retirement, or augmented benefits because of "delayed" retirement (see § 11.2(b)), the surviving spouse would receive the deceased spouse's reduced, or augmented, benefit.

But if the surviving spouse has not yet reached "full retirement age," his or her benefits will be actuarially reduced based upon the number of months remaining until such "full retirement age." A surviving spouse is eligible for benefits starting as early as age 60, and the minimum benefit is 71.5% of the deceased worker's actual benefit. A surviving spouse who begins receiving benefits any time after age 60, but before "full retirement age," receives a percentage of the worker's benefit that varies with that person's "full retirement age." The minimum benefit level remains 71.5%, but the 28.5% difference is spread ratably over the period between age 60 and the person's "full retirement age." For purposes of this computation—and *only* for this computation—"full retirement age" is determined by treating the person as if he or she had been born two years earlier than was the case.

This rather strange calculation can be illustrated as follows: assume that Philip is a surviving spouse who is 60 years old in 2006. His actual year of birth is 1946, but for this purpose, he is treated as having been born two years earlier—in 1944. According to

the table at § 11.2, his "full retirement age" therefore is 66 years. The period between age 60 and this
"full retirement age" is 72 months (6 years × 12
months). If Philip starts receiving benefits before
his "full retirement age," those benefits will be
reduced by .396% (28.5% divided by 72 months) for
every month the benefits begin before that age.

These surviving spouse benefits are payable only
if the surviving spouse was married to the worker
at least nine months before the worker's death,
though this rule is waived if the worker's death was
accidental. In any case, benefits to a surviving
spouse generally are paid only if that person is not
presently married. So if Freda married Simon after
the death of her first husband, Gene, Freda is not
eligible for spousal benefits based on Gene's work
record. On the other hand, after being married to
Simon for one year, Freda is eligible for spousal
benefits based on Simon's work record.

There is an exception to this rule for remarriages
that occur after someone is 60 years old. Basically,
such remarriages do not disqualify someone from
receiving benefits as a surviving spouse. So, if Freda
was at least 60 years old when she married Simon,
she can still receive surviving spouse benefits based
on Gene's record. But when Freda becomes eligible
for spousal benefits based on Simon's record (i.e.,
after Freda and Simon are married one year), Social
Security will automatically pay her whichever benefit is greater—as Gene's surviving spouse, or as
Simon's current spouse. She will not receive both
benefits.

A surviving spouse who is not yet 60 years old may be entitled to a "mother's" or "father's" benefit, if the surviving spouse has in his or her "care" a child of the deceased worker who is either under 16 years old or disabled. Such a benefit is payable without regard to the surviving spouse's age and is equal to 75% of the deceased worker's PIA. As is usually the case, when the surviving spouse becomes entitled to benefits on his or her own work record (i.e., at age 62) or as a surviving spouse generally (i.e., at age 60), Social Security automatically pays whichever benefit is largest. On the other hand, remarriage terminates a "mother's" or "father's" benefit, unless the new spouse is also entitled to some type of Social Security benefit.

Finally, there is a one-time payment of $255 to a surviving spouse. If a person dies without leaving a surviving spouse, this $255 goes to any "dependent" children who otherwise qualify for children's benefits, as discussed below.

b.   *Children's Benefits*

Children of a retiree can receive benefits if they are under 18 years of age, under 19 years of age and still attending elementary or high school, or over 18 years old but became mentally or physically disabled prior to reaching age 22. See 42 U.S.C. § 402(d)(1). A child for this purpose includes not only adopted children and stepchildren, but also children born out of wedlock. To receive Social Security benefits, children must be unmarried and "dependent" upon the retiree for their support.

Moreover, grandchildren can also qualify for "children's" benefits, if they satisfy the other criteria, including "dependency" upon the retiree for support.

A child's benefit is generally half of the retired worker's PIA, but there is a family limit that caps the amount that Social Security will pay on any one worker's account. The more children that one has, the less each one gets, since the total remains the same. This "family maximum" is determined in the year the worker is 62 years old. It is based upon the worker's PIA and utilizes a four-part formula with three annually adjusted "bend points." The formula for workers who became 62 years old in 2006 was as follows:

150% of the first $838 of PIA, +

272% of the PIA between $838 and $1,210, +

134% of the PIA between $1,210 and $1,578, +

175% of the PIA over $1,578.

As with all benefits, the "family maximum" is increased every year by Social Security's cost-of-living adjustments.

The "family maximum" does not affect the retired worker's own benefit, only the derived spouse's and children's benefits. So if Ron's PIA were $2,000, his "family maximum," using the bend points for 2006, would be $3,500.40 (rounding down to the next-lower 10). Ignoring cost-of-living adjustments, at "full retirement age," Ron would receive $2,000 per month, and his wife, Nancy, and

their young son, Cary, would split the remaining
$1,500.40 ($3,500.40 − $2,000) evenly. But for the
"family maximum," Nancy and Cary would each
receive $1,000, half of Ron's $2,000. Instead, their
benefit will be only $750.20 each ($1,500.40 divided
by 2). And if Ron and Nancy had two children
qualifying for benefits, the $1,500.40 would be split
three ways, with one-third for Nancy and one-third
for each of the two children.

Upon the death of the retired worker, the children's benefits for any child who still qualifies (i.e.,
unmarried and "dependent" upon the retiree) becomes 75% of the retiree's PIA until the child
outgrows his or her age-based eligibility. The "family maximum" continues to apply in this circumstance, but there would no longer be a worker's
retirement benefit being drawn against this "maximum," needless to say.

c.   *Divorced Spouse's Benefits*

A person who was married at least ten years to a
worker can receive one-half of that worker's PIA as
a divorced spouse. 42 U.S.C. § 416(d)(1), (4). As is
the case with a spousal benefit, a divorced spouse
must be at least 62 years old, and will face actuarial
reductions from the half-share if he or she has not
yet reached "full retirement age." Similarly still, a
divorced spouse of a deceased worker can receive
survivor's benefits as early as 60 years of age, but
these benefits will equal the worker's actual benefit
only if the surviving divorced spouse has reached
"full retirement age." If not, reductions similar to

those that affect a surviving spouse will apply. Finally, a surviving divorced spouse who is not yet 60 years old may receive a "mother's" or "father's" benefit equal to 75% of the deceased worker's PIA, if the surviving divorced spouse has in his or her "care" a child of the worker who is under age 16 or is disabled—just like a spouse. See generally § 11.4(a) regarding a spouse's benefits.

Unlike a spouse, however, a divorced spouse can receive Social Security benefits even though the worker from whom the divorced spouse's benefit is derived has not yet started to receive benefits. The worker, in this circumstance, must be at least 62 years old, and the divorce must have been final for at least two years. The two-year finalization requirement does not apply, however, if the worker has reached "full retirement age." For example, assume that Donald is 63 years old and that his "full retirement age" is 66 years. Although Donald could receive "early" retirement benefits from Social Security, assume that he has chosen not to do so. Nevertheless, his ex-wife, Ivana, may receive benefits as a divorced spouse once their divorce has been final for two years. But if Donald was already 66 years old, Ivana could receive such benefits immediately upon the divorce, if she otherwise qualifies.

In further contrast to a spouse's benefit, a divorced spouse's benefit is *not* subject to the "family maximum" limit that was described in connection with children's benefits. See § 11.4(b). Nor do benefits paid to a divorced spouse, or divorced spouses, affect the "family maximum" or the benefits of the worker's current spouse. Divorced spouse benefits, in other words, are calculated independently of a worker's spousal and children's benefits.

As to the divorced spouse, if he or she had more than one marriage that lasted at least ten years, Social Security automatically selects the ex-spouse's earnings record that yields the largest benefit. The divorced spouse's own earnings record will also be considered if it produces a higher benefit. On the other hand, to receive a divorced spouse benefit, the recipient must be unmarried. Marriages that occur after a person is 60 years old, however, do not disqualify a person from receiving benefits as a divorced spouse. So if Ivana, age 55, married Charles after divorcing Donald (in the preceding example), Ivana would no longer qualify for a divorced spouse's benefit derived from Donald. But if she had been at least 60 years old when she married Charles, she would still be eligible for benefits derived from Donald.

d. Parent's Benefits

An older person who receives at least half of his or her support from a son or daughter who has died may receive parent's benefits derived from that son or daughter's Social Security account. For this purpose, "parent" includes an adoptive parent or a stepparent who became such before the child in question was 16 years old. The support test considers expenditures for food, shelter, routine medical care, and other necessities. In addition, the parent generally must not have married since the child's death, although certain marriages do not terminate the receipt of such benefits. If a parent meets these various qualifications, the benefit amount is 82.5% of the deceased child's PIA, or 75% of that PIA if more than one parent is receiving benefits from that child's account. 42 U.S.C. § 402(h). In any case, if the older person would receive a larger Social Security benefit based upon his or her own work record, the older person receives the larger benefit.

§ 11.5 Effect of Earnings After Retirement

Social Security imposes a "retirement earnings" test on certain recipients who perform compensated work while receiving retirement benefits. 42 U.S.C. § 403. Reduced to its essence, this test limits the amount of earnings that a retiree can receive before his or her Social Security benefits are reduced. This test applies, however, only to those recipients who have not yet reached their "full retirement age." Persons who have reached that age may earn whatever they can without facing any reduction in their Social Security benefits.

The "retirement earnings" test looks exclusively at income from performing personal services. It completely ignores income from any other source, be it interest, dividends, rentals, annuities, pension plan distributions, capital gains, or the like. Thus, a person could have $400,000 in investment income without suffering any reduction in his or her Social Security benefits, since that income was not earned by performing personal services. This level of income would, however, subject most of the recipient's Social Security benefits to Federal income tax, as described in § 11.6. But the benefits themselves would not be reduced.

a. Scope of "Earnings"

The types of income that trigger benefit reductions include any form of wages, salaries, bonuses paid by an employer, commissions, director's fees, and net earnings from self-employment. For this purpose, all remuneration for labor is counted, whether paid in cash or in kind, and without regard to de minimis thresholds like the $1,500–per-year (in 2006) rule for domestic work (babysitting, housecleaning, etc.) or the $400–per-year floor for self-employment income. Nor is the annual cap on wages subject to Social Security's payroll tax relevant; *all* earned income is counted. Even work in "noncovered" employment counts as earnings for this test.

On the other hand, deferred compensation is excluded, as long as the recipient is able to show that the funds in question were in fact earned before Social Security benefits were received. Similarly, royalties attributable to patents and copyrights that were obtained before retirement are excluded, even though those royalties are received after retirement. But if the patent or copyright was obtained after retirement, the corresponding royalties represent earnings for purposes of this test. Yet, fees for jury duty are not counted, by specific provision.

Earnings in a self-employment context include income for any regular services that are performed in the ongoing management or operation of a trade or business, if those services can be related to the income received. Mere ownership of a business, however, does not transform the profits from that business into "earnings" for purposes of Social Security benefit reduction. On the other hand, distributions to shareholders of so-called "S corporations" may be treated as "earnings" if those shareholders performed services for their corporations.

b. *Applicable Thresholds*

The amount that a Social Security recipient can earn without having his or her benefits reduced depends upon the recipient's age. Persons who will not reach their "full retirement age" during the year in question can earn up to an annually adjusted amount without losing any benefits. In 2006, that amount was $12,480. Earnings above this threshold, however, reduce a person's Social Security benefits by $1 for every $2 of such earnings.

Persons who reach their "full retirement age" during the year in question can earn up to an annually adjusted amount each month before that date without losing any benefits. In 2006, that amount was $2,770. Earnings above this threshold reduce the recipient's benefits by $1 for every $3 of such earnings, but only for the months prior to that person's reaching his or her "full retirement age." Clearly, this version of the retirement earnings is much less significant than the version that applies to those persons who did not reach their "full retirement age" during the year in question. Of course, persons receiving Social Security benefits before their "full retirement age" have already sustained permanent benefit reductions, as explained in § 11.2(a). The retirement earnings test reduces those benefits still further.

c. Impact on Benefits

The mechanics of this provision can be illustrated as follows: assume that Sandra is 63 years old and earns $20,480 as a consultant. Assume further that her Social Security retirement benefit would be $10,000 per year but for the retirement earnings test. Since she will not reach her "full retirement age" during this year, Sandra faces the lower earnings threshold—$12,480 in 2006—in determining her "excess" earnings, which are $8,000 ($20,480 − $12,480). She then divides this excess by two to determine the amount by which her Social Security benefits are reduced—namely, $4,000. Her Social Security benefit, therefore, becomes $6,000 ($10,000 − $4,000).

In other words, the $8,000 of earnings over the applicable threshold cost Sandra $4,000 in lost Social Security benefits, an implicit tax of 50% on those earnings. Moreover, these earnings are taxable income, so they bear Federal income tax, probably at the 15% rate. A particularly ironic twist makes Sandra liable for the Social Security taxes (6.2% + 1.45% for Medicare = 7.65%) on this income as well. As a result, Sandra faces an effective tax rate of nearly 73% on the $8,000 of earnings in excess of the applicable threshold (50% benefit reduction + 15% Federal income tax + 7.65% Social Security tax = 72.65%).

Sandra's effective tax rate would have been still higher if she had enough income from nonwage sources to move her into the 25% Federal income tax bracket. On the facts presented, in 2006, Sandra would need only $10,170 of pension and investment income to find herself in that position. Earnings beyond that point would face an effective marginal tax rate of 83%. Note that these tax rates ignore state income taxes, even though most states impose such taxes.

Finally, all of these calculations assumed that the Social Security benefits themselves were not subject to tax. That is usually the case, but oftentimes those benefits are taxable. See § 11.6. When that is the case, the effective tax rate rises still higher, possibly beyond 100%!

Sandra will have one consolation, however. If she received "excess" earnings before reaching "full retirement age," the "early" retirement discount that reduces her Social Security benefit will be recalculated when she reaches "full retirement age" to take account of benefits that she lost before that date. So if Sandra loses the equivalent, say, of eight months of benefits, she will be treated as if she retired eight months later than she actually retired, and the "early" retirement discount factor will be recalculated accordingly. Corresponding adjustments will also be made to anyone who receives derivative benefits on the basis of Sandra's account.

d.   Effect on Derivative Benefits

Social Security's "retirement earnings" test is applied on an individual, rather than a household, basis. In other words, if Harry and Louise are married and Harry has "excess" earnings, those "excess" earnings would affect his worker's retirement benefits, but Louise's earnings would generally not be considered in applying the earnings test to Harry. On the other hand, if Harry's Social Security benefit is a spousal benefit that is derived from Louise's work record, a reduction of Louise's worker's benefit will also affect Harry's spousal benefit. In fact, a worker's "excess" earnings will affect the benefits of any person who receives derivative benefits from that worker's account. (See generally § 11.4 regarding derivative benefits.) If Harry also had "excess" earnings, his spousal benefit would be reduced once, because of Louise's "excess" earnings, and again, because of Harry's own "excess" earnings.

One exception to this pattern applies to persons who receive Social Security benefits as a divorced spouse. A divorced spouse's benefit is not affected by "excess" earnings received by his or her ex-spouse, if the divorce has been final for at least two years. The Social Security benefits of the divorced spouse will, however, be affected by his or her own "excess" earnings, as is the case generally.

§ 11.6   Taxation of Benefits

For most recipients of Social Security retirement benefits, no Federal income tax is imposed upon their receipt. But approximately one in four recipients is subject to a two-tiered tax on Social Security benefits that is based on a recipient's overall income. I.R.C. § 86(a). This tax is triggered by income from *any* source, including capital gains, and even nominally tax-exempt interest—unlike the retirement earnings test, which is concerned exclusively with *earned* income. (See generally § 11.5.) Thus, even a person with no earned income, or with earned income that is below the applicable "retirement earnings" threshold, might owe Federal income tax on his or her Social Security benefits, depending upon that person's income from all other sources. And a person with earned income in excess of those thresholds might face such taxation in addition to the reduction of benefits that those "excess" earnings already caused.

a.   Provisional Income

The triggering formula for Federal income tax on Social Security benefits is "adjusted gross income" (AGI), plus tax-free interest income, plus one-half of the recipient's Social Security benefits. I.R.C. § 86(b). If a person's benefits have been reduced because of "excess" earnings, those reduced benefits are used in this formula. For example, assume that Ellen's Social Security benefits would have been $6,000 per year but for "excess" earnings that reduced those benefits to $5,000. For purposes of this tax, one-half of those reduced benefits, or $2,500, will be used in this formula. Note that tax-free interest income, which is commonly referred to as "municipal bond" interest, remains tax-free, but it is included in the triggering formula to determine how much, if any, of a person's Social Security benefits will be subject to tax. The result of this formula is often described as "provisional income."

b.   First Tier

Once provisional income is computed, it is compared to thresholds of $25,000 for single persons and $32,000 for married couples filing joint returns. I.R.C. § 86(c)(1). Those thresholds are *not* indexed for inflation. Therefore, an increasing percentage of older persons may find themselves above these thresholds over time. Be that as it may, the excess of "provisional income" over the relevant threshold is computed, and one-half of this excess is then treated as taxable income. In the case of married couples, it does not matter which spouse receives the Social Security benefits or which spouse has the relevant "provisional income."

To illustrate, assume that Andy and Kathy have pension, dividend, and corporate bond interest income of $24,000, in addition to tax-exempt interest of $6,000, and Social Security benefits of $13,000. Their "provisional income" would be $24,000 + $6,000 + $6,500 (one-half of their Social Security benefits of $13,000), or $36,500. This figure exceeds their threshold as a married couple of $32,000 by $4,500. Therefore, one-half of this $4,500 excess—

namely $2,250—is taxable. The other $10,750 of their Social Security benefits ($13,000 − $2,250) faces no Federal income tax. Thus, the major portion of this couple's Social Security benefits is tax-free.

The tax code's formula effectively raises the taxable portion of Social Security benefits as a recipient's income rises, following general notions of tax progressivity based upon taxpayers' presumed ability to pay. For example, if Andy and Kathy's income other than Social Security were $34,000 instead of $30,000, the taxable portion of their benefits would be $4,250 ($34,000 + $6,500 [one-half of their benefits] = $40,500 − $32,000 threshold = $8,500 divided by 2 = $4,250). The additional $4,000 of income, in other words, exposed an additional $2,000 of Social Security benefits ($4,250 − $2,250) to income taxation. Under the operation of this first tier of taxation, however, no more than one-half of a person's Social Security benefits (here, $6,500) is ever taxed.

c. Second Tier

To obtain still greater tax progressivity, this first tier of taxation is supplemented by a second tier that utilizes the same formula for "provisional income," but applies it against a set of higher thresholds. Those thresholds are $34,000 for single persons and $44,000 for married couples filing jointly. I.R.C. § 86(c)(2). These thresholds are also not indexed for inflation, so the proportion of Social Security recipients who must face this second tier is also likely to rise over time.

Mechanically, "provisional income" *up to* these higher thresholds is applied as explained above. Then, 85% of the excess of "provisional income" over these thresholds is added to the first tier result. So, if Andy and Kathy have "provisional income" of $48,000, the taxable portion of their Social Security benefits is computed as follows:

(a).   First tier: $44,000 − $32,000 =
       $12,000 × 50% = $6,000
       (but never more than one-half of
       their benefits—here, $6,500) $6,000

(b).   Second tier: $48,000 − $44,000
       = $4,000 × 85% = $3,400
       Taxable Portion $9,400

This process effectively phases in the taxable portion of one's Social Security benefits as one's income rises, until a maximum of 85% of those benefits are taxable. In other words, regardless of how high Andy and Kathy's income might get, no more than 85% of their Social Security benefits, or $11,050 ($13,000 of benefits × 85%) would ever be subject to Federal income tax.

As to the taxation of Social Security benefits by those states that impose an income tax, there is no consistent treatment. Some states exempt such benefits from their income tax, regardless of the recipient's income. Others tax a portion of these benefits, with some states following the Federal formula and some states utilizing different approaches.

§ 11.7   Disability Benefits

As noted at the beginning of this Chapter, the official name of the Social Security program is Old–Age, Survivors and Disability Insurance. Thus far, this Chapter has dealt with the Old–Age and the Survivors aspects of Social Security, so the focus here is the Disability portion of that program. From an elder law perspective, of course, the Old–Age and Survivors portions are the most critical aspects of Social Security. The Disability program is much more important to younger persons. Indeed, disability benefits cease when a recipient attains "full retirement age," and Social Security's Old–Age program provides retirement benefits after that point. Nevertheless, some overview of the disability provisions of Social Security is appropriate, even in a volume that is primarily focused on older persons.

Disability benefits are payable to disabled workers as young as 21 years old. To qualify as "disabled," however, one must be unable to perform "*any* substantial gainful activity by reason of any medically determinable physical or mental impairment." 42 U.S.C. § 416(i)(1)(A) (emphasis supplied). This inability is determined by medical examinations, as well as vocational tests that assess whether an applicant can be retrained for some type of employment. Numerous factors are considered in this latter inquiry, including the applicant's age, past work experience, level of formal education, years since completion of that education, literacy, and ability to communicate in English. There is a presumption, however, that earning an average of less than an annually adjusted amount indicates an inability to perform "substantial gainful activity." In 2006, this amount was $860 per month, or $1,450 per month if the person was "statutorily blind." In any case, this inability must be expected to last at least one year or to result in the applicant's death. A person's status as "disabled," moreover, is reviewed periodically until that person attains "full retirement age," at which time such status is no longer relevant.

If a person is "disabled" according to these standards, the person can receive benefits equal to his or her full "primary insurance amount" (PIA), regardless of that person's age. (See generally § 11.3 regarding PIA.) Accordingly, a disabled person who is at least 62 years old, but not yet of "full retirement age," should apply for "disability" status, because disability benefits are generally not reduced on account of age—unlike retirement benefits. See § 11.2(a). Moreover, if a person receives Social Security disability benefits for 24 consecutive months, he or she is automatically enrolled in Medicare, the Federal government's health care program, without regard to the person's age. See generally Chapter 4 regarding Medicare.

In any case, if a disabled person already receives workers' compensation payments or disability benefits from some governmental program other than Social Security, the combination of these payments and Social Security's disability benefits cannot exceed 80% of that person's earnings for the year prior to his or her becoming disabled.

To receive disability benefits under Social Security, a person must be "fully insured," i.e., have at least 40 "quarters of coverage." See § 11.1(a). In addition, a person must have earned at least 20 "quarters of coverage" during the 40–quarter period that preceded the onset of that person's disability. Special rules mitigate this requirement for workers who become disabled before the age of 31.

Once the various requirements are met and the disability has been proven to the government's satisfaction, benefits are payable starting with the sixth month after the disability ensued and continuing through the second month after it ends. When a disability recipient dies or reaches "full retirement age," disability benefits cease.

Finally, derivative benefits are payable to the spouse, divorced spouse, children, and grandchildren of the disabled person, if they meet the eligibility requirements and limitations that apply to derivative benefits generally. See § 11.4 regarding such benefits. In addition, a surviving spouse or a surviving divorced spouse who is disabled can receive benefits as early as age 50, instead of the usual requirement of age 60. These benefits equal 71.5% of the worker's PIA, without regard to the specific recipient's age.

§ 11.8   Appeals Procedures

Benefits available under any of the component programs of Social Security must be applied for directly. The application process is handled by the Social Security Administration's (SSA) numerous

field offices and generally involves providing proof
of eligibility for the specific benefits being sought.
Determinations of old age and survivors benefits
are relatively straightforward and extensively com-
puterized. Disability benefit determinations are often more complicated because of the medical and
vocational tests that govern entitlement to these
benefits. But regardless of the specific type of benefit in question, SSA employs a four-step appeals
process for persons who want to contest the agency's determinations. Each step concludes with a
written notification of the result and includes a 60–
day period during which a claimant may file for
further redress. The written notice also describes
the applicable appeals process from that point on.

The first step is "reconsideration" by SSA of its
initial determination. This "reconsideration" is
done by an employee of SSA who was not involved
previously with the claimant's application for benefits. New evidence may also be submitted at this
point.

The second step is a "hearing" before an administrative law judge within the SSA. The claimant
need not be present at this hearing but is allowed if
he or she so chooses. The hearing procedure is fairly
informal, with direct questioning by the judge of the
claimant and his or her witnesses.

Should a claimant wish to go further, the third
step is a review of the administrative law judge's
decision by the "Appeals Council" of the SSA. The
Appeals Council can choose not to review a decision

of the administrative law judge. Alternatively, the Council can remand the file to that judge for further review, or simply hear the case itself and render its own decision.

Finally, a claimant can seek judicial review in a Federal district court. This is the only step that is outside the SSA itself.

Throughout these various proceedings, a claimant may appoint someone to represent his or her interests. Such a representative can be an attorney, but need not be. Union officials, employers, and other qualified advocates often fill this role. Some legal service organizations also provide assistance in this process, usually at no cost to the claimant. In some circumstances, SSA will pay attorneys' fees to claimants who prevail against the agency in the appeals process.

CHAPTER 12

SUPPLEMENTAL SECURITY INCOME (SSI)

The Supplemental Security Income program (SSI) is a Federal welfare program created in 1974 that provides monthly cash benefits to eligible elderly, blind and disabled individuals. Funded through the Department of Health and Human Services and administered by the Social Security Administration (SSA), SSI is designed to insure a minimum monthly benefit to eligible individuals and couples. Almost every state provides additional monthly payments to recipients of SSI.

§ 12.1 General Eligibility

To be eligible for SSI, an applicant must be a resident of the United States and a citizen or a qualified alien. Residents of Puerto Rico are not eligible. Applicants for SSI must be prepared to offer proof of residency such as a tax return, rent receipt, utility bill or similar documents. Proof of citizenship can be established by a certified copy of a birth certificate or baptismal record, a passport, or naturalization certificate.

The Welfare Reform legislation enacted in 1996 severely limited the rights of noncitizens to SSI benefits. No illegal alien is eligible for SSI. Even legal aliens are not eligible unless they meet the requirements of a "qualified alien", who are defined as permanent residents, asylees, or refugees who meet certain criteria. Refugees and asylees are eligible for five years from arrival in the United States or from the date asylum granted; active-duty Armed Forces personnel and honorably discharged veterans (generally with 24 months of active duty) and their spouses and dependent children; and permanent resident who have worked or are credited with 40 qualifying quarters of coverage for Social Security purposes. Legal aliens who were receiving SSI on August 22, 1996, continue to receive benefits.

A resident of a public institution is ineligible for SSI. A public institution is defined as a residence that furnishes room and board (it may or may not provide treatment) regardless of whether anyone pays for the residence. A county operated nursing home, for example, would be a public institution whose residents would not be eligible for SSI. If, however, Medicaid pays 50% or more of the costs of a patient in a public hospital, a nursing home or other extended care facility, the resident is eligible for SSI benefits of $30 per month ($60 for a couple if both are institutionalized). Community residences that serve 16 or fewer residents are not considered public institutions. For example, individuals would be eligible for SSI if they were residents of a community home for eight older, mental health patients.

a. Income Eligibility Requirements

Individuals age 65 or older (and younger individuals who are blind or disabled) who meet the SSI income and resource tests are eligible for monthly cash benefits. An individual with net annual countable income in excess of $7,236 in 2006 or $603 a month (the dollar amount is adjusted annually for inflation) is ineligible for SSI. Both spouses are ineligible if their combined income exceeds $10,848 in 2006 or $904 a month (adjusted annually for inflation).

If the individual's annual income is below the annual eligibility limit, the individual will be eligible for SSI in every month that his or her income is below the SSI benefit amount. SSI benefit amounts are adjusted annually for inflation. In 2006, the maximum monthly benefit for an unmarried individual was $603; for married couples it was $904. An individual is ineligible for SSI for any month that his or her countable income exceeds the maximum benefit.

Eligible individuals with countable income have their SSI benefit reduced one dollar for every such dollar of countable income. For example, Teresa, age 66, has $100 of countable income. As a single individual in 2006 she would have been eligible for $603, but the benefit would have been reduced by her $100 of countable income, so that she would have received $503 per month of SSI. An individual may be ineligible for SSI in one month because of excessive income, but become eligible again the next month if the excess income is spent (i.e., does not become an excess resource) and his or her income falls below the benefit amount.

SSI eligibility is based upon *countable* income (and resources). The SSI Regulations define countable income "as anything you receive in cash or in-kind that you can use to meet your needs for food or shelter. In-kind income is not cash, but is actually food or shelter or something you can use to get one of these." Countable income includes both earned income and unearned income. Earned income is income from gross wages or net earnings from self-employment. All other income is considered unearned and includes dividends, interest and even gifts. In-kind income may be earned (e.g. payment for services) or unearned (e.g. a gift). Regardless of the source or the form, if the in-kind item is food or shelter, it is countable income for SSI purposes. Conversely, in-kind support that is not food or shelter is not income for determining SSI eligibility. Thus, a gift of groceries is countable income, but the gift of a television is not (though it becomes a countable resource).

SSI eligibility is determined monthly based on the countable income in the month that passed two months previously. Thus, SSI eligibility for March is determined by January's countable income. For initial eligibility, however, the first month's income for which SSI benefits are requested is used. If the claimant applies for benefits in July for example, July income is used to determine eligibility for July, August and September. The same rule applies to the first month of eligibility that follows a period of ineligibility.

SSI eligibility is based upon "countable" income, which consists of all of the applicant's earned and unearned income, both cash and in-kind. Certain income is then excluded in determining eligibility and the amount of the monthly benefit. First, $20.00 a month is subtracted from unearned income, or if unearned income is less than $20.00, the total unearned income is subtracted from earned income. Next, an exclusion of $65.00 a month is subtracted from earned income, and one-half of the remainder above that initial $65.00 is also excluded from countable income.

To illustrate, assume Carol, who is single, age 70, receives $100.00 a month in Social Security retirement benefits and works part-time, earning another $215.00 per month. Her countable income is determined as follows:

Total Unearned Income:	$100
Exclusion	– 20
Total Countable Unearned Income	$80
Total Earned Income:	$215
Exclusion	– 65
	$150
Less One-half Countable Earned Income	– 75
Total Countable Earned Income	$ 75

> Total Countable
>   Income (Earned +   + 80
>   Unearned) $155

Only $155.00 is counted in determining whether Carol is eligible for SSI. Assuming that she meets the resource eligibility tests, she will receive the current monthly SSI payment less $155.00, or in 2006, $603 − 155 = $448.

b. *Resource Eligibility Requirements*

Individual applicants are ineligible for SSI if they have more than $2,000 in countable resources. Couples are permitted countable resources of $3,000. Individuals with excess resources are expected to use them for their support (referred to as "spend down") until the value of their resources is below the eligibility limit. Under SSI, "resources" are defined as "cash, liquid assets, and any real or person property that an individual owns (or has the right, authority or power to liquidate) and could convert to cash to be used for support and maintenance."

Income and principal of self-settled trusts created on or after January 1, 2000, are counted as available resources. An individual is considered to have established a trust if any of individual's assets are transferred to the trust other than by will. If the individual transfers assets to an irrevocable trust that also contains assets of the spouse or a third party, the portion of the trust assets attributable to individual or the spouse are countable resources.

The attribution of trust assets occurs regardless of why the trust was established, the discretion of the trustee, or any restrictions on trust distributions. Any income of the trust attributable to the individual is considered unearned income for purposes of calculating SSI eligibility.

All the assets of a revocable trust are considered resources of the individual who established the trust and the assets of an irrevocable trust are considered resources to the extent that the assets of the trust could be distributed to the individual. However, a d4A payback trust or d4C pooled (community) trust established to create Medicaid eligibility are not counted as resources in the calculation of SSI eligibility.

Some assets are partially or totally excluded from the eligibility test. They include the home (personal residence), and household goods and personal effects (personal jewelry and wedding or engagement rings are also excluded). The value of medical equipment is also not counted as a resource. If the home is sold, the sale proceeds are not counted if used to purchase another home within three months. The value of one car needed for transportation for the individual or a member of the household. The individual's equity in any other car is a countable resource.

A home is any shelter in which the SSI applicant has an ownership interest and uses (or his or her spouse uses) as a principal residence. A jointly owned house that is not the personal residence of the applicant is not a countable resource if it is the home of the joint owner. For example, Dan and his sister, Dawn, inherited their parents' home in which Dawn lives. Dan applies for SSI. The jointly owned house will not count as a resource in determining Dan's eligibility so long as Dawn lives in the house.

Up to $6,000 of property used in a trade or business essential to self-support is not counted if it produces a return of at least 6%. This includes buildings, equipment, inventory, and supplies. Non-business property essential for self-support (such as tools or equipment used in employment) is also excluded. For example, Michelle owns an outdoor display cart worth $2,000 used to display the home-made dolls that she sells. Neither the cart nor her inventory of dolls are counted in determining her eligibility.

The value of burial spaces for the applicant, his or her spouse, or any members of the applicant's immediate family are excluded from countable resources. Also excluded are amounts up to $1,500 specifically set aside for the burial expenses of the individual or his or her spouse. This includes burial funds, trusts, pre-paid contracts or even cash or savings specifically designated for burial expenses. The exclusion of burial funds, however, is reduced by the face value of any otherwise excluded life insurance policies on the life of the applicant or his or her spouse.

Insurance on the life of the applicant or his or her spouse is considered a countable resource only if the face value exceeds $1,500 (term and burial policies are not counted). If the face value of all policies exceeds $1,500, the cash surrender value of the policies is a countable resource.

If excluded resources are lost, damaged or stolen, any cash received as compensation is not counted if it is used to repair or replace the excluded resources within nine months of receipt. Disaster assistance is excluded as a resource.

The receipt of a lump sum such as an inheritance or tort settlement is considered income in the month received. Any portion retained into the next calendar is counted as a resource.

Applicants who meet the income eligibility requirements, but who have excess resources can become eligible for SSI payments if they agree in writing to dispose of those excess resources at current market value. The proceeds from the sale must be used to repay any SSI benefits received while the excess resources were being disposed of. Excess personal property must be disposed of within 3 months, and real property within 9 months, or longer if the applicant makes reasonable efforts to sell.

To receive SSI, an application must be filed at a Social Security office or other authorized Federal or state office. (An application for Social Security benefits is *not* an application for SSI though the applicant must apply for any other Social Security benefits for which the applicant or his or her spouse is eligible.) Normally the applicant must sign the application, but if that is not possible, another can sign and file an application for the applicant. For example, if John is in the hospital, his friend Alan can sign the application on John's behalf. The individual may be required to produce evidence of their right to file for another. Guardians, for example, must submit a certificate issued by the court evidencing their authority.

SSI benefits are not retroactive, though eligibility for benefits begins with the first day of the month of the date of application. Even if formal application is not filed, any writing that expresses an intent to file for SSI benefits will count as establishing the date of eligibility. The applicant, however, must file a formal written application within 60 days. Under certain conditions, even an oral request for SSI may establish an eligibility date if a written application follows within 60 days.

Applicants for SSI are required to provide detailed information, including a statement of income and resources, written authorization for the SSA to investigate bank accounts, proof of income and assets, a copy of a birth certificate or other proof of age, and proof of living arrangements such as receipts and utility bills. Applicants who knowingly provide false information or omit material information may have benefits suspended up to six months for the first offense, 12 months for a second offense and up to 24 for months for subsequent offenses.

c.   Resource Transfer Rules

The transfer of resources for less than fair value may cause a loss of eligibility for SSI benefits. Upon application for SSI the applicant must account for any transfers for less than market value for the 36 month period proceeding the date of application. Resource transfers within the 36 month look-back period can create a period of ineligibility. The length of the penalty period is determined by dividing the value of the uncompensated transfer by the total amount of the individual's combined monthly federal SSI benefit and any state supplementary payment with the number of months of penalty being rounded to the nearest whole number. The resulting penalty period begins to run in the month of the transfer. There is no limit on the number of ineligible months due to the transfer of resources. If a married applicant makes a transfer that results in a period of ineligibility, and later the spouse becomes eligible for benefits, the penalty is apportioned between the SSI applicant and th spouse. Transfers that were not made with the intent of qualifying for benefits can be reversed if the resources are returned to the transferor. Where the application of a transfer penalty would work a hardship, the SSA can waive the imposition of the penalty.

If a resource is held jointly, any action taken that reduces or eliminates the SSI applicant's ownership or control of the resource will be considered a transfer and if for less than fair value could result in an imposition of the transfer penalty.

The receipt of a lump sum such as a inheritance is treated as income in the month received. As such it can be transferred without penalty during the calendar month received. If, however, any amount is retained into the next calendar month and then transferred for less than fair market value, the amount transferred is considered a resource and a period of ineligibility may result.

Certain transfers are excepted from the transfer penalties. Transfer to or for the sole benefit of the spouse do not create a period of ineligibility. Other exempt transfers include the transfer of a home to a spouse, a child under age 21 or who is blind or disabled, a sibling with an equity interest who has resided in the home for at least one year immediately prior to the transferor entering an institution, such as a nursing home, or to a child who resided in the home for a period of at least two years immediately prior to the transferor entering an institution and who provided care to the transferor which delayed the transferor's entry into an institution.

§ 12.2   Benefits

The maximum monthly SSI grant as of January 2006 was $603 for unmarried individuals and $904 for couples. Benefit amounts are adjusted annually for inflation. Individuals living in nursing homes or other institutions with more than 16 residents receive only $30 a month from SSI for their personal use.

All but six states supplement SSI benefits by providing additional monthly benefits. The Social

Security Administration administers the payment for about half the states, the rest of the states administer and pay the benefits themselves. The six states that do not provide additional SSI benefits are Arkansas, Georgia, Kansas, Mississippi, Tennessee, and West Virginia.

Any income from any other source reduces the amount of the SSI benefit. Income of an ineligible spouse is deemed to be income of the applicant. Countable cash income reduces SSI dollar for dollar. In-kind income also reduces SSI benefits. (See ¶ 12.1(a)).

If a SSI recipient lives in the household of another and receives free food and shelter, the value of these items is held to be worth one-third of the Federal SSI benefit rate ($603 in 2006), and the monthly benefit is reduced accordingly. The actual value of the items is irrelevant as the presumption of value is irrebuttable.

If the recipient receives in-kind support and maintenance and the one-third reduction does not apply, the value of the items is presumed to equal one-third of the SSI benefit plus any amount left of the $20 "any income" exclusion. This presumption, however, is rebuttable if the recipient can prove that the fair market value of the items is less than the presumed value. If the fair market value is more than the presumed value, the presumed value governs and the fair market value is ignored.

For example, Erik lives with his cousin, Cara. He pays no rent, but does pay for his share of the food. The value of the rent is presumed to be equal to ⅓ of the monthly benefit of $603 or $201 plus $20 for a total of $221. Erik's monthly benefit check will be reduced by that amount unless he can prove that the fair market value of the free room is less than $221. If the free room was worth only $120 a month, Erik's monthly benefit check would be reduced only by $120.

Married individuals who live with their spouse receive benefits at the couple's rate even if only one spouse qualifies. For example, Jose and Joan are married. Jose is age 67 while Joan is only 60. If Jose qualifies for SSI because they have less than $3,000 in resources and if their combined income is less than $904 a month (in 2006), they are eligible for SSI.

Couples need not be legally married under state law, but are considered married for SSI purposes if they hold themselves out to be so to the community. If they are separated for six months, however, each eligible spouse is paid at the individual rate.

CHAPTER 13

VETERANS' BENEFITS

"If a man shalbee sent forth as a souldier and shall return maimed, hee shalbee maintained completely by the collonie during his life."

§ 13.1 History

Veterans' benefits in America can be traced back to the above-quoted 1636 colonial statute drafted by the Pilgrims that carried over the nascent English tradition of providing benefits to its country's soldiers. After America won its independence, the Continental Congress strengthened the tradition by promising to provide government securities to those who fought in the Revolutionary War. Widows and orphans first began to receive benefits in 1836. Veterans became eligible for medical benefits starting in 1861.

In response to the greatly increased number of veterans, veterans' benefits increased dramatically in the aftermath of World Wars I and II. In 1930, the Veterans' Administration, now the Department of Veterans Affairs (VA), was established to administer and oversee benefit distribution. Over time, disability compensation, vocational rehabilitation, and education assistance came into being.

The Vietnam War, which added over eight million men and women to the list of veterans, placed great demands on the veteran's benefits system. The traditionally informal, nonadversarial structure of the benefits system was poorly equipped to handle this influx, and complaints mounted about how veterans benefits were handled. As a result, in 1988 Congress passed the Veterans' Judicial Review Act (VJRA) that provided a formal structure for veterans to litigate their benefit claims. The VJRA created the U.S. Court of Veteran Appeals (CVA), a Federal court that will play a pivotal role in shaping future developments in veterans benefits.

§ 13.2   Eligibility Requirements

Veterans, their spouses, parents and children are all potentially eligible for benefits. A detailed statutory structure determines who is eligible. (The Federal law is found in 38 U.S.C. § 101 et seq.).

a.   Veterans

A veteran is defined as "a person who served in the active military, naval, or air service, and who was discharged or released therefrom under conditions other than dishonorable." "Active military, naval, or air service" includes: (1) active duty, (2) training for active duty during which disability or death is incurred in the line of duty, and (3) inactive duty training during which disability or death is incurred in the line of duty. Detailed requirements for each of the three categories are set out in the statute.

For Veterans Administration (VA) purposes, military service must be identified as either wartime or peacetime, an important distinction because of the advantages for veterans of wartime service. At present the recognized periods of war are: the Spanish–American War, the Mexican border period, World War I, World War II, the Korean Conflict, the Vietnam Era, the Persian Gulf War and IRAQI conflict. Any service during these periods constitutes wartime service without regard to whether the veteran actually participated in the war.

Veterans who enlisted in military service on or after September 8, 1980 are subject to a minimum length of service requirement for eligibility for VA benefits. In general, they must have served on active duty for 24 months unless discharged earlier because of a service-connected disability.

Another eligibility requirement is that a disability *cannot* have been brought about through the veteran's willful misconduct, which "involves deliberate or intentional wrongdoing with knowledge of or wanton and reckless disregard of its probable consequences." Common forms of willful misconduct that can preclude disability benefits include alcoholism, drug addiction, venereal diseases, and suicide.

b. Nonveterans

Surviving spouses, children, and parents of veterans are also eligible for benefits.

A "surviving spouse" is a person of the opposite sex who, at the time of the veteran's death, was the veteran's spouse in a valid marriage, and had lived continuously with the veteran from the date of marriage to the date of death. An exception to the continuous living requirement exists if the veteran obtained or caused a marital separation. (Remarriage by the surviving spouse precludes eligibility.)

A "child" is a person who is unmarried, and (1) under 18 years of age, or (2) before reaching the age of 18 years has become permanently incapable of self-support, or (3) is pursuing a course of instruction at an approved educational institution (up until the age of 23). The child may be a stepchild, legally adopted, or illegitimate.

A "parent" is a natural or adoptive mother or father, or someone who "stood in the relationship of a parent to a veteran at any time before his or her entry into active service."

§ 13.3 Benefits

Veterans are eligible for disability benefits, which are referred to as "compensation" arising from a service-connected disability or death. Compensation benefits amount to over ten billion dollars annually. Nonservice-connected disability benefits are called "pensions." A veteran cannot concurrently receive both compensation and a pension even if eligible for both. Compensation and pensions are also available to spouses and dependents of deceased veterans.

a. *Compensation*

Veterans who served either in war or peace are entitled to disability compensation if: (1) they were discharged under conditions other than dishonorable, (2) their disability was incurred in the line of duty, and (3) the disability is not a result of their own willful misconduct.

To obtain compensation for a disability, a veteran must have incurred the disability "in the line of duty." The line of duty is bracketed by one's entry into and exit from military service. Any disability incurred or aggravated during that time frame is compensable. A veteran whose knee is injured in a softball game while in the service is just as eligible for disability compensation as a veteran whose knee is injured in combat.

There are five primary ways to establish that a disability is service-connected.

First, a service connection exists if the condition was incurred or aggravated co-incident with the veteran's service. A current disability can be considered service-connected back, i.e. an in-service disability, if the current disability was chronic, or if the symptoms caused by the original disability were consistently recurrent (known as "continuity of symptomatology").

Second, a condition that preexisted the veteran's service, that was aggravated during service, is considered to have a service connection. However, the increase in disability must be something that is beyond the natural progression of the condition, and the aggravation must be more than just a temporary worsening of symptoms.

Third, because the law presumes that veterans entered the service in sound condition, there is a presumption of a service connection for certain conditions that were not manifested during service. For example, if the veteran served in Vietnam, certain tropical diseases such as dysentery, malaria and yellow fever are considered to be service related even if there is a lack of evidence that establishes that they were incurred while the veteran was in service.

Fourth, a service connection is established if the disability is a secondary result of another service-oriented condition.

Finally, a service connection is established if the disabling condition was a consequence of any VA-provided health care. For claims arising after September 1, 1997, there must be proof of VA fault or negligence in the provision of care.

Once the service connection is established, compensation benefits are paid according to the individual level of disability. The VA employs a disability percentile schedule to determine a veteran's level, from zero, or no disability, to 100%, or total disability. (The schedule of disability percentages measures the impairment of a veteran's average earning capacity.) The schedule is divided into increments of 10%, with the monthly benefit increasing as the percentage increases. In 2006 the disability payments ranged from $112 per month to $2,393 per month. Higher benefits are paid for listed anatomical losses. (Amounts are adjusted periodically by Congressional action.)

Eligible spouses and dependents of a veteran who has a disability of at least 30% are eligible for additional compensation benefits. Similarly, veterans with extreme disabilities, including those who are housebound, or who need regular aid and assistance, are eligible for supplemental benefits. These payments are collectively known as Special Monthly Compensation (SMC).

A finding of total disability results if, according to the ratings schedule, the veteran is 100% disabled. Alternatively, the veteran may be classified as having individual unemployability (IU). Whereas the schedule of disability rating percentage is an objective measure, IU is a subjective one. A veteran is considered IU if unemployable even though an average person with the same disability would still be able to secure gainful employment. To that end, IU takes into account subjective personal circumstances such as education and prior employment history. The VA, however, may not consider the veteran's age or nonservice-connected conditions when attempting to determine eligibility for IU benefits.

To qualify for IU status, the individual veteran must have at least a 60% disability, or if the veteran has two or more disabilities, the combined rating must be 70% or more. Due to the inherently subjective manner of IU determination, as well as cost considerations, the VA is reluctant to recognize total disability arising from IU.

Spouses, dependent children, and parents are also eligible for compensation benefits if a veteran's death was service connected. The two main benefits programs are Death Compensation and Dependency and Indemnity Compensation (DIC). A third program, the Restored Entitlement Program of Survivors (REPS) may also provide assistance.

Dependency and Indemnity Compensation (DIC) provides benefits to survivors of veterans whose service-related deaths occurred after January 1, 1957. DIC also is payable to survivors of a veteran whose death was not service-connected if at the time of death the veteran had been rated 100% disabled for at least ten years due to a service-connected condition. Compensation amounts under DIC are based on the highest pay grade attained by the veteran while in service.

The Restored Entitlement Program (REPS) is a Social Security program created to restore Social Security benefits that had been cut in 1981 to survivors of veterans whose service-connected death occurred before August 13, 1981. REPS payments are offset by Social Security payments on a dollar-for-dollar basis.

b. *Pensions*

Compensation is based almost solely on a service-connected disability or death. In contrast, veterans' pensions are based on need and are designed to supplement the income of disabled veterans. Though pension benefits are lower than compensation benefits, eligibility does not depend on the disability being service-connected.

There are significant eligibility restrictions for pensions.

First, the veteran must be discharged or released under other than dishonorable conditions. Second, the veteran must meet active service requirements. That is, the veteran must have: (1) served for 90 days or more during one or more periods of war, or (2) served for 90 days or more, and at least one of those days was during a period of war; or (3) served for any length of time in a period of war and gotten released or discharged due to a service-connected disability. Third, the veteran must have minimum income. Fourth, the veteran must be permanently and totally disabled. Fifth, the disability must not be a result of the veteran's willful misconduct.

Three different pension programs exist: Old–Law Pension, Section 306 Pension, and the Improved Pension program.

The Old–Law Pension applies to veterans who became eligible prior to July 1, 1960. A key provision of Old–Law Pension is that it does not count the income of the veteran's spouse. Today, however, no one may apply for Old–Law Pension benefits and those receiving them may elect to switch over to the Improved Pension program (see below).

The Section 306 Pension program covers veterans who served from July 1, 1960 to December 31, 1978.

It also does not count the income of the veteran's spouse, but it does count unearned income such as Social Security. Again, no veteran or survivor may apply for these benefits today, and a Section 306 beneficiary may elect to switch to Improved Pension benefits.

The Improved Pension program became effective on January 1, 1979 and is open to new applicants. In determining eligibility Improved Pension counts all kinds of income, including that of the veteran's spouse. To be eligible for the Improved Pension program the veteran must be disabled and financially needy.

Because the pension programs are need-based, the VA requires all applicants and recipients to file annual Eligibility Verification Reports (EVRs). An EVR reports the previous year's income and anticipates the current year's. Both net worth and income are considered when determining pension eligibility. The VA establishes a Maximum Annual Pension Rate (MAPR) that is used to determine the threshold of countable income. If a claimant's countable income exceeds the MAPR, pension benefits are denied.

To be eligible, veterans under age 55 must be totally disabled. Total disability, as with compensation benefits, is measured by the percentile schedule or by individual unemployability.

Veterans age 55 and older must have the following disability ratings: veterans aged 55 to 59 with two or more disabilities must have the combined ratings of 60%. Veterans over age 60 must have a 50% combined rating for two or more disabilities. Veterans who meet these requirements, and who can prove that consequently they cannot obtain substantial gainful employment, meet the total disability requirement.

Prior to the 1990 Budget Act, veterans age 65 and over were presumed to be permanently and totally disabled. That is no longer the case. For all claims for Improved Pension filed after October 31, 1990, the presumption is inapplicable, and the disability must be proved.

Surviving spouses and dependent children are also eligible for pension benefits under rules similar to those governing the Improved Pension program. This pension program is comparable to the DIC program. Though survivors do not have to be disabled, the maximum income rate for survivors is much lower than the rate for veterans. Survivors whose income exceeds the maximum rate can reapply for death pension benefits should their income later decrease.

c. *Other Benefits*

Veterans and certain of their family members are entitled to burial in a national cemetery. Government headstones or grave markers are also available. In addition, if a veteran's death was the result of a service-connected disability or if the veteran died while on active duty, an allowance up to $2,000 for burial expenses is provided, plus a limited reimbursement for associated expenses. Veterans who were receiving compensation or pension benefits and who die from a nonservice-connected disability are entitled to a burial allowance of up to $300, a $300 plot internment allowance plus $55 for transportation.

Veterans are not automatically eligible for hospital care. The VA is required only to furnish medical care for veterans with a service-connected disability, for veterans who are entitled to disability compensation, for former prisoners of war, for veterans exposed to a toxic substance or radiation, and for veterans of the Mexican border period or World War I.

Veterans with nonservice-connected disabilities are eligible for VA medical assistance only if they are unable to afford medical care. A VA determination that a veteran is unable to pay for medical care must be based on a finding that the veteran is eligible to receive medical assistance, that the veteran is receiving pension benefits, or that the veteran's attributable income is below the income guidelines. Veterans with nonservice-connected disabilities and those with incomes higher than the threshold described above "may" receive care at VA hospitals or nursing homes depending on the availability of resources and facilities.

The VA is also authorized, under certain conditions, to provide disabled veterans with automobiles and adaptive equipment, trained guide dogs for the visually impaired, or prosthetic devices and rehabilitative aids.

§ 13.4   VA Procedures

a.   Filing a Claim

A veteran considering filing a claim with the VA for benefits should file it as early as possible, since payment of benefits begins from the time the claim is filed. There is no penalty for filing a frivolous claim, and a claimant will not be sanctioned even if the claim had no merit.

A veteran need not file a formal claim in order to ensure the earliest possible payment. If the veteran writes a letter to one of the 58 VA regional offices (VAROs) notifying them of an intent to file a claim for benefits, the payment date is set. The letter need not be specific, so long as it identifies the type of benefit sought. Of course, because a letter is only an interim claim, a formal claim must then be filed, but by using an informal application a veteran can effectively lock in the earliest possible payment date.

The VA makes a distinction between "original" and "reopened" claims. Whenever a claim is formally filed for the first time, it is considered an original claim. There can be only one original claim for each claimant. Any subsequent claims are considered to be "reopened," and no formal application is required. Once a veteran files an original claim using VA Form 21–526, Veteran's Application for Compensation or Pension, the veteran may notify the VA of any subsequent claims simply by writing a letter.

Under the Veterans' Judicial Review Act of 1988 (VJRA), the VA has a duty to assist claimants in preparing evidence for their claims. The U.S. Court of Veterans' Appeals (CVA) has interpreted the assistance to include, minimally, the duty to search and produce records and to conduct medical examinations.

All original claims are processed through one of the 58 VAROs. Those offices make the initial decision to award or deny claims, and are thus known as agencies of original jurisdiction. A VA medical facility may also be the agency of original jurisdiction if it makes a decision concerning a claimant's eligibility for care. If the VARO requires more evidence or other information, the claimant generally has 60 days to produce it. If the 60 days expire without compliance by the claimant, the claim will be disallowed. If the VARO denies the applicant's claim, it must provide a written explanation containing the reasons for the denial, a summary of evidence considered, and the claimant's appeal rights.

The first step in appealing VARO denial is to file a Notice of Disagreement (NOD) at the VA office that notified the claimant of the adverse decision. There is a one-year deadline for filing a NOD, which begins from the mailing date of the VARO explanation.

Once a NOD is filed, the VARO issues a Statement of the Case (SOC). The SOC is designed to provide the claimant with an understanding of the

VARO's decision, and includes specific information concerning the evidence, laws, and rationale behind the decision. The claimant, after receiving the SOC, has 60 days or the remainder of the one-year deadline from the mailing of the VARO decision, whichever period ends later, to file a VA Form I–9, a Substantive Appeal. This is also known as a formal appeal, which serves three purposes. First, it transfers jurisdiction from the VARO to the Board of Veterans' Appeals (BVA). Second, because the Substantive Appeal is mandatory, it puts the VA on notice as to the claimant's specific appellate arguments. Third, a Substantive Appeal will inform the BVA whether the claimant desires a BVA-level hearing, and the location of such a hearing.

There is a 60–day filing deadline starting from the date of the mailing of the SOC for filing a formal appeal. In contested claims, the deadline is 30 days from the date that the SOC is mailed.

b. Board of Veterans Appeals (BVA)

After the filing of a Substantive Appeal with the VARO, the case must be transferred to the BVA. The BVA, which is completely independent of the Veteran's Benefits Administration, is comprised of 67 members, headed by a chairperson. The 66 members (excluding the chairperson) are divided into 22 three-member panels, each of which is called a section. Decisional review of the agency of original jurisdiction is de novo and does not require any deference to the VARO's decision.

The most common type of BVA review is based solely on the written record. A claimant, however, may request a personal hearing before the BVA. There are three separate hearing possibilities at the BVA level. A BVA field hearing is held before a VARO hearing officer (HO). Only if the HO determines that new and material evidence exists, can the VARO's decision be changed. Otherwise, the record from this field hearing is sent to a BVA panel for later view. Another choice is a BVA hearing in Washington, D.C. before one of the three-member sections. This is known as a formal hearing, and it is uncommon, due to travel costs and time considerations. Finally, a claimant may request a hearing before a traveling section of the BVA. The traveling panel consists of three BVA members from separate sections, plus an attorney, but the number of such traveling panels is severely limited.

For appeals certified and transferred to the BVA after June 14, 1990, there is a 90–day deadline to submit new evidence, request a personal hearing, or change counsel. The time limit begins to run from the date of the mailing of the VARO's notification that the appeal has been certified. Extensions of the deadline for good cause are allowed.

After the BVA makes its final decision, the adversely affected claimant has three options. A claimant may file a motion for reconsideration by the BVA. There is no time limit for submission of such a motion. Second, a claimant may reopen the claim at the VARO due to the introduction of new and material evidence, or because the BVA's denial was the product of error. Again, there is no time limit for reopening a claim. Finally, under the provisions in the VJRA, a claimant may appeal a BVA decision to the Court of Veterans' Appeals (CVA).

An adversely affected claimant has 120 days from the date of the BVA decision to file an appeal with the Court of Veterans Appeals. Only a final BVA decision may be appealed. If for example, the BVA remands a case to the VARO, it is not considered final, and the claimant must wait until the case is brought before the BVA again. Also, only BVA decisions decided after November 18, 1988 (the date of the VJRA's enactment) are appealable.

Final CVA decisions can be appealed to the Federal circuit courts within 60 days of the decision. If an adverse Federal circuit decision is handed down, a claimant may petition the United States Supreme Court to hear the case.

CHAPTER 14

PENSION PLANS

As noted in Chapter 11, Social Security is the foundation of most retirees' financial security, as it provides benefits to more than nine out of ten retirees. But it was never intended to be the sole source of such financial well-being, only a basic standard. A common metaphor for retirement financing is the three-legged stool, one of whose legs is the Social Security system—a nearly universal leg, in fact. A second leg is a person's individual investment assets, be they stocks, bonds, mutual funds, bank certificates of deposit, savings accounts, investment real estate, and the like. The third leg in this metaphor is an employer-based pension plan. Such plans typically are part of an employee's compensation package and presently cover almost half of all retirees. These plans are the focus of this Chapter.

§ 14.1   Scope of Pension Plan Coverage

The Federal tax code affirmatively encourages the creation of pension plans by permitting employers to deduct their payments to the pension plans in the year made. Employees, by contrast, do not report any income from this employee benefit until they retire and actually receive income from the plan. By then, presumably, an employee is in a lower tax bracket because he or she is no longer employed. But the point remains that a sum paid into a pension plan can grow much faster than a comparable sum paid as additional wages, since wages are taxed before they are invested. In addition, the investment income that accumulates in a pension plan during the employee's employment is not taxed to the employee, until it is actually distributed to that person or to some designated beneficiary, another major tax benefit. Also, the pension plan itself is exempt from tax, thereby enabling the investment income that it receives to compound without diminution by current taxation. As a consequence of these provisions, employer-provided pensions are an unusually attractive component of the compensation package, both for employers and for employees.

Nevertheless, pension coverage of employees is far short of universal, having hovered around 50% for several decades. Employer-provided pensions are more often found in manufacturing industries than in retail or service-oriented businesses. Larger employers are more typical providers, as are unionized companies. These categories are not mutually exclusive, of course, but the plain import is that pension coverage is less typical in those sectors of the U.S. economy that seem to be growing the fastest—namely, smaller employers, in nonunionized settings, engaged in retail and service businesses. The principal exception is public sector employment, which is generally growing *and* typically provides pension coverage. Still, for the current generation of retirees, pension coverage is still the rule, if only barely so.

Finally, it should be noted that any given retiree may be covered by several pension plans, depending upon his or her work history. As long as a retiree spent at least five years with an employer offering a pension plan, Federal law requires that the plan cover that retiree. The benefits will, of course, reflect the term of that employment, but at least some coverage must be provided for each such employee, who is thereby said to be "vested" in the plan. Thus, if Janet worked for three different employers for ten years each, she would be entitled to benefits under three pension plans, even though she will not actually collect any benefits until she reaches the plans' "normal retirement age," which generally is 65 years.

§ 14.2   Defined Benefit Plans

The older of the two basic types of pension plan is the "defined benefit plan." Such a plan defines what *benefits* an employee will receive upon retirement, usually in the form of a series of monthly payments that lasts until that employee's death. This series of payments is called an "annuity" and serves as a promise that the employee, once retired, will not outlive the pension, since the payments continue as long as the retiree is alive. In many cases, payments will be paid even after a retired employee's death to that person's spouse until his or her death, but at a minimum, pension payments continue throughout the lifetime of the retired person.

The amount of the payment itself is typically a function of several factors. The most common factors are years of service with the employer, the employee's age at retirement, and some salary base. The salary base might be the average of the most recent three or five years, might include overtime or bonuses, and might consider accrued vacation pay or unused sick leave. The range of possible formulae is endless, but most such plans try to reward employees with lengthier periods of service and often those with higher earnings as well. This last feature attempts to compensate for the proportionately lower payments that middle and upper income employees receive through the Social Security system's benefit calculation methodology. See generally § 11.3. The emphasis on employment longevity—usually expressed as increasing percentages of the salary base depending upon years of service—accords with an employer's desire to use pension plans to reduce staff turnover and to help retain experienced personnel.

Be that as it may, defined benefit plans promise specified benefit levels that are geared to an individual employee's work history. The benefits do *not* depend upon the amount that the employer puts into the plan or the investment success or failure of the plan itself. If a pension plan prospers, any individual employee's benefits are usually not augmented. Similarly, if a plan's investments do poorly, the employee's benefits remain intact. Of course, in this latter situation, the employer may be called upon to put additional funds into the pension plan to compensate for the investment shortfall, but that is where the risk of investment failure resides in a defined benefit plan—on the employ*er*.

If an employer is unable to make up the shortfall, the retiree's benefits are protected by a Federal agency. This agency is charged with ensuring the payment of defined benefit plan pensions: the Pension Benefit Guaranty Corporation, or PBGC. Similar to the Federal agencies that ensure deposits at financial institutions, the PBGC collects premiums from pension plans to enable it to cover shortfalls that the originating employers are unable to rectify.

Employees enrolled in defined benefit plans are not totally without risk, however. First, the benefit level protected by the PBGC is not unlimited. Rather, the protection applies to a monthly benefit of no more than an annually adjusted figure. In 2006, that limit was $3,971.58. Any promised benefit above this limit is not covered by the PBGC.

Second, some defined benefit plans are not covered by the PBGC, because the sponsoring employer was exempt from the PBGC and its originating legislation, the Employee Retirement Income Security Act (ERISA). Among the most prominent employers excluded from ERISA are governments at all levels and church-based employers that do not choose to be included. The Federal government, of course, may ultimately be able to print its way out of any shortfall, but the other excluded employers have no such option. In fact, many of the most severely underfunded defined benefit plans are run by state and local governmental units.

Absent this default risk, an individual employee's benefit level is readily determinable. There are no segregated accounts for individual employees, but their work history and other factors can be easily determined, and the benefit formula can then be applied. Deferring retirement may add additional high wage years to the salary base, as well as additional years of service. It also reduces the number of years over which benefits are paid and the possible erosion of those benefits due to inflation— an important consideration since most defined benefit plan benefits do not adjust their payouts for post-retirement inflation. But the point remains that a prospective retiree's pension benefit is not directly linked to a pension plan's assets when the plan is a "defined benefit" plan.

§ 14.3 Defined Contribution Plans

The second general type of pension plan is a "defined contribution plan." Such plans define the amount of an employer's *contribution* to an employee's pension plan, but make no promises about what level of benefits that contribution will eventually provide. Instead, each employee has an "account" that includes the employer's payments into the plan, plus the investment earnings generated by those payments. Under some plans, employees can add to their accounts, sometimes on a tax-deductible basis, but sometimes not. In either circumstance, the amount designated for any individual employee is set aside in a segregated account, and the value of that account can be calculated at any point in time. The actual pension benefits that will be paid to the employee, however, cannot be determined until that employee retires and chooses to "annuitize" the account; that is, until the account balance is transformed into a series of lifetime monthly payments.

The amount of those monthly payments, moreover, is largely a function of the investment success or failure of the individual retiree's account. There is no guarantee as to any minimum level of benefits, and the PBGC plays no role in ensuring the value of the benefits to be received. Indeed, the amount in the account may actually fall below the amount of the original contributions if the investment performance of the account has been negative overall. Correspondingly, if the account in a defined contribution plan shows great investment success, there is no limit or ceiling on the amount of the pension benefits that can be obtained. But the point remains that the risk of investment failure in such plans resides with the *employee*, and not the employer. It is largely for this reason that defined contribution plans have become increasingly more common and today represent the overwhelming majority of new pension plans being created, especially among smaller employers.

As to the employer's contributions to such plans, the amount is generally some percentage of an employee's salary. Better-paid employees, therefore, have larger sums set aside on their behalf in such plans. As one's salary increases, moreover, the amount contributed by the employer usually increases as well.

How those funds are invested varies with the specific plan. Sometimes, an employer offers an employee a choice of two or more investment pools or funds, each specializing in some specific investment medium, such as stocks, bonds, money market instruments, overseas investments, or fixed-rate contracts called "guaranteed investment contracts." An employee then chooses how to invest the employer's defined contribution that was made on his or her behalf. Different plans have different rules about allocating one's account among various investment options and about switching among those options, including minimum amounts required and limits on the frequency of such switches. The range of choices available also varies considerably from one employer to another. But the bottom line is the same—the defined contribution plan format represents a major shifting of responsibility for one's financial well-being in retirement to employees.

§ 14.4 Distribution Options

When a worker retires, one of the most significant decisions that he or she must make involves how to receive the pension benefits that have accrued. One option is to take the entire account in one payment, a so-called "lump sum distribution." In a defined contribution plan, this is simply the value of the employee's account. Defined benefit plans also have this option, but the calculation of the lump sum distribution is less straightforward and is usually set forth in the plan's descriptive contract or other formal agreement. For many retirees, a lump sum distribution represents the largest pool of investable resources that they have ever encountered in their lives. Some will use such distributions to start new businesses, pay medical bills, or for some other purpose. Moreover, lump sum distributions are generally taxable upon receipt. See § 14.7.

The more commonly selected option for pension plan distributions, however, is an annuity—a series of monthly payments that lasts for a specified period. This period may be expressed in a number of years as an "annuity for a term certain," a fixed-term annuity. Alternatively, the period can extend until the death of the payee, a "single life annuity." This option usually produces less income each month than a fixed-term annuity, because the annuity payor assumes the risk that the particular payee might live longer than the average life expectancy at his or her age. On the other hand, a lifetime annuity provides the retiree with the security that he or she will receive a monthly pension check as long as that person is alive. This proposition assumes, of course, that the annuity payor itself remains solvent—*generally* a fairly safe assumption.

Another option is the "joint and survivor annuity," an arrangement for monthly payments to continue over *two* lives. That is, a payment is made monthly for the duration of the retiree's life and then continues for the duration of a designated survivor's life, generally that of the retiree's spouse. Because this period is usually longer than just one life, the monthly payment under a "joint and survivor" annuity will be less than under a single life annuity. On the other hand, the retiree has the satisfaction of knowing that the monthly payments will continue to support his or her spouse after the retiree's death.

In certain circumstances, however, a married retiree might prefer the larger payments that are available under a single life annuity. For example, the retiree's spouse might already have sufficient financial resources, perhaps even an employer-provided pension plan in his or her own right. Or, the spouse's health history may make it unlikely that he or she will outlive the retiree. There is little reason, in those situations, to accept the lower payments that joint and survivor annuities entail.

An example will illustrate the choices presented. Assume that Wayne's pension plan entitles him to $50,000 per year, or $4,167 per month, as a 65–year old retiree. If he wants the payments to continue over the remaining life of his 60–year old wife, Loretta, the monthly payment drops to $3,335. Note that this lower payment takes effect at the start of the annuity. In other words, Wayne gives up $832 per month ($4,167 − $3,335) throughout *his* lifetime, in exchange for the $3,335 monthly payment's continuing after his death as long as Loretta is alive.

An intermediate option is a "joint and 50% survivor annuity." This option offers initially higher payments than a customary "joint and survivor" annuity, because the payments decrease by 50%—rather than remain undiminished—after the death of the first annuitant. Under the preceding facts, Wayne would receive $3,705 per month under this option, and Loretta would get $1,853 (half of $3,705) after Wayne's death. A much younger spouse would affect these computations more significantly.

In any case, the statute requires most pension plans to pay out benefits of married employees as joint and survivor annuities, with the survivor's portion being at least 50%. A single life annuity may be elected only if the retiree and his or her spouse agree in writing to a waiver of spousal rights.

§ 14.5   Income Taxation of Periodic Pension Payments

When pension payments are made over a period of time, the retiree reports their receipt as income as they are received. In effect, the pension acts as a salary substitute and is subject to Federal—and usually state—income tax in the same manner as salary income, complete with periodic withholding of taxes from each payment. Deferral of this compensation from a person's earning years to one's retirement period usually has the benefit of a lower tax bracket in retirement than would have been the case during the employee's working years. That downshift in tax brackets does not always happen, especially if tax rates are raised generally as one reaches retirement. In any case, the mere deferral of tax—even at the same tax rate or bracket—is a significant economic benefit, particularly when the period of deferral is 20 years or more. But the point remains that pension payments are taxed when they are received.

This tax treatment also applies, incidentally, to other sorts of tax-favored retirement savings mechanisms; e.g., Keogh plans for self-employed individuals, so-called "tax sheltered annuities" under I.R.C. § 403(b), tax-deferred accounts under I.R.C. § 401(k), and pre-tax (i.e., deductible) individual retirement accounts (IRA). It does not apply, however, to Roth IRAs, which first became available in 1998, or to "Roth contributions" to § 401(k) and § 403(b) plans, which first became an option in 2006. Withdrawals from these accounts are usually tax-free if the funds have been in the accounts at least five years. I.R.C. § 408A, § 402A. Most current retirees do not have Roth accounts, but these accounts will become more relevant over time as current employees retire.

Some retirees may "convert" their regular IRAs into Roth IRAs to obtain the latter's tax-free treatment. Such conversions, it should be noted, trigger immediate taxation of the regular IRA's *entire* balance. To convert a regular IRA into a Roth IRA, a taxpayer (whether single or married) cannot have adjusted gross income (AGI) of more than $100,000 in the year of conversion, not counting the IRA balance being converted. This $100,000 AGI threshold does not apply, however, after 2009.

In some pension plans, employees make after-tax contributions. That is, some employee contributions to defined contribution plans are made from funds that were subjected to tax when the funds were earned. When payments are received from such plans, the investment earnings on those contributions are taxable, but not the contributions themselves. Accordingly, it becomes necessary to split these payments into two components: investment profit, which is taxable, and recovery of the taxpayer's capital ("basis"), which is tax-free.

This bifurcation is accomplished by dividing the after-tax contributions ("investment in the contract") by a factor to determine the amount of each monthly payment that is received tax-free. The remainder of each payment is taxable. The factor itself is derived from the following table, which is based upon the age of the recipient when the payment period begins:

Age	Factor
Under 56	360
56–60	310
61–65	260
66–70	210
Over 70	160

I.R.C. § 72(d)(1)(B)(iii). For example, assume that Jessica is 65 years old and annuitizes her pension when her after-tax contributions are $52,000. The insurance company or other payor determines that she can receive $6,000 per year (actually $500 per month) for the rest of her life. She divides her $52,000 of after-tax contributions by the table factor for age 65, namely 260, and derives $200 as the result. This is the amount that Jessica can exclude from taxation each month, so she pays tax only on the remaining $300 ($500 monthly payment − $200 excluded).

Once a person recovers all of his or her basis, subsequent payments are taxable in full. I.R.C. § 72(b)(2). So, after Jessica in this example receives her 260th monthly payment, she will have recovered her entire "investment in the contract" tax-free ($200 per payment × 260 payments = $52,000). Thereafter, she is taxable on the entire $500 she receives each month.

On the other hand, if a person dies before recovering all of his or her basis, the unrecovered amount is deductible on that person's final income tax return. I.R.C. § 72(b)(3). Assume, for example, that Jessica in the preceding example died at age 83 after receiving 216 monthly payments (age 83 − age 65 = 18 years × 12 months per year). As a result, she recovered $43,200 tax-free ($200 excluded each month × 216 monthly payments). Since her "investment in the contract" was $52,000, she may deduct $8,800 ($52,000 − $43,200) on her final tax return.

To address this situation from a nontax perspective, some insurers and other annuity payors offer a refund feature. The variations that insurance companies can create are endless, but refund features generally return the portion of an employee's contributions that was not paid out before that person died. While these refunds reduce the amount that would otherwise be deductible, a refund is worth more than a tax deduction.

In lieu of a refund arrangement, some retirees arrange for benefits to be paid to a designated beneficiary after they die. Such "joint and survivor" annuities make monthly payments as long as *either* the retiree or the named beneficiary is alive. The taxation of these arrangements employs the same methodology described above but utilizes a different table, one that is based on the *combined* ages of the two recipients, as follows:

Combined Ages	Factor
Under 111	410
111–120	360
121–130	310
131–140	260
Over 140	210

To illustrate, assume that Jessica from the preceding example provides that her annuity be paid after her death to her son, Peter, who is 40 years old when Jessica's annuity starts. Accordingly, her "investment in the contract" (namely, $52,000) is divided by a table factor of 410, reflecting the combined ages of Jessica (65) and Peter (40), or 105. As a result, $126.83 of each monthly payment is received tax-free, and the remaining $373.17 ($500 received − $126.83 excluded) is taxable.

This table-based methodology—whether for single or joint lives—does not apply in two circumstances. First, if the annuity provides for a fixed number of payments, the "investment in the contract" is simply divided by that number. So, if Jessica's annuity called for 300 payments of $500 each, her $52,000 "investment in the contract" would be spread ratably over this 300–month period. Thus, $173.33 ($52,000 divided by 300 months) would be tax-free, and the remaining $326.67 ($500 received − $173.33 excluded) would be taxable.

Second, the table-based methodology does not apply if the primary annuitant (Jessica, in the preceding examples) is 75 years old or older when the annuity starts. In that circumstance, the life expectancy methodology that applies to annuities generally (i.e., not associated with pension plans) will determine how the monthly payments are split into their tax-free and taxable components. See I.R.C. § 72(b)(1), (c)(3)(A). But if the annuity provides fewer than five years of guaranteed payments, the table-based methodology will apply, regardless of the primary annuitant's age.

§ 14.6 Special Penalty Taxes on Periodic Payments

As noted in § 14.1, pension plans are favored with unusually attractive Federal tax treatment. The flip side of this treatment, however, is a multitude of restrictions that attempt to ensure that the Federal tax code's largess is used as Congress intended—namely, to encourage employment-based savings for an employee's retirement. Most of these restrictions and limitations affect the *employer's* side of pension plans and therefore need not be discussed in this volume. But there are two major limitations on pension plan distributions, enforced by substantial tax penalties, that affect pension plan *recipients* and their pension benefit planning. Basically, these penalties apply to pension benefits that are received too soon or too late.

a. *Premature Distributions*

The first of these penalties ensures that pension plans are used primarily to save for retirement. This goal is achieved by imposing a 10% excise tax on distributions received before an individual is 59½ years old. I.R.C. § 72(t)(1), (2)(A)(i). This penalty is imposed in addition to taxing the distribution itself.

To illustrate, assume that Margie takes $10,000 out of her Keogh self-employment plan account, individual retirement account, tax-sheltered annuity, or some other tax-favored retirement savings vehicle. She will owe her regular income tax (Federal tax of, say, $2,500 + state tax of, say $600 = $3,100), plus a $1,000 excise tax ($10,000 × 10%), for a total tax of $4,100 ($3,100 + $1,000) out of the $10,000.

Note that the excise tax is payable only on the portion of the withdrawal that is subject to tax. So, to the extent that a withdrawal represents a return of contributions made on an after-tax basis (i.e., no deduction was allowed), that portion is not taxable, nor subject to the 10% penalty. Accordingly, a distribution from a Roth IRA is tax-free to the extent of such contributions. Moreover, a Roth IRA distribution is treated as coming first from these after-tax contributions. I.R.C. § 408A(d)(1)(B).

A related wrinkle applies to persons with more than one regular (i.e., non-Roth) IRA. When a person withdraws funds from a regular IRA, all of that person's regular IRAs are combined and treated as a single IRA to determine how much of the withdrawal represents after-tax contributions. As a result, the amount that can be received free of tax—or penalty, for that matter—may be very different than if the specific IRA in question were being considered alone.

More generally, there are several exceptions that avoid the 10% penalty, even though the recipient is under age 59½. In these situations, the recipient still includes the withdrawal in his or her taxable income (except to the extent of contributions to a Roth IRA), but there is no 10% penalty.

The first such exception applies to distributions made after the death of an employee. I.R.C. § 72(t)(2)(A)(ii). Another exception covers recipients who are "disabled," meaning persons who are not able to "engage in any substantial gainful activity by reason of any medically determinable physical or mental impairment which can be expected to result in death or to be of long-continued and indefinite duration." I.R.C. § 72(m)(7). For these two exceptions, a distribution from a Roth IRA is also entirely tax-free, as long as the funds have been in the account at least five years.

A further exception applies to recipients who begin annuitization; i.e., persons who are collecting periodic payments over their life expectancies, including those using joint life expectancies with a designated beneficiary. I.R.C. § 72(t)(2)(A)(iv). Such persons, of course, receive relatively smaller amounts, because starting an annuity before age 59½ means using longer life expectancy figures and getting correspondingly smaller payments each month. But if a person is willing to accept this trade-off, the 10% penalty is not imposed.

Finally, the 10% penalty does not apply to distributions that do not exceed the amount of a person's medical expenses that would qualify as an income tax deduction (i.e., over 7.5% of that person's adjusted gross income), even though no deduction is actually claimed. I.R.C. § 72(t)(2)(B).

Two other exceptions apply only to distributions from pension plans *other than* IRAs. The first such exception covers a person who is at least 55 years old and has separated from the service of his or her employer, voluntarily or otherwise. I.R.C. § 72(t)(2)(A)(v). The other such exception applies to persons receiving payments pursuant to certain divorce-related court orders. I.R.C. § 72(t)(2)(C).

On the other hand, there are two exceptions that apply *only* to distributions from IRAs. The first such exception allows withdrawals of up to $10,000 over a lifetime, if the funds are used within 120 days of their withdrawal to purchase a "principal residence" by a "first-time homebuyer." I.R.C. § 72(t)(8). While most retirees would not fit this description, a child or even a grandchild of a retiree can qualify. Thus, Selma could withdraw $10,000 from her IRA to buy a condominium for her daughter, Beverly, as long as Beverly has not owned a principal residence during the preceding two years. This withdrawal is still taxable to Selma (unless it is from a Roth IRA), but the 10% penalty does not apply.

The other IRA-only exception covers withdrawals that are used to pay "higher education expenses," including tuition, room and board charges, fees, and books. I.R.C. § 72(t)(7). As with the homebuying exception, this provision can apply to expenses incurred by a retiree's child or grandchild. So, Selma in the preceding example could withdraw unlimited funds from her IRA to pay college costs that are incurred by either her daughter Beverly, or Beverly's daughter (i.e., Selma's granddaughter), Stephanie. This provision calls off the 10% penalty, but the withdrawal itself is still taxable—except to the extent of contributions to a Roth IRA.

b. Delayed Distributions

The second major penalty applies at the other end of retirement planning. In general, persons who are at least 70½ years must begin receiving pension payments, or they will be taxed on their failure to do so. Specifically, anyone who does not receive the "minimum required distribution" owes an excise tax of 50% of the difference between such distribution and the amount actually received, if any. I.R.C. § 4974(a). At an effective tax rate of 50%, the benefits of further deferral are largely lost. This 50% penalty can be waived by the Internal Revenue Service, if the retiree proves that the failure to make the "minimum required distribution" was due to "reasonable error" and is being rectified.

The "minimum required distribution" is an annuitized amount beginning on April 1 of the year after the year in which a person becomes 70½ years old. So, if Rick's 70th birthday is March 15, 2007, he became 70½ on September 15, 2007, and his annuitization must begin on April 1, 2008 at the latest. On the other hand, if his 70th birthday were November 1, 2007, he would not be 70½ until May 1, 2008, and his annuitization would not need to start until April 1, 2009.

Annuitization is not required, however, if a person is still working, regardless of that person's age. So, if Martha does not retire until she is 82 years old, no penalty will apply as long as her distributions start by April 1 of the year following her retirement. This delayed starting date is not available to persons with regular IRAs. Roth IRAs, on the other hand, are not subject to the 50% penalty, so they need not be annuitized while the account holder is alive. I.R.C. § 408A(c)(5).

The "minimum required distribution" is calculated by dividing the balance in the person's account at the preceding year-end by a factor derived from a special IRS table. This factor is based on the life expectancy for the taxpayer's age reached during the year the distribution is required. In part, this table follows:

Age	Factor	Age	Factor
70	27.4	83	16.3
71	26.5	84	15.5
72	25.6	85	14.8
73	24.7	86	14.1
74	23.8	87	13.4
75	22.9	88	12.7
76	22.0	89	12.0
77	21.2	90	11.4
78	20.3	91	10.8
79	19.5	92	10.2
80	18.7	93	9.6
81	17.9	94	9.1
82	17.1	95	8.6

To illustrate, assume that Sally's 70th birthday is September 1, 2007. She reaches age 70½, therefore, on March 1, 2008, and her first required distribution is for the year 2008, though it need not actually be taken until April 1 of the following year, 2009. In any case, during Sally's first distribution year (2008), she turns 71 years old, so she will use an age of 71 to find the applicable factor in the IRS table. According to this table, Sally's factor is 26.5, which is then divided into her account balance as of the preceding year-end, December 31, 2007. If that balance was, say $300,000, Sally's "minimum required distribution" for 2008 is $11,321. Thereafter, the "minimum required distribution" will be calculated by dividing the account's balance as of the preceding year-end by the applicable factor in the IRS table for a person with the age of the taxpayer in that year. So, in 2009, Sally will be 72 years old on her birthday that year, and the applicable factor from the IRS table therefore is 25.6.

There is one exception to the methodology just described that applies when a retiree has a spouse who is more than ten years younger. In that circumstance, the applicable factor is obtained from a table that is based on the joint life expectancies of the retiree and his or her spouse. Once that factor is determined, however, the mechanics are the same.

When the account holder dies, whoever succeeds to the account as the designated beneficiary has several choices. The typical option is to withdraw the entire balance in the account and pay taxes on that amount. Alternatively, the beneficiary can withdraw smaller amounts over a period of years to minimize the immediate tax liability and to continue the tax-deferred growth of the account in question. At a minimum, the beneficiary must withdraw an amount equal to the account balance divided by his or her own life expectancy, determined from the single life expectancy table that the IRS uses for annuities generally. This requirement applies to a designated beneficiary of a Roth IRA as well, even though those accounts were not subject to the minimum distribution rule while the account holder was alive.

If the sole beneficiary is the surviving spouse of the account holder, other alternatives exist as well. The surviving spouse may transfer the account balance into his or her own IRA and simply treat this amount as part of that person's IRA. Similarly, the surviving spouse can elect to treat the inherited IRA as his or her own IRA.

§ 14.7 Lump Sum Distributions

Under the provisions of many pension plans, a participating employee can receive a single payout of his or her entire interest in the plan. Such payouts are called "lump sum distributions" and can occur in a variety of circumstances. A participant may be leaving the employ of a particular employer and may want to sever all ties, emotional as well as financial, with that employer—particularly if the termination of the employment relationship was involuntary or was otherwise unpleasant. Alternatively, an employee might regard the investment options that are provided by the employer as too restricted. In that case, he or she may prefer to manage the investment of his or her funds directly, or through an investment advisor that is selected by, and is answerable to, that employee. In still other circumstances, an employee might need the funds currently to meet ongoing day-to-day expenses, without considering the less immediate demands of retirement planning.

Regardless of the originating reason, receipt of a lump sum distribution presents the recipient with an array of options. If a recipient simply uses the money for current consumption, it will be included in that person's income for tax purposes, thereby terminating the tax deferral conferred by the pension plan. Instead, a recipient might choose to extend the benefits of tax deferral by "rolling over" the funds into some other pension plan, typically an individual retirement account (IRA), within 60 days of receiving the lump sum distribution. As to "rollovers" generally, see § 14.8.

To the extent that a distribution is not "rolled over," some part of it—usually all—is taxable. An employee does, however, receive back his or her after-tax contributions free of any tax, but the rest is taxable. If larger distributions are included in a recipient's taxable income in the year of their receipt, the graduated income tax rate schedule will expose these distributions to the highest parts of that rate schedule. The result is often more tax being owed than if the funds had been received in a more regular fashion.

Taxpayers who were born before 1936 may use a one-time option called "forward averaging" to moderate the impact of the graduated rate schedule. This option provides that the tax on a lump sum distribution will be computed *as if* it were received over a period of ten years, thereby reducing the impact of a large distribution received in a single taxable year. But once this tax is so computed, it is payable in full in the year of receipt.

a. Eligibility for Forward Averaging

To be eligible for "forward averaging," several requirements must be met. First, the recipient must have participated in the pension plan that is making the distribution during at least five taxable years prior to the year of distribution. Time in a plan that transferred funds directly to the distributing plan counts towards fulfilling this five-year requirement.

Second, the distribution must represent the employee's entire interest in the pension plan. Moreover, if an employer has several "similar" plans, the distribution must cover the employee's interest in *all* such "similar" plans. For this purpose, pensions plans are treated as one category of "similar" plans, but profit-sharing and incentive-savings plans are a separate category. Stock bonus plans are considered still another separate category. Furthermore, if an employee receives more than one lump sum distribution during the taxable year, forward averaging must be applied to all such distributions received, even if they derive from pension plans that are not treated as "similar" plans for this purpose.

Third, the lump sum distribution must be paid within a single taxable year of the recipient. A lump sum distribution, in other words, need not actually be paid in a lump sum, strictly speaking. A calendar year recipient who receives half of his or her interest upon termination in May and the balance by year-end qualifies for forward averaging.

Finally, the election must cover the entire lump sum distribution. So, if part of a lump sum distribution was "rolled over" to an IRA, for example, forward averaging is not available for *any* part of that distribution.

b. *Mechanics of Forward Averaging*

If a person qualifies for forward averaging, that person will usually want to elect its provisions for three reasons. First, the forward averaging mechanism treats a lump sum distribution as if it were received in ten equal annual installments, thereby moderating the impact of the graduated tax rate structure. On the other hand, this methodology employs the tax rates of 1986, rather than the generally lower tax rates that apply today. As a result, forward averaging yields a lower tax than would otherwise obtain, but not as much lower as one might expect.

Second, the tax under this method is computed assuming that the recipient has no other income, whether that is true or not. In other words, forward averaging begins at the bottom of the graduated rate structure, a major advantage to recipients with other taxable income in the year of receipt.

And finally, a taxpayer may elect to apply a 20% "capital gain" rate to the portion of the lump sum distribution that is attributable to pre–1974 participation in the pension plan. Forward averaging then applies to the portion of the distribution that is attributable to post–1973 plan participation. A distribution is split into its pre–1974 and post–1973 components by comparing the number of years that an employee participated in the plan before 1974 to that person's total plan participation years.

Reduced to its essentials, forward averaging divides a lump sum distribution by ten, computes the tax on this one-tenth using the 1986 tax rates for unmarried taxpayers (available in the Instructions to current IRS Form 4972), and then multiplies this tax by ten to derive the tax due. This tax is then paid in the year of distribution, notwithstanding the assumption of a ten-year payout schedule in its calculation.

In any case, the one-tenth methodology is employed solely to determine the tax on the lump sum distribution. It is a computation separate and apart from the recipient's general tax computation. This separation ensures that the distribution does not create collateral tax consequences for the recipient based on an elevated level of income, such as the taxation of a person's Social Security benefits. See § 11.6 regarding the taxation of those benefits.

c. Enforcement By Withholding Taxes

Lump sum distributions that are not "rolled over" in their entirety are subject to income tax withholding. Trustees of qualified pension plans and tax sheltered annuities (but not IRAs), are required to withhold 20% of a lump sum distribution as prepaid income taxes. I.R.C. § 3405(c). This withholding mechanism does not make such a distribution taxable; it merely *collects* a potential tax. If a distribution is not taxable—say, because it was "rolled over" into an IRA within the requisite 60 days—then the taxes withheld are applied against the recipient's other tax liability, or may even be refunded.

On the other hand, no withholding is required if funds are transferred *directly* from one pension plan to another or to the recipient's IRA. The important point is having the recipient avoid possession of the funds. The Regulations provide that a check can be delivered to an employee without having taxes withheld, if the check is made payable solely to the new pension plan. There is also a de minimis rule that exempts distributions of less than $200 from the withholding requirement. Considering the ease with which major IRA operators can arrange direct trustee-to-trustee transfers, the withholding requirement usually presents few difficulties to recipients of lump sum distributions. Moreover, pension plan administrators must provide written notice to recipients of the options available to them, including the possibility of direct transfers between trustees, at least 30 days before a distribution is made.

If, however, funds are distributed to an employee, a major trap for the unwary is presented. Assume that Laura is scheduled to receive a lump sum distribution of $100,000 and that she has not authorized any direct rollover of funds to another pension plan. Accordingly, the disbursing plan's administrator will send $20,000 as withheld tax to the Internal Revenue Service on Laura's behalf and will remit the other $80,000 directly to her. If Laura does decide to establish an IRA and transfers the

$80,000 she received to that IRA within the required 60 days, that $80,000 will not be subject to tax. But the $20,000 that she never received and therefore did not put into her new IRA will be treated as a taxable distribution. Accordingly, she will owe Federal income tax and possibly state income tax on $20,000 of taxable income. And if Laura is not yet 59½ years old, she will also owe $2,000 of penalty tax ($20,000 × 10%) on the premature distribution of pension funds—subject, to be sure, to the usual exceptions applicable to this penalty. See § 14.6(a). The $20,000 that was already withheld should more than cover this tax liability, but for Laura to avoid being taxed on the $20,000, she would need to send $20,000 from other sources to her IRA, thereby funding it at the full $100,000. In contrast, a direct rollover of the entire $100,000 would have avoided this difficulty entirely.

d. *Employer Stock*

If a retirement account contains stock of a retiree's former employer, additional considerations apply to a lump sum distribution from that account. While the retiree can usually rollover this account into an IRA, as explained in § 14.8, the retiree might also be able to withdraw the securities and hold them thereafter as nonretirement assets. The tax benefits of taking the securities can be considerable, if they have appreciated in value since they were acquired.

To illustrate these options, assume that Nicole has employer stock worth $300,000 in her § 401(k) account that cost $30,000 when it was acquired by the retirement plan. If Nicole transfers this stock into an IRA, no tax is due at that time. When amounts are withdrawn from this account, however, they will be taxed at ordinary income rates, which can be as high as 35% (in 2006). I.R.C. § 72(a), § 408(d)(1). But if Nicole withdraws the stock from her § 401(k) plan, she will pay tax only on the stock's acquisition cost—$30,000 on these facts. I.R.C. § 402(e)(4). While this amount will be taxed as ordinary income, Nicole might be eligible to apply the "forward averaging" methodology explained in § 14.7(b). That methodology is not available to withdrawals from an IRA.

In any case, the real benefit of this approach is the tax on the unrealized appreciation—$270,000 in this case ($300,000 value of stock − $30,000 cost). This gain is taxed when Nicole sells the stock, but at the long-term capital gains tax rate, which generally is 15%. Moreover, this rate applies even if Nicole did not hold the stock long enough to otherwise qualify for the "long-term" rate. Treas. Reg. § 1.402(a)–1(b)(1)(i) (1994).

And if the stock appreciates after being distributed from the retirement account, that gain will also be taxed as capital gain—either short-term or long-term, as the case might be. Continuing with the previous example, assume that Nicole held her stock two years after receiving it from her § 401(k) account, and sold it for $375,000. The $75,000 of post-distribution gain ($375,000 sale price − $300,000 value when distributed) would be taxed as long-term capital gain. In contrast, if Nicole had rolled this stock into an IRA, *all* of her gain would be taxed as ordinary income.

If Nicole does not sell the stock before she dies, her decision to take the stock out of her retirement account has additional benefits for her heirs. Using the facts set forth above, the $270,000 of unrealized gain at the time the stock was distributed will be taxed as long-term capital gain, and the $75,000 of post-distribution gain will not be taxed at all, due to the step-up-in-basis rule. I.R.C. § 1014(a)(1). See § 10.2 regarding that rule. In contrast, if Nicole had rolled her stock into an IRA, her heirs would pay tax at ordinary income rates on *both* gains—the pre-distribution gain of $270,000 and the post-distribution gain of $75,000.

§ 14.8 Rollovers

Older people usually depend upon pension plan distributions to help finance their retirement living expenses, and accordingly apply such distributions to their current consumption needs. But sometimes, a particularly large pension distribution is not yet needed for such expenses, and reinvestment may be desired, particularly on a tax-deferred basis. To accomplish such reinvestment, pension plans generally permit direct transfers between plan trustees, which is clearly the most efficient way to "roll over" a pension distribution. If a distribution were made instead to the plan participant, 20% would be withheld as taxes, as described in § 14.7(c). Moreover, the distribution would itself be taxable to the extent that it is not "rolled over" into a new pension plan within 60 days of receipt of the distribution. I.R.C. § 402(c)(3). Direct plan-to-plan transfers, therefore, are clearly the pathway of choice to implement a rollover of one's retirement funds.

While "rollovers" are probably of greatest interest to older people in the context of lump sum distributions, they are not restricted to such distributions. Virtually any distribution can be rolled over to a new pension plan or an individual retirement account (IRA), as long as the particular plan in question is willing to accept such distributions. Many plans do not.

Certain distributions, however, are not eligible for tax-free rollovers. This category includes "minimum required distributions" for persons over age 70½. See § 14.6(b). After all, the rationale of the "minimum required distribution" rule is that the benefits of tax deferral have been obtained long enough, so further deferral via rollovers would not be appropriate. Also ineligible for rollovers are distributions that are part of a series of substantially equal annual payments that are being made over a fixed period of at least ten years, or over a person's life expectancy (or joint life expectancy, as the case may be). Finally, any distribution that is made on account of an employee's "hardship," as defined by the retirement plan, is ineligible for rollovers. I.R.C. § 402(c)(4)(C).

Ex-employees often have the option of leaving their pension accumulations with their former employers. This option automatically accomplishes the objective of continued tax deferral without further ado. On the other hand, ex-employees might not want any continuing financial tie to their former employers, particularly if their parting was less than happy. Moreover, the investment performance of an employer's plan, its financial soundness (if it is a defined benefit plan), or the range of investment options that it provides (if it is a defined contribution plan) might encourage a departing employee to take his or her funds elsewhere. In all of these cases, leaving one's distribution with the former employer might not be an appealing alternative.

If the employee obtains employment with a new company that offers a pension plan, that employee might want to roll over the distribution into the new employer's plan. This method also accomplishes the desired tax deferral, but it is subject to a similar array of investment-oriented considerations. Moreover, if the distribution from the former employer has already been received, 20% will have been withheld as taxes, and satisfaction of the 60–day rule for rollovers might be problematic. Older persons in particular often need more than 60 days to locate another job, so they may want to leave the funds with their former employer until new employment is obtained—if that option is permitted, of course.

Regarding lump sum distributions, there is a further consideration relating to the forward averaging methodologies described in § 14.7(b). Only lump sum distributions from "qualified plans" are eligible for forward averaging. "Qualified plans" include most pension and profit-sharing plans, salary deferral plans described in I.R.C. § 401(k), and tax-sheltered annuities described in I.R.C. § 403(b), *but not* IRAs. So, if a lump sum distribution is rolled over into an IRA, even in part, that distribution is thereafter ineligible for forward averaging. Instead, the entire distribution should be rolled over into a special IRA, sometimes called a "conduit IRA" or a "rollover IRA," and then rolled over at some later date into a "qualified plan." Following the steps of this tango will preserve the distribution's eligibility for forward averaging. Care must be taken, however, to prevent any other funds—from another qualified plan or from additional contributions—from being commingled in this rollover. Only if the rollover IRA is kept distinct from other investments, including other IRAs, will it be able to retain forward averaging as an option once it is rolled over into a new "qualified" pension plan.

CHAPTER 15

AGE DISCRIMINATION IN EMPLOYMENT

§ 15.1 History of the ADEA

The Age Discrimination in Employment Act (ADEA) was passed by Congress in 1967 to protect older Americans from discrimination in the workplace. The ADEA protects workers age 40 or over from being discriminated against on account of their age by an employer in hiring, discharging or in terms of compensation or the conditions of employment. Mandatory retirement on account of age (except for narrow exceptions) is barred by the ADEA. Although the ADEA has undergone significant changes over the years, its goal remains to "promote employment of older persons based on their ability rather than age; to prohibit arbitrary age discrimination in employment; [and] to help employers and workers find ways of meeting problems arising from the impact of age on employment." 29 U.S.C. § 621(b).

Since its initial passage, the ADEA has been amended several times. In 1974, federal, state, and local government employees were brought under the protection of the Act. In 1984, enforcement of the ADEA was transferred from the Department of

Labor to the Equal Employment Opportunity Commission (EEOC). Originally, the ADEA protected employees from age 40 to age 65, but a 1978 amendment raised the upper limit to age 70. The upper limit was removed in 1986, so that Act now protects workers age 40 or older. In 1990, the Older Workers Benefit Protection Act declared that an employer could not refuse to hire older workers due to the higher costs that might arise because of an employee benefit plan. Most recently, in 1996, the ADEA was amended to permit public employers to discriminate on the basis of age in the hiring and mandatory retirement of firefighters and law enforcement officers.

§ 15.2 Who is Protected?

The protections of the ADEA are applicable only to employers, including charitable or nonprofit, with 20 or more employees as well as states, local governments, and governmental agencies that employ 20 or more employees. (Employers with fewer than 20 employees may be subject to state anti-age discrimination laws.) The employer must have 20 or more employees for each working day of the week for 20 weeks (not necessarily consecutive) to meet the 20–employee requirement. Part-time employees, thus, will not be counted for determining whether the employer is covered by the ADEA. If, however, the employer is covered, then *all* employees including part-time and temporary employees are protected by the ADEA.

To determine whether an individual is an employee, the court looks at the facts and circumstances. Outside consultants or independent contractors are not employees. If there is doubt as to whether an individual is an employee or an independent contractor, the reality of the relationship, rather than the title, will govern. An individual is an employee if the employer can dictate the time, place and manner of employment, furnishes tools and equipment, and controls the individual job performance.

Under the ADEA, partners, directors, or owners of businesses are not considered to be "employees," and are not protected. While that is clear, the definition of partner is less certain. In *Caruso v. Peat, Marwick, Mitchell & Co.* (S.D.N.Y.1987), the defendant accounting firm labeled a number of its employees as partners. The court found, however, that many of the so-called "partners" were actually employees for purposes of an ADEA action. The so-called "partners" could not control or operate the business, engage in profit-sharing, and did not enjoy significant job security. Regardless of their title, the "partners" were held to be employees for purposes of application of the ADEA.

The 1974 amendment extended the ADEA to include federal, state and local government employees. The U.S. Supreme Court upheld the constitutionality of the amendment in the 1983 case of *EEOC v. Wyoming* (S.Ct.1983). The Court held that the amendment did not "directly impair" a state's ability to operate government and so did not violate the Tenth Amendment doctrine of state immunity.

The ADEA applies to the domestic U.S. operations of foreign employers and to U.S. citizens who work for American corporations in foreign countries.

In addition to conventional employers, both unions that maintain a hiring hall or that are an exclusive bargaining agent and have 25 or more members are subject to ADEA. Public employee unions are similarly covered. Employment agencies are also subject to the ADEA. An employment agency is defined as an entity or person who procures employees for employers. The agency need not itself employ any minimum number of employees.

Because of tribal sovereignty, Indian tribes are not subject to the ADEA.

§ 15.3   Who is not Protected?

While almost universal in its coverage of employees age 40 or older, the ADEA does exempt a few employees. The ADEA does not protect an individual who "is employed in a bona fide executive or a high policymaking position" if such employee is entitled to annual nonforfeitable retirement benefits worth at least $44,000 per year. This exception permits employers to terminate higher paid executives and thereby create an orderly plan of progression in the higher executive ranks. The Regulations explain that the exemption applies *only* to a few top-level employees and never to middle management, even if they meet the retirement income requirement. Moreover, the employer has the burden of proving whether an employee meets the criteria.

A "bone fide executive" is primarily a manager with discretionary powers who directs the work of other employees, and who has the authority to hire and fire. Employees who are not executives may be exempted from the ADEA if they are in a "high policy-making position." These are employees who lack direct line authority, but who play a significant role in determining company policy. Examples include chief economists or chief research scientists who have significant intellectual or policy input by virtue of their access to the executive decision makers.

Firefighters and law enforcement personnel (prison guards and police officers) are exempted from the ADEA's protection because of concern that older individuals may not be able to adequately perform the job duties and if they should fail, they might put others at risk.

§ 15.4 Employees: Proving Illegal Discrimination

Only about 10% of the employee claims under the ADEA allege age discrimination in hiring. In most cases, employees who are not hired may not even know why they were not hired, and their level of indignation is often lower than that of a terminated employee. Hence, there are many fewer suits alleging age discrimination in the decision not to hire. Applicants are also discouraged from suing because the case for discrimination in hiring is difficult to prove. It is not sufficient for the claimant to show that a younger applicant was hired. Rather, the claimant must prove that age was the determining factor in the employer's decision not to hire. ADEA-recognized discrimination is proved when a "but-for" test is satisfied: but for the claimant's age, the claimant would have been hired. Unless the employer leaves a "paper trail" that proves the illegal age discrimination, or unless the employer's hiring practices clearly evidence age discrimination, the complaint is likely to fail.

The great majority of age discrimination complaints filed under the ADEA arise from employees claiming that they were terminated on account of their age. While there is seldom written proof of age discrimination in job termination cases, a "smoking gun" does sometimes exist in the form of internal memoranda and other correspondence. However, as the ADEA has become better understood, employers usually take precautions to avoid creating incriminating documents. Still, direct evidence of discriminatory attitudes is occasionally uncovered, and, if it is reasonably linked to the termination or failure to hire, the applicant will have established his or her case.

Even if written evidence cannot be found, however, a prima facie case of age discrimination may be proved through circumstantial evidence. In *McDonnell Douglas Corp. v. Green* (S.Ct.1973) the United States Supreme Court established a four-part, prima facie test to be used to prove cases under Title VII of the Civil Rights Act of 1964 that bars discrimination on account of race, religion and sex. The test has been adopted by courts in cases involving allegations of age discrimination. Adapted to the ADEA, an applicant, to establish a prima facie case, must prove:

(1) The individual belongs to the protected group (age 40 or over).

(2) The applicant applied for or was employed in, and was qualified for a job for which the employer was seeking applicants.

(3) Despite the applicant's qualifications, he or she was rejected.

(4) After the rejection, the position remained open, and the employer sought applications from persons with similar qualifications or filled the position with a younger person with comparable qualifications.

If these four facts are established, the burden of proof shifts to the defendant-employer. Unless the employer can prove that the discharge or refusal to hire was for nondiscriminatory reasons, the plaintiff will win.

In response, the employer may claim that the discharge was for nondiscriminatory reasons. The employer must prove that the proffered reason was in fact the basis for its decision. The reason need not be an admirable one, nor an intelligent one, so long as it provides a legal, nondiscriminatory basis for the decision.

If the employer offers a legal reason for its decision, the employee must respond by arguing that the employer's explanation was merely a pretext and was not the true reason for the decision. Ultimately, a jury will decide the merits of the case.

Other means are available to prove an age discrimination case. A few cases have been proven by statistics that seem to indicate a pattern of dismissal on account of age. Usually, however, the issue is an individual case of discrimination and statistical evidence is of little assistance. Generally, the plaintiff must provide specific evidence that he or she was terminated because of age. For example, if an employer chooses to reduce the number of upper management positions, the fact that the dismissed employees are, on the average, older than the remaining employees, proves little since older employees tend to occupy the upper management positions.

Statistics can help support a case based upon a disparate impact claim. To establish a prima facie case of disparate impact, the plaintiff must (1) identify the specific practice or criteria being challenged; (2) show that it had a disparate impact upon older, protected employees; and (3) prove that the criteria was not related to job performance. In rebuttal, the employer can argue that the dismissal did not have a disparate impact on older employees. Alternatively, the employer can concede that the policy disproportionately harmed older workers, but offer a legitimate business reason that explains the use of a policy that had a disparate impact on older workers. For example, the employer might have reduced its

workforce by eliminating a level of middle management, most of whom were over age 40. Though a
case of disparate impact, the company had an independent, legal reason for the policy and so was not
liable under the ADEA.

Some employers, in a cost-cutting attempt, severely cut back the number of employees or, as it is
called, implement a "reduction in force." Often a
reduction in force results in the termination of a
disproportionate number of employees over age 40.
However, merely citing this statistical evidence does
not establish the plaintiff's prima facie case if the
dismissed employees were not replaced, but had
their duties assumed as additional responsibilities
by other employees. To win a prima facie case of age
discrimination only by statistical evidence, the
plaintiffs must prove both that they were dismissed
and that they were replaced by younger employees.

§ 15.5   Employer Defenses

The ADEA allows an employer to take an action
that is otherwise prohibited if the decision to take
that action is based on "reasonable factors other
than age." 29 U.S.C. § 623(f)(1). The Reasonable
Factors Other than Age (RFOA) provision is somewhat of a catch-all for employers. Older workers
may be fired or not hired for a number of reasons
without violating the ADEA. Personality conflicts,
insubordination, rule violations, health problems,
and decreases in productivity are all acceptable
grounds for dismissal or for a refusal to hire an
older employee. So long as the action is not taken

on the basis of age, the ADEA has not been violated. For example, an older employee may be fired because of an inability to perform productively even if age is a contributing factor to the poor job performance.

Employers can discriminate against older employees "where age is a bona fide occupational qualification reasonably necessary to the normal operation of the particular business." 29 U.S.C. § 623(f). Known as the BFOQ defense, it is only rarely allowed. Its success has been limited to those jobs that are very physically strenuous or jobs that involve public safety, e.g., airplane pilots. *Western Air Lines v. Criswell* (S.Ct.1985).

An employee may counter a BFOQ defense by arguing that the employer should have relied on individual testing procedures to evaluate job competency rather than using a blanket prohibition against older employees. Unless the employer can successfully prove that individual employee testing would not suffice, the employee will win.

In general, employers are given great latitude in operating their businesses. They may hire or dismiss employees for a variety of reasons so long as they are not violative of state or federal law. Many ADEA cases arise when an employer reduces the size of its workforce, which is legal if it was not a pretext for discriminating against older workers. Courts will not interfere when an employer chooses to dismiss excess employees. The ADEA does not require affirmative hiring of older workers, nor does it mandate more favorable treatment of older workers. It only protects older workers against discrimination on the basis of their age.

§ 15.6   Enforcement of the ADEA

Administrative remedies must be pursued before an age discrimination lawsuit may be filed. If the employee's state has a law that prohibits age discrimination, the aggrieved employee must file a complaint with the proper state agency. Within 300 days of that filing, the employee must also file a complaint with the Equal Employment Opportunities Commission (EEOC). After the filing, the claimant is required to wait 60 days before filing a lawsuit. If the employee's state does not have a law that prohibits age discrimination, the employee must file a complaint with the EEOC within 180 days of the discriminatory event. Again, a claimant must then wait 60 days before commencing a civil suit. If the EEOC commences a lawsuit based on the employee's complaint, the employee may not commence a private suit. If, after 60 days the EEOC has not sued, the employee may sue, and even if the EEOC later sues, the employee's action may continue.

The statute of limitations in ADEA cases is two years for nonwillful violations and three years for willful violations. The statute begins to run from the date of notification of termination or other discriminatory act.

If the complaint goes to trial, the employee may request a jury trial. Most plaintiffs prefer a jury because they are thought to be sympathetic to claims of age discrimination.

§ 15.7 Remedies

A number of remedies are available to the employee who successfully proves an age discrimination case. In addition to back pay, the ADEA allows reinstatement or, when appropriate, front pay (future damages in lieu of reinstatement). The court may also issue an injunction to bar future violations. The employee has a duty to mitigate damages, but the employer bears the burden of proving that an employee failed to mitigate. A successful plaintiff is usually awarded attorney's fees, but damages for pain and suffering, as well as punitive damages, are not allowed. In the case of a willful violation of the ADEA, the plaintiff can be awarded "liquidated damages" equal to twice the amount of pecuniary loss.

§ 15.8 Taxation of Monetary Remedies

Damages, including backpay and liquidated damages, awarded under the ADEA are included in the gross income of the employee. Since August 21, 1996, Section 104 of the Internal Revenue Code excludes from income compensation for injuries or sickness, but only if awarded on account of personal injuries or sickness. Damage awards under the ADEA clearly do not qualify for the exclusion. In 1995, the Supreme Court in *Commissioner v. Schleier* (S.Ct. 1995) held that all compensation awarded under the ADEA was taxable.

§ 15.9   Other Issues

The Older Workers Benefit Protection Act of 1990 amended the ADEA so that an employer cannot use the existence of an employee benefit plan as a justification for failing to hire or involuntarily retiring older employees. Under employee benefit plans, older employees often cost the employer more than younger employees, such as for health insurance premiums. Even so, employers may not refuse to hire older employees in an attempt to reduce their costs, nor can an employer reduce or terminate employee fringe benefits because of the employee's age. However, the employer can legally spend the same amount for each worker on benefits even if that buys fewer benefits for the older worker.

Because the ADEA has all but eliminated mandatory retirement, some employers encourage voluntary "early" retirement. Such a program is lawful only if it is genuinely voluntary and non-discriminatory. If the plan is only a subterfuge for mandatory retirement, it violates the ADEA.

Employers frequently offer early retirement benefits. The employee is offered a generous "bonus" for retiring, and warned that if not enough employees voluntarily retire, some will be terminated. Even though the purpose of these inducements is to encourage the retirement of older employees, they do not violate the ADEA because they favor the older employee by giving them an attractive option. The employer may legally limit the eligibility for the early retirement benefits to older employees.

In light of the ADEA's protections, employers often require an employee who accepts early retirement to sign a waiver of rights freeing the employer from any liability under the ADEA. Such waiver is valid only if it was voluntarily signed, with full knowledge of all rights, and for adequate consideration. Under the ADEA (as amended in 1990), a waiver is valid only if the employee was advised in writing to consult with a lawyer, was given 21 days to consider the agreement, and had seven days to revoke a signed agreement. The waiver also must clearly state the rights and claims being waived by the employee.

CHAPTER 16

ELDER ABUSE AND NEGLECT

§ 16.1 Introduction

Americans have come to realize the extent of domestic violence in our society. Initially parental abuse of children was discovered. Later there came a growing understanding of spousal abuse. Finally, the abuse and neglect of the elderly has drawn increased attention.

Elder abuse is the sustained physical or psychological assault of an older person. Abuse and neglect are distinguished from mere criminal behavior by their repetitive nature. A single incident of physical assault or verbal abuse is generally not considered to be elder abuse and neglect. Because of its repetitive nature, almost all elder abuse arises between individuals with some ongoing relationship. Often it is a case of a caregiver abusing the older person, though it is not limited to such relationships, since neighbors or relatives who do not live with or assist the abused individual can also be guilty of abuse.

§ 16.2 Incidence of Elderly Abuse and Neglect

It is estimated that more than one and a half million older Americans are abused each year, equal to approximately 5% of all age 65 or older. The actual numbers of abuse are unknown, but it is believed most incidents are never reported.

After states began to take action against elderly abuse, the number of reported cases rose significantly, indicating a high degree of unreported abuse.

One of the difficulties in estimating the incidence of elderly abuse is the lack of any bright line definition of what is abuse and neglect. Even states that define it by statute cannot agree. In the end it is less of an issue of just how many people are abused, than that there are victims and, in any event, far too many victims.

§ 16.3 Definitions

As indicated, there are no fixed definitions of elder abuse and neglect, but the following are probably as close to a generalized agreement as any. Abuse can be defined as a physical or mental mistreatment or injury that threatens or harms an elderly person. Abuse can take place either by actively injuring the older person, or by inaction that permits that person to be injured. Neglect refers to a willful refusal, by a caregiver or any person with a duty to provide care, to provide services necessary to maintain an elderly person's physical or mental health. Exploitation refers to the financial abuse of individuals by the repeated improper or illegal use of their assets. Finally, the term "self neglect" is often used to refer to the refusal or inability of elderly persons to provide for themselves with the resources or services necessary for their physical or mental well-being. Whether self neglect should be considered a form of abuse and neglect is problematical. It is probably better perceived as an indication of individuals who lack the necessary capacity to take care of themselves or that they suffer from a mental illness.

Much of what is called physical abuse takes the form of threats, with only an occasional actual assault. Physical abuse is any conduct that results in mental distress or physical injury. It can be active, in the sense of striking the victim, or it can be passive in the form of neglect that could include the deliberate withholding of medication or food or care if necessary for the elderly person. Physical abuse also includes sexual assaults, which, though relatively uncommon, are a significant and serious form of abuse.

Psychological abuse can also be extremely dehabilitating to elderly individuals. It can range from simple name calling and shouting to protracted dehumanization through repeated assaults on the other individual's personality and ego. Psychological abuse is generally used to coerce the elderly individual into behaving in ways acceptable to the abuser or to destroy his or her free will in regard to their life choices or property management. The most common form of psychological abuse is to threaten to put the elderly person into a nursing home if that person does not behave in the way demanded by the abuser.

Some abuse takes place under the general category of "violation of rights," referring, for example, to forcing an elderly person to move in with the abuser against that person's will. It may also mean locking the older person in his or her room, denying basic privacy or refusing to let the older person complain to others or seek assistance.

The numerical breakdown of abuse by categories is uncertain. Because so much abuse is unreported there are no firm estimates as to the amount and type of abuse. Most studies indicate that neglect is the most common form of abuse followed by physical abuse. Together these two probably make up over half of all abuse, with financial exploitation, emotional abuse and other, miscellaneous forms of abuse making up the remainder.

§ 16.4   Noninstitutional Abusers

Abuse and neglect occur in both institutional settings such as a nursing home or an assisted living facility, and also in the community, most commonly in the victim's home. In the case of institutional abuse, the abuser is either the institution or its employees. In the case of noninstitutional setting abuse, the abuser is most often the caregiver, because a caregiver is usually one of the few people who has repeated interaction with the abused individual and thus the opportunity to commit repeated assaults.

In some instances the caregiver is also the guardian of the victim, and thus has special control over the victim's life and property. (For a discussion of the powers of a guardian, see Chapter 9, Guardian-ship.) Older persons are also abused by spouses, though such abuse might better be thought of as spousal, rather than elder, abuse.

Children, grandchildren, nieces, nephews, and siblings are often the abuser, because their kinship provides them access to the older person and per-mits them to carry on the abuse. Neighbors or "friends" often insinuate themselves into the older persons' lives and take advantage of that closeness to abuse or exploit them. The abused person often puts up with the abuse or exploitation for fear of losing what benefits the abuser provides, or, in extreme cases, because the abuser prevents the abused person from notifying anyone else of the abuse or neglect. For example, an abusive nephew lives with his aunt. Though he does help her around the house, he takes all her money and repeatedly threatens to have her declared incompetent and moved into a nursing home. As a result, the aunt is a virtual prisoner in her own home. Though she could call the police for help, she does not because she does not want her nephew to go to jail for fear that if he does, she will have to move into a nursing home. Another common example is that of a neigh-bor who begins by doing favors for an isolated older person and ends by stealing his or her assets.

As the preceding examples illustrate, most abus-ers profit from their abuse, often financially. In some instances the abuse is designed to hasten the victim's death, so that the abuser can inherit or steal their property. Some abuse merely for the psychological "payoff" that comes from tormenting their victim. Either the abuser is pathological or is taking "revenge" upon the victim for real or imagined slights.

Much abuse by caregivers is a form of control. By abusing the older person, the abuser seeks to break down resistance, to make the caregiver's role easier or merely to enjoy dominating another person.

Because abuse is a form of control, it is not always clear what is abuse and what is merely firm control. For example, if a caregiver yells at their abused person, is this abuse or is it merely an unfortunate pattern of control? Neglect is one thing, but merely ignoring the incessant demands of a bedridden older person is quite another. To an outside observer, a caretaker who shouts at the older person, who is short tempered, who mumbles threats of "you ought to be in a nursing home," and who provides less than optimum care might seem abusive. In his or her defense, the caregiver might claim that the older person is difficult, demanding and unappreciative, and that as a volunteer, the caregiver is doing as well as can be expected. Clearly there is no bright line test between merely what is merely subpar care or what is abuse. On the other hand, at some point slack caregiving shades into abuse and neglect.

Neglect is the most common form of abuse by caregivers. Sometimes it is passive, meaning an unconscious or unintended failure to fulfill caregiving obligations. If the caregiver simply does not realize the needs of the individual, neglect can occur. For example, Angie, is caring for her grandmother, Margaret, who suffers from diabetes. Though Angie tries to be a good caregiver, her ignorance of her grandmother's medical needs causes her to fail to provide a proper diet and so intensifies the effects of the diabetes.

Active neglect is more culpable. It includes deliberate abandonment or refusal to provide essential health and nutritional needs. For example, withholding food either to control or torment the person is a typical example of active neglect.

Neglect can only occur if there is a duty of care that arises out of a legal relationship. Spouses have a legal obligation to care for one another, and a few states impose a duty of care for parents upon adult children, though such statutes are rarely enforced. A duty to care for another more commonly arises from a contractual relationship or from creating a reliance expectation. For example, Dan agrees to care for his Uncle Carl because his Uncle has promised to leave his house to Dan. If Dan subsequently fails to care for Uncle Carl, he could be guilty of neglect as well as be in breach of the agreement. Reliance of an older person on another for care is very common. If, for example, Melissa begins to help her Aunt Lucy when Lucy becomes bedridden, Melissa cannot simply cease to show up without making some provision for Lucy's care. Having made Lucy dependent upon her, Melissa has the responsibility to see that Lucy is not abandoned. If she fails to ensure that Lucy is taken care of, Melissa is guilty of neglect.

§ 16.5 Institutional Abuse and Neglect

Abuse and neglect frequently occur in institutional settings. Institutional abuse and neglect usually are not the result of a policy of the institution, but are rather individual acts by employees. Here again, the abuse is connected to control, an employee may slap or hit a patient "in order to make them behave." Denial of privileges or threats of future harm are used to keep patients "in line." Employees of the facility may steal money or property from the residents, or may insist upon bribes for care promised in the facility's contract with the resident. (See discussion of patient care in Chapter 7, Nursing Homes, Rights and Responsibilities.) In a few unfortunate cases the institution actively promotes, or at least turns its eye from abusive employee misbehavior. The facility may encourage the excessive use of restraints to handle patients who act out, are violent or have a tendency to wander off the premises. Alternatively, the facility may neglect its residents by failing to meet basic standards of nutrition, care and cleanliness.

Board and care homes for the elderly have been cited by a Congressional Committee as constituting a "national disgrace." Residents of board and care homes are often older persons suffering from a lack of capacity who need assistance, but not the medical care provided in nursing homes. Such individuals often have few assets and may have no friends or relatives to watch out for them. As a result of their isolation and diminished capacity, board and care home residents are frequently abused or neglected.

In board and care homes that serve the very poor, abuse often occurs because the home lacks the ability to perform better. What seems to be active abuse may merely be the result of inadequate finances or bad management. Other home operators are more culpable. To increase its profits, the home may provide substandard living conditions, inadequate nutrition or isolate the residents from the world, making them virtual prisoners. In other cases, the home owner will steal the assets and incomes of the residents who are often too frail or demented to complain to the authorities.

§ 16.6 Causes of Abuse and Neglect

Though the causes of abuse and neglect are many, it is often simply an expression of evil. Some abusers have a pathological need to hurt others, and take particular pleasure in tormenting defenseless older persons. In other cases the abuse results from caregivers breaking down under the strain of their responsibilities and turning their anger and frustration against the older person. In fact, it is estimated that in noninstitutional settings the major precipitating factor of abuse is stress, which leads to despair, anger and resentment, which in turn are expressed as abuse or neglect.

The financial and emotional pressures of caring for older individuals can be very burdensome. Guardians who are responsible for an older incapacitated person often lack adequate training or supervision, and may resort to abuse either out of anger or ignorance. Guardians and caregivers may be unaware of available social services and other forms of support. Feeling isolated and unappreciated, they may neglect the older person, hoping that his or her death will terminate the seemingly endless obligation of care.

Some abuse is simply revenge. Adult children, for example, sometimes retaliate against their older parents for abuse committed against them as children. Others do not even consider it to be retaliation, but simply consider violence as a normal and acceptable way of dealing with other persons, particularly if they are uncooperative or burdensome.

Many abusers suffer from alcohol or drug dependency, and much of the abuse occurs when the abuser is drunk or on drugs. Other abusers, particularly, financial abusers, exploit the elder person as a means of obtaining money to purchase drugs or alcohol.

Finally, many caregivers are financially dependent upon the older person. This creates a sense of anger and resentment that is expressed as exploitation, physical abuse, or neglect. Phil, for example, may beat his aged mother even though (or perhaps because) she gives him money to buy drugs.

Institutional abuse often results from too few staff, low wages and inadequate training. Too often the employees of the facility take out their resentment on the patients or, lacking proper training,

know no other way to handle patients other than by
violence or threats. Attempts to screen employees
by checking on criminal records have proven only
partially successful in screening out inadequate employees. Better training and better wages would
probably go a long way towards reducing institutional abuse. Increased state supervision and vigor-
ous enforcement of laws and regulations designed to
protect nursing home residents also would reduce
abuse. (See Chapter 7, Nursing Homes: Rights and
Responsibilities.)

Abuse and neglect in board and care homes could
be lessened by better state supervision and by more
careful screening before licensing potential board
and care home operators. If the residents of board
and care homes could afford to pay more, they
would probably be treated better. Additional state
financial support for low income board and care
home residents would undoubtedly improve their
care.

§ 16.7 Legislative Responses

The primary responsibility for protecting the
rights of the elderly rests with the states. Every
state has some active program to protect the right
of elderly citizens, though the average amount
spent by states for elderly anti-abuse programs is
very modest. The only Federal funding for state
protective services comes from the social services
block grant that over the years have been reduced
by direct cuts and eroded by inflation.

Federal grants are made to state agencies on aging which in turn make subgrants to or contract with area agencies on aging (AAAs). The state agency on aging serves as a general coordinator of all services and programs related to the assistance of elderly people within the state. The state agency designates service areas within the state to be serviced by the AAAs, each of which serves as the primary planner and coordinator of all aging-related services in the designated area. An AAA, in turn, may make subgrants to or contract with service providers to provide specific services to elderly people within the area. Such services typically include: supportive services, congregate meals services, home delivered meals services, in-home services, preventative health services, and outreach services.

Congress enacted the Older Americans Act Amendments of 1987 that requires state Area Agencies on Aging to assess the need for elder abuse prevention services. Each state was to create a state plan on aging that would enact elder abuse prevention activities within the state. The Federal act, however, did not provide any significant Federal money to enable states to carry out these duties that include public education to identify and prevent abuse, a plan to receive reports on incidents of abuse, provide outreach conferences and referrals to other sources of assistance and to law enforcement or public protective service agencies.

Of course, most elder abuse is criminal activity and is already outlawed by various laws against assault and battery, blackmail or extortion. In addition a number of states have enacted specific statutes that criminalize abuse of the elderly.

Traditional criminal statutes have not proven effective. In many cases the abused individual is reluctant to use the criminal justice system, particularly if the abuser is a family member or caregiver. The resulting publicity, shame and emotional cost often prevents any steps being taken. Finally, the persons who are abused often fear that if their abuser/caregiver is prosecuted they will lose any source of assistance and be forced to move to an institution, such as a nursing home. There is also the issue of whether the overloaded criminal justice system can respond quickly enough to the problem. The time between the initial complaint and eventual punishment can be long, and the victim's fear of retaliation by the abuser is always present.

Victims of elder abuse can resort to civil remedies including restraining and protective orders as well as the right to civil suit for damages, although the latter usually has little practical significance. Every state and the District of Columbia have specifically provided for restraining orders and protective orders against intra-family abuse. These statutes, generally referred to as Domestic Violence Acts, permit the victim to obtain a court order ordering the defendant to refrain from the abuse to vacant the household. Most of the statutes permit monetary compensation to the victim.

Unfortunately not every state's intra-family violence statute can be used by the elderly. In a few states, the remedies are available solely to an abused spouse, or the remedy is conditioned upon the filing of a divorce or separation petition. Obviously these statutes are useful only for abused elderly spouses. Even if the abuser is the spouse, an older victim may not be willing to file for divorce or separation in order to get a protective order or temporary restraining order.

Fortunately most state Domestic Violence Acts do provide protection for elder abuse victims in the form of a protective order or injunction. A protective order by itself, however, will not necessarily protect the elderly victim from abuse. Typically, only the victim is authorized to file a complaint. Unfortunately, too many older victims are unable to get to court or fear a court action would only worsen the situation by increasing animosity or result in institutionalization. Even if the older person does file under the Act, there may not be adequate services available once he or she is removed from the abusive environment. There are very few elderly abuse victim shelters, leaving the victims almost no alternative except institutionalization or abandonment.

§ 16.8   Adult Protective Services

With encouragement although not financial assistance from the Federal government, every state has passed some form of an adult protective services act. These statutes are designed to provide a comprehensive response to the abuse of older persons. Adult protective service legislation includes a definition of elderly abuse and neglect, means to uncover elderly abuse, a state response to the abuse, and punishment for the abuser.

All states define elderly abuse to include physical harm, although some distinguish between willful infliction of physical abuse and negligent infliction by failure to prevent the physical abuse. Many, but not all states, define abuse to include mental anguish or psychological injury. Among those, some states require that the psychological abuse be severe enough to require medical attention. The failure to include psychological abuse is probably attributable to the fear that to include such abuse would unnecessarily expand the numbers of abuse beyond the ability of the state to respond and might well criminalize activity that is best considered deviant behavior, but not activity that rises to a level warranting state intervention. A few states recognize unreasonable confinement as elder abuse, and some even include intimidation. Sexual abuse is sometimes considered general abuse, or it sometimes appears as a separate category of abusive behavior. Neglect is almost always covered in adult protective service laws. It is typically defined as a failure to provide, or the deprivation of, basic needs, including food, shelter and care for physical and mental health. Some states include all forms in neglect, including those caused by negligent behavior; others require a degree of willfulness. A minority of states include self neglect as a variety of neglect that justifies state intervention under the adult protective service statutes.

Financial exploitation is also included under the definition of abuse. It includes the illegal or improper use of an elderly individual's resources or property for the benefit of the exploiter or another's.

Many of the adult protective services laws contain requirements for mandatory reporting. These statutes require professionals to report known or suspected cases of elderly abuse. Professionals usually include health care and social service individuals such as law enforcement officers, social workers, physicians and nurses. Some states have detailed lists of those persons required to report. Others mandate anyone, professional or otherwise, who has knowledge or cause to believe that abuse has occurred, to report the incident.

Generally, state statutes grant immunity from civil or criminal liability to a mandatory reporter, although some extend the protection only to the extent that the report was made in good faith. A few states provide that individuals who know of abuse and fail to report it can be prosecuted. Even states that do not require mandatory reporting nevertheless guarantee anonymity or confidentiality for reporters of abuse. Some states permit limited disclosure of the identity of the reporter of abuse under particular circumstances. Confidentiality is needed because individuals otherwise might hesitate to report abuse for fear of retaliation or civil or criminal liability.

A number of states keep a centralized listing of all abuse reports and information about any subse-

quent investigation. By maintaining a central registry, states hope to avoid the fragmentation of information or a failure to follow up on repeated reports
of potential abuse.

The need for confidentiality for abuse reports,
whether in a central registry or not, is great. As a
result, almost all states restrict the access to abuse
records. They are not public documents and information gathered during investigation is not open to
public scrutiny. Some states have absolute confidentiality, others provide that the information may be
released with the victim's permission.

A few states permit expungement of records of
abuse that are determined to be inaccurate or un-
substantiated. Obviously, the failure to expunge
such false reports can be highly damaging to the
alleged abuser. On the other hand, expungement
may inadvertently clear the record of a guilty party.

Most adult protective services laws do not contain
penalties against the abuser. States, which do have
adult protective service penalties, usually provide
that abuse and neglect is a form of misdemeanor for
which the abuser can be fined or imprisoned. A few
states classify certain abuse as a felony with consequently stricter penalties.

All states statutes provide some sort of initial
investigation upon receipt of report of alleged
abuse. Who carries out the investigation varies from
state to state with most naming Department of
Human Services, Social Service Agencies or Welfare
Department as the investigatory agency. A few

states require the local law enforcement agency to investigate while others have assigned the job of investigation to a different agency depending upon the form of the alleged abuse. If, for example, the abuse is considered to give rise to imminent bodily harm, the referral may be made to the appropriate law enforcement agency or the district attorney's office.

After an investigation is completed or if the older person requests assistance, most state adult protective service statutes permit the provision of a variety of services. The goal is to provide such services as might be necessary to terminate the abuse and to meet the care needs of the older individual. Usually the services include a combination of health, social, psychological, medical and legal assistance, coordinated in a manner that meets the individualized needs of the victim.

The majority of states permit the services to be provided even if the older person has not consented. In particular, many statutes permit provision of services to incapacitated individuals whose person or property may be in danger. The involuntary provision of services to an older person is controversial. Many commentators object to the provision of services under the claim that the individual is guilty of self neglect. A common example would be an older woman who is found living in her home with a dozen or more cats with no heat and apparently not maintaining her own physical well-being. Under many state adult protective service statutes, a state could force its way into the home, remove the animals and either force the woman to take care of herself or move her into another facility for her care. Such intervention into an individual's life engages the competing values of autonomy for the individual versus protection for an individual with diminished capacity.

INDEX

References are to Pages

425

†